The TRADITIONAL FURNITURE MAKER

David Bryant

B. T. Batsford Ltd, London

To Mark and Sarah

Acknowledgements

I would like to express my sincere thanks to all those who offered their help and guidance during the preparation of this book. In particular I am indebted to the following country houses, their owners, curators and administrators, who allowed me to measure up the selected furniture items.

Mr and Mrs T. Richards, Gawsworth Hall, for the plank chest and carved oak coffer (Chapters 1 and 2); Mr Richard Ryder for the thrown chair in Rufford Old Hall, National Trust (Chapter 3); Rufford Old Hall, National Trust for the Chippendale chair (Chapter 4); Manchester City Art Gallery for the William and Mary chest of drawers and hooded rocking cradle at Wythenshawe Hall (Chapters 5 and 6); The American Museum in Bath, Claverton Manor, for the Sausage chair and Shaker rocking chair, also for the photographs of these items, and that of Claverton Manor (Chapter 7 and 8); Erddig, National Trust for the walnut tea table and George III mahogany whatnot (Chapters 9 and 10); Mr Hal Bagot, Levens Hall, for the walnut side table and George III mahogany tray (Chapters 11 and 12); Mr and Mrs R. Gillow-Reynolds, Leighton Hall, for the Gillow dining table and the Queen Anne chair (Chapters 13 and 14); Dunham Massey, National Trust, for the Pembroke table and the quartetto tables (Chapters 15 and 16); Mr and Mrs William Bromley-Davenport, Capesthorne Hall, for the Hepplewhite dining chair and American double chest (Chapters 17 and 18); Mr Randle Brooks, Peover Hall, for the mahogany 'D' end dining table (Chapter 19); Tatton Park, National Trust, for the Sheraton elbow chair and rosewood octagon worktable (Chapters 20 and 21); the Trustees of the Chatsworth Settlement for the Kent chair and George III bedside cupboard (Chapters 22 and 23); Mr Charles Legh, Adlington Hall, for the Regency games table and Sheraton dressing table (Chapters 24 and 25); Mr Hugh Cavendish, Holker Hall, for the Silver table, the dumb waiter and the Hepplewhite four-post bed (Chapters 26, 27 and 28); Mr Michael Flower, Arley Hall, for the Regency sofa table and rosewood centre table (Chapters 29 and 30).

I also owe thanks to Mr Michael Wisehall, a local antique dealer, for kindly checking the manuscript, and to Mr R. Shepherd for the front cover photograph and help and advice on photographic matters. Finally my thanks go to my wife and long-suffering children, who patiently accepted that father should go on trips to 'Australia', as they referred to my sorties to country houses, and permitted me to shut myself in my den rather too often whilst I was working on this project.

© David Bryant, 1990
First published 1990

ISBN 0 7134 5954 9

Typeset by Servis Filmsetting Ltd, Manchester and printed in Great Britain by The Bath Press, Avon

for the Publishers
B. T. Batsford Ltd
4 Fitzhardinge Street
London W1H 0AH

Contents

Preface

This book originated partly from a growing interest in country houses and antique furniture, and also because I sensed there was a need for a reference book of fine period furniture designs presented with fully detailed drawings, which would be appreciated by craftsmen wishing to reproduce them.

It was decided that if the job was to be done well, I could not do better than to seek the assistance of the owners of some of Britain's country houses, within whose rooms is an enormous variety of fine traditional furniture. The thirty designs in this book are measured from originals in some of England's finest country houses which have participated in this project. The selection is to a degree regional, for the simple reason that I live in the north-west of England. It is, however, representative of furniture you will find in country houses elsewhere.

The range of period furniture designs includes tables, chairs, chests, and miscellaneous other items, carefully chosen to appeal to craftsmen of all levels of ability. Thus there are designs for simple items such as a mahogany tray and a whatnot, intermediate-level pieces such as Sheraton and Hepplewhite dining chairs, and more demanding furniture, such as an inlaid octagon worktable, a four-post bed, etc.

The furniture selection has also borne in mind the houses we live in today. The emphasis is on practical designs that will suit the modern scene, and pieces that can be matched together. For this reason, ornate gilt-style furniture has not been included. Some furniture designs are described as Chippendale, Hepplewhite, and Sheraton etc; however, unless otherwise stated, this does not imply that these renowned craftsmen were responsible for the manufacture of the piece in question, only that the item is in the period style attributed to them.

In general, the furniture items are prefaced with details of the house from which they have been selected. Information is also given, where appropriate, on the design evolution of the item under discussion. From the constructional point of view, it has been assumed that the craftsman woodworker has acquired the necessary skills, eg joinery, marquetry, woodturning, and so on. The text is therefore limited to a suggested order of assembly, and notes on the construction that may not be revealed entirely by the drawings. Where there may be obvious difficulties, eg making a double twisted leg, these aspects have been amplified.

The drawings have sufficient detail to enable the reader to make a facsimile reproduction of the original. Metric measurements are now widely accepted in the UK, and it was decided to adopt metric dimensioning on the design drawings rather than imperial. A metric drawing is much tidier to read, and once you have become accustomed to the system it is generally easier to work with. A conversion table is included at the end of the book. If there is a shortfall in the drawings then the mistake is mine, but as you can imagine on a project such as this, it is not an easy task to be totally error free.

Preparing this book has been a thoroughly enjoyable experience, and it is earnestly hoped that readers will try making up some of the furniture designs, and will benefit from the information contained herein. Finally, all the furniture items are on display at the houses concerned, so if you wish to view the originals they are there to see – plus a lot more besides!

David Bryant
Knutsford 1990

Chapter 1

Elm plank chest

The ancient manor of Gawsworth Hall in Cheshire, with its picturesque half-timbered elevations, is the country seat of the Roper-Richards family. This is the first country house from which two furniture designs have been selected, an early seventeenth-century elm plank chest and a carved oak coffer, also of this period.

The earliest references to a manor at Gawsworth are from Norman times, when it was in the ownership of the de Orreby family. For nearly 350 years, until 1662, the Fittons were in residence. They were succeeded by the Earls of Macclesfield, and then the Earls of Harrington. The Roper-Richard's family has been resident since 1937.

Gawsworth Hall, as it stands today, dates principally from the second half of the fifteenth century. The building was originally quadrangular, but was extensively altered and reduced in size during the late sixteenth century by Charles Gerard, the second Earl of Macclesfield.

The house has some unusual claims to fame. Mary Fitton lived at Gawsworth, and it is said she was the 'Dark Lady' of Shakespeare's sonnets. It was also the scene of the famous duel between Lord Mohun and the Duke of Hamilton in 1712, fought over the ownership of the Gawsworth estates. Both duellists were killed. The last professional jester, Samuel Johnson, lived in the house, and lies buried in the spinney known as 'Maggotty Johnson's Wood', nearby.

A visit to Gawsworth is thus a time to relive its special character and past history. You might even begin to wonder what other secrets the first furniture design, the *seventeenth-century elm plank chest*, might have to reveal if only it could talk.

Early chests and coffers are of two forms: a six-plank type of construction which has no jointing; and a framed type consisting of interconnecting rails with fielded panels in between. Gawsworth has both, and the plank chest design shown in Fig 1.2 can be seen above the principal staircase.

1.1 *Gawsworth Hall*

1

Elm plank chest

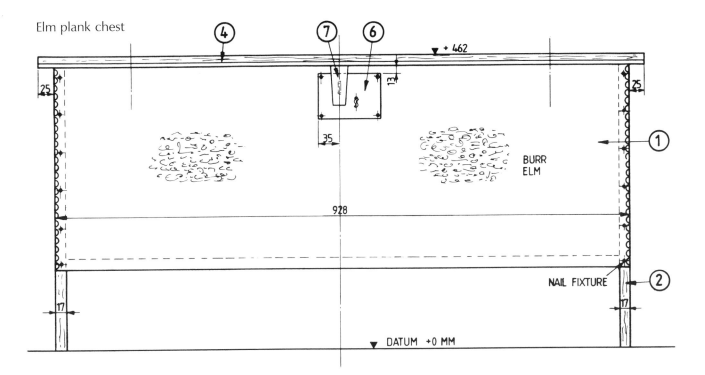

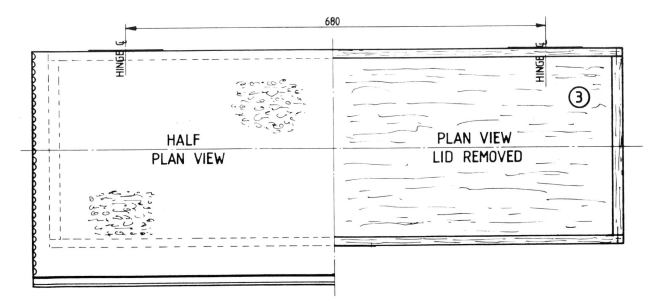

1.2 *General arrangement of plank chest*

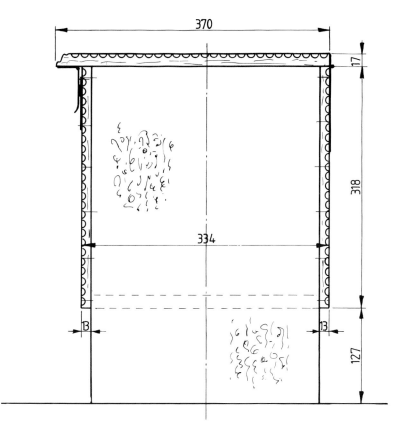

370

17

318

334

127

13

13

Parts list

Item	No	Material	Dimensions (mm)
1 Side	2	Burr elm	318 × 13 × 928 long
2 End	2	Burr elm	308 × 13 × 445 long
3 Bottom	1	Elm	308 × 17 × 894 long
4 Lid	1	Burr elm	370 × 17 × 978 long
5 Hinge	2	Steel	Make to suit
6 Lock plate	1	Steel	102 × 70 × 1 thick
7 Hasp	1	Steel	Make to suit

1.3 *Elm plank chest*

Plank chests are plain and simple and have scant regard for the movement of wood as it dries and seasons. Furniture design in the early seventeenth century was still at an early stage, and joiners did not fully understand the hygroscopic nature of wood. The nailed panel fixture is evidence, too, that it was a time before glues were invented. (See Therle Hughes 'Cheese glue from milk curds 1710, bone glue patent', *Old English Furniture* p 24–5). In the six-plank arrangement the legs are an extension of the end boards and the members are nailed together. In their day, they were probably cherished pieces, and despite their age many have survived remarkably intact. Some, like the Gawsworth example, are plain, while others have Gothic, Tudor or Jacobean carvings, usually on the front, and sometimes also on the ends. The end boards typically finish with a vee form to effectively make four legs, though this example does not have this feature. Verifying the authenticity of carved chests can be difficult because the Victorians sometimes applied carving to original plain coffers.

If you are interested, there are other examples of plank chests in Rufford Old Hall (NT) near Ormskirk, and in Wythenshawe Hall, South Manchester there are two seventeenth-century German coffers with heavy metal strapping. There are also numerous other originals in our country houses elsewhere.

Construction

The general arrangement of the plank chest is shown in Fig 1.2. The plan view with the lid removed shows its basic simplicity. The construction is quite straightforward and little need be said about it. The original is made from an attractive piece of burr elm, though other material such as oak, ash or a fruit wood could be used. Because of its jointless construction, it is suggested that well-seasoned wood is used to minimize the effects of humidity changes, which could promote crack formation. The only carving is in the form of simple edge scallops along each vertical face where the front meets the ends, and along the end faces of the lid. The beaded shape of the front edge of the top can either be routed or alternatively formed using a scraper.

The wrought iron hinge details are given in Fig 1.4. These are to some degree a reconstruction because in the original some lock and hinge parts are missing. The suggested details are based on ironware patterns typical of the period.

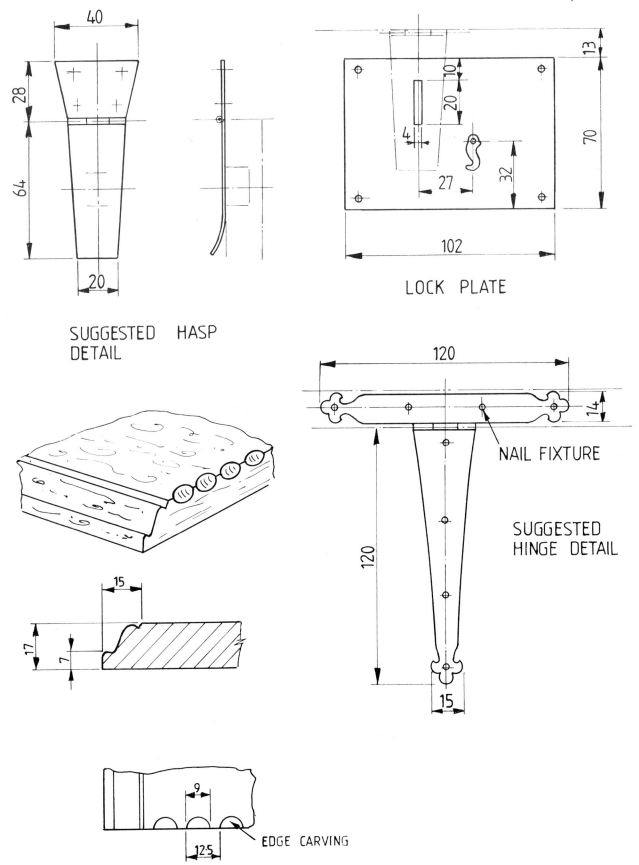

40

28

64

20

SUGGESTED HASP
DETAIL

LOCK PLATE

13

10

20

4

27

32

70

102

120

14

NAIL FIXTURE

SUGGESTED
HINGE DETAIL

120

15

15

17

7

9

12·5

EDGE CARVING

1.4 *Hinge and lock details*

Chapter 2

Carved oak coffer

Many of the furniture items in Gawsworth Hall date from its rebuilding and alteration in the Elizabethan and the late Stuart periods. One of the earlier pieces in the dining room is an impressive sixteenth-century refectory table standing on eight carved, bulbous legs with plain, stretcher rails, and in the drawing room, the principal living room of the house, is a later William and Mary bureau. In the Solar is a sixteenth-century four-post bed, known as the 'Boswell Bed' with elaborate marquetry on the tester and a boldly carved headboard. The Hall Room, the principal bedroom of the house used by the Fitton families, contains another four-post bed from the William and Mary period (1690–1702). Above the principal staircase hangs a Waterford chandelier (c. 1780).

The long room includes a small, sixteenth-century credance table, and also a richly carved Oak coffer (c. 1650). The latter has arched panels to the front and side, a plain hinged top and stands on padded feet. Inside is a lidded candle box compartment.

Construction

The oak coffer is of pegged frame construction with fielded panels. Compared to the plank chest in Chapter 1, this method of assembly allows timber

2.1 *Carved oak coffer*

movement with minimal risk of cracking. The general arrangement is shown in Fig 2.4, and sections through the chest in Fig 2.5. The construction consists of four corner posts (1), connected by front and back rails (2), (3), (4) and side rails (5), (6). Vertical muntins (7) and (8) subdivide the frame to give three panels on the front and two on the ends. In many coffers the corner stiles are carried through to the floor to provide the feet for it to stand on, but in this case they stop short, and the chest stands on padded feet.

It is thought that the chest originally stood on the foot pad (14) only, and that the spacer pieces (15) may have been added at a later date. Miscellaneous

2.2 *Front panel carving*

2.3 *Side panel carving*

details of the corner posts, candle box and pad feet are given in Fig 2.6.

Carving

The cabinet maker clearly gave some design thought to ease of construction in separating as far as possible the carving aspect from the carcase work. In this respect the majority of the carving is by means of applied strips and mouldings which can be independantly prepared in the workshop and then added to the chest as work progresses.

Corner posts and muntins

The corner posts and muntins at the front have an applied facing strip (20) with a reeded pattern as in Fig 2.6. To the side and rear the corner posts, rails and muntins have a scratch moulding detail as in Fig 2.8. Figs 2.4 and 2.5 show the extent of this, and the rails and posts to which it is applied.

Top rail decoration

The top rails on both the front and sides have the same decoration in the form of two applied moulding strips (16) and (17), with an interlacing geometric pattern in between. Moulding (16) has a repeating gouge cut pattern with a centre raised bobble, and below this a narrow flat face with a line of angular corrugations interposed with star punching. Moulding (17) has simple gouge carving incised along its length. The circular geometric pattern between the two mouldings is carved into the surface of the rail. The centre buttons are surrounded by a flat scroll border incised with alternating nicks and star punching. The background surrounding the geometric pattern is stipple punched.

Bottom rail decoration

The bottom rails on the front and side are faced with applied mouldings (18) and (19). These are plain without carving. Standard techniques for making these, such as routing and scraping, can be employed. Moulding (19) serves to hide the bottom planks (13) (see Fig 2.5 section 'CC').

Front panel carving

The applied decoration to each front panel consists of a pilaster arrangement (23), (24) and (25) on either side, above which is a panel (21) carved with a semi-circular arch enclosing a geometric pattern. The latter is similar to that carved on the top rail, except that the centre is a floral motif instead of a bobble, and the scroll border is pin punched, not star punched. The arch panel is carved with a foliate motif in each corner. A stipple punched background surrounds the carved leaf and the outside of the circular geometric pattern.

Side panel carving

The applied ornamentation to the side panels follows the same principles as for those on the front, the only difference being that the pilaster strips (26) and arch panels (22) have a gouge-cut fish scale motif instead of the circular geometric pattern used on the front.

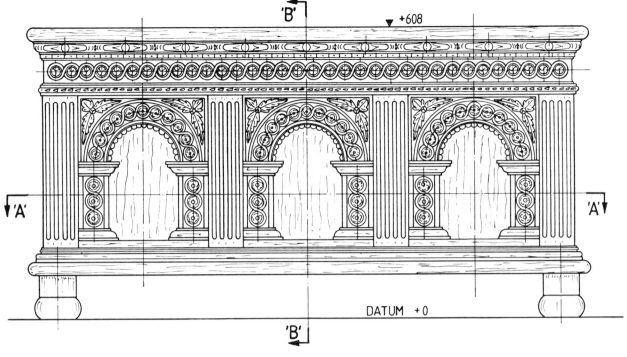

FRONT ELEVATION

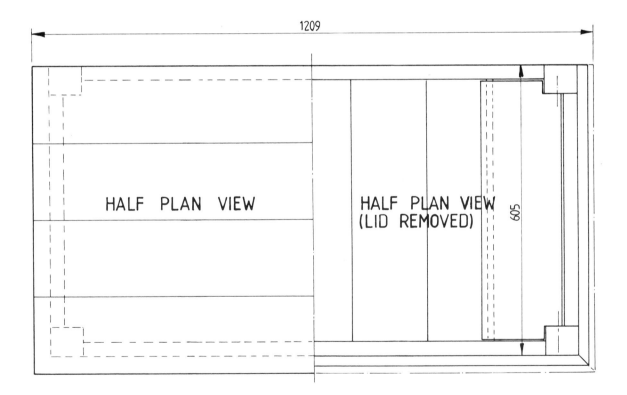

2.4 *General arrangement of coffer*

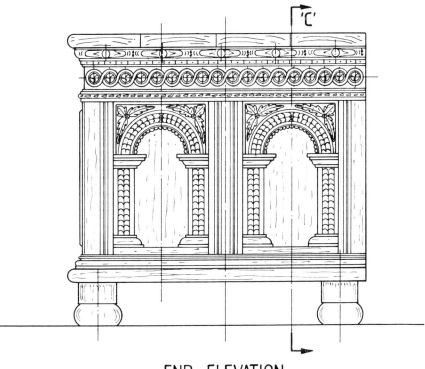

END ELEVATION

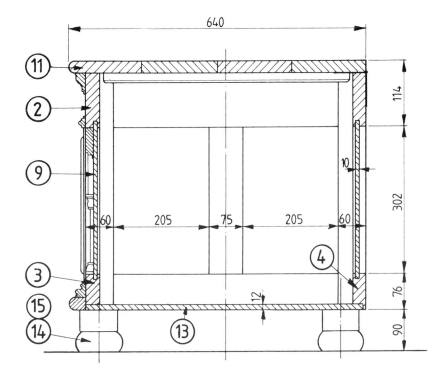

SECTION 'BB'

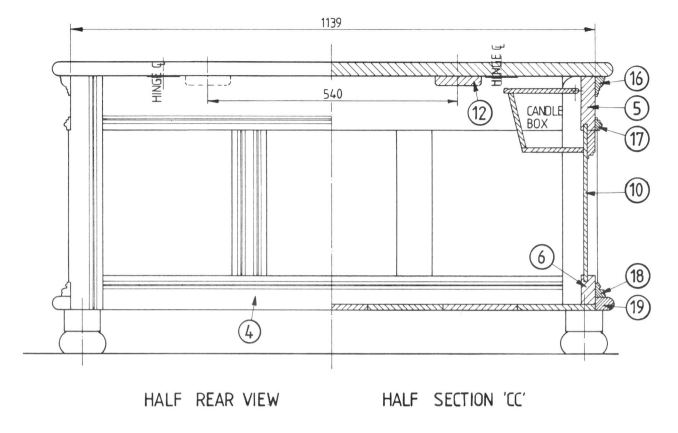

HALF REAR VIEW   HALF SECTION 'CC'

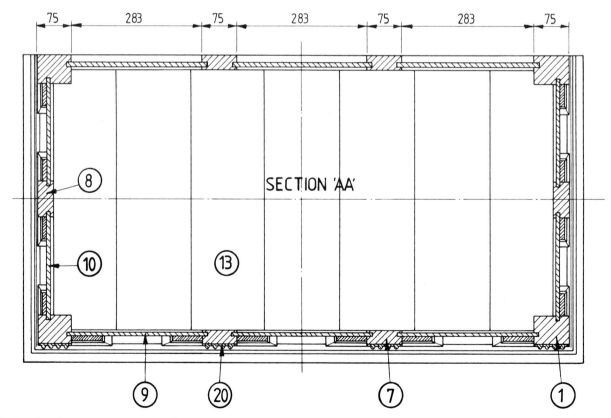

SECTION 'AA'

2.5 *Sectional arrangements of coffer*

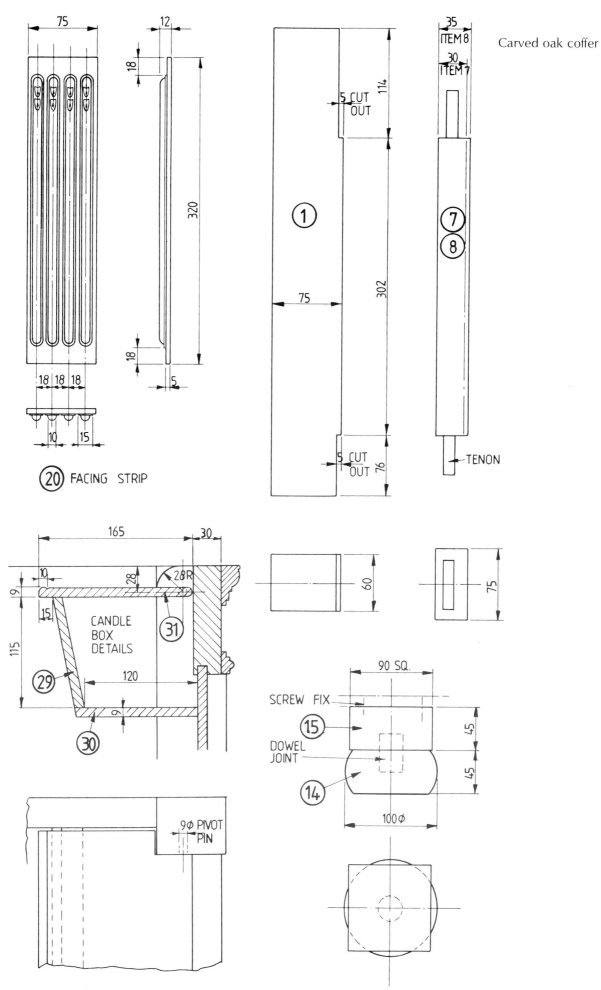

Carved oak coffer

20 FACING STRIP

CANDLE
BOX
DETAILS

SCREW FIX

DOWEL
JOINT

9Ø PIVOT
PIN

TENON

2.6 *Miscellaneous details*

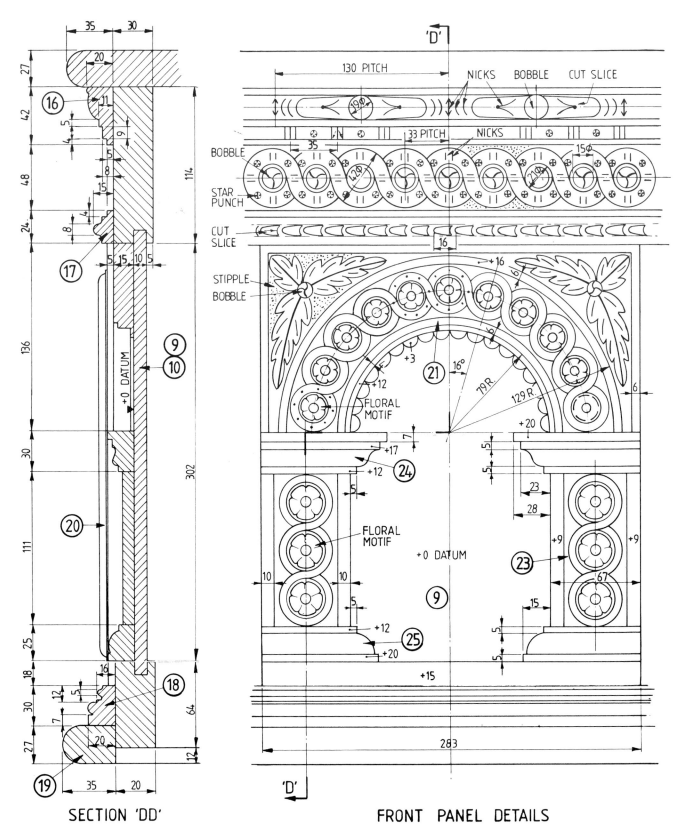

SECTION 'DD'

FRONT PANEL DETAILS

2.7 *Front panel details*

Parts list

Item		No	Material	Dimensions (mm)
1	Corner stile	4	Oak	75 × 60 × 492 long
2	Top rail (1)	2	Oak	114 × 30 × 1100 long
3	Bottom rail (1)	1	Oak	64 × 30 × 1100 long
4	Bottom rail (2)	1	Oak	76 × 30 × 1100 long
5	Top rail (1)	2	Oak	114 × 30 × 585 long
6	Bottom rail (3)	2	Oak	64 × 30 × 585 long
7	Muntin (1)	4	Oak	75 × 30 × 480 long
8	Muntin (2)	2	Oak	75 × 35 × 480 long
9	Panel (1)	6	Oak	303 × 10 × 322 long
10	Panel (2)	4	Oak	225 × 10 × 322 long
11	Lid	1	Oak	160 × 27 × 1209 long (4 pieces required)
12	Lid cross-beam	2	Oak	100 × 20 × 530 long
13	Bottom	1	Oak	163 × 12 × 600 long (7 pieces required)
14	Foot pad	4	Oak	105sq × 45 long
15	Spacer pad	4	Oak	90sq × 45 long
16	Edge moulding (1)	1	Oak	42 × 20 × 2600 long total
17	Edge moulding (2)	1	Oak	24 × 16 × 2600 long total
18	Edge moulding (3)	1	Oak	30 × 20 × 2600 long total
19	Edge moulding (4)	1	Oak	35 × 27 × 2600 long total
20	Facing strip	4	Oak	75 × 12 × 320 long
21	Arch panel (1)	6	Oak	283 × 16 × 136 long
22	Arch panel (2)	4	Oak	205 × 16 × 107 long
23	Pilaster strip (1)	6	Oak	67 × 10 × 111 long
24	Pilaster crown (1)	6	Oak	30 × 20 × 95 long
25	Pilaster foot (1)	6	Oak	25 × 20 × 87 long
26	Pilaster strip (2)	8	Oak	45 × 10 × 140 long
27	Pilaster crown (2)	8	Oak	30 × 20 × 70 long
28	Pilaster foot (2)	8	Oak	25 × 20 × 65 long
29	Candle box front	1	Oak	120 × 9 × 545 long
30	Candle box bottom	1	Oak	130 × 9 × 545 long
31	Candle box lid	1	Oak	165 × 9 × 545 long
32	Hinge	2	Steel	200 × 150 × 2 thick plate
33	Lock	1	Steel	70 × 20 × 100 long approx
34	Screws	–	Steel	Miscellaneous

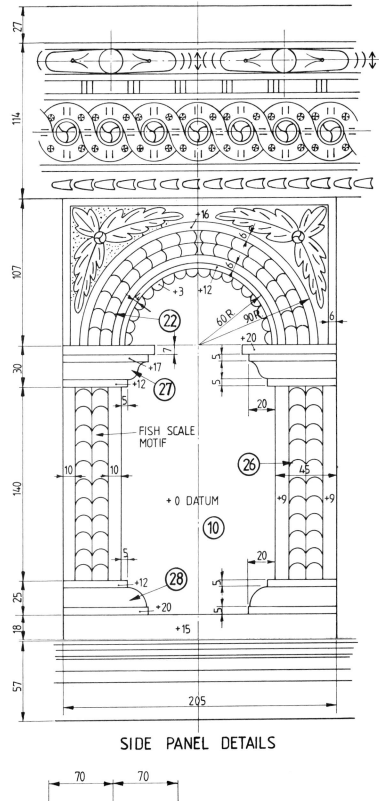

SIDE PANEL DETAILS

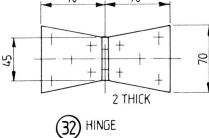

32 HINGE

SCRAP DETAIL OF SCRATCH MOULDING OF SIDE & REAR RAILS & MUNTINS.

2.8 *Side panel details*

Chapter 3

Thrown chair

In considering the choice of two furniture designs from Rufford Old Hall, Lancashire, a medieval half-timbered manor, I decided to pick two chairs to represent the old and newer parts of the building. From the medieval hall I chose a thrown chair (c. 1600), and from the Carolean wing I selected a Chippendale dining chair (c. 1750). The origins of Rufford Old Hall are rather earlier than both of these, and date from around the thirteenth century when the Manor of Rufford passed by marriage from the Fyttons to the Heskeths. In Elizabethan times the Heskeths were among the wealthiest Lancashire landowners. Rufford remained under their custodianship for more than 500 years until the present century. In 1936 it was presented to the National Trust by the first Lord Hesketh.

Like many halls, Rufford has undergone changes, additions and subtractions. The original building was

built to a typical medieval plan, with the main hall connected at each end to an east and west wing. The oldest part, the Great Hall, was built between 1416 and 1458 by Sir Thomas Hesketh, and survives virtually unaltered to this day. The west wing, which contained the family apartments, disappeared some centuries ago. The east wing, housing the kitchen and servants' quarters, was rebuilt in brick in 1662 with alterations made in 1821.

Of particular note is the hammer-beam roof construction of the Great Hall, supported on massive cantilever wall trusses, and of noble proportions. At the east end of the room is an elaborately carved screen, or 'sphere', which originally would have served to protect the body of the hall from draughts coming from the doorways. At the west end is the high table and one can imagine the lord of the manor presiding here, sitting in one of the 'thrown' chairs

3.1 *Rufford Old Hall*

14

displayed in this room. This is the furniture design now detailed.

The 'thrown' chair was an Elizabethan chair form which developed a distinctive style of its own. Quite different from the heavy, square-legged mortice and tenon jointed chair construction, it consisted of an assembly of turned spindles interconnected by taper dowel joints. The simplest triangular ones were of plain, practical form, but many were also highly elaborate, with a profusion of turned spindles decorated with bobbins, knobs and finials, etc. These were important chairs, perhaps made for the lord of the manor, and considered a seat of honour for visiting guests. They are sometimes referred to as turned or bobbin chairs, for obvious reasons. The hardwoods commonly used were ash, elm, walnut and fruitwoods. Oak was not used because it was harder and less amenable to turning. It is possible that the chair form evolved in part due to the early craft guilds, which jealously guarded the skills of their members. Because of guild rivalry, it was difficult to mix joinery and turnery, and hence the 'thrown' chair

3.3 *Corner post detail*

is almost totally spindle turned. It is of note that a turner's charter was granted in 1604.

Some authorities suggest that four-legged thrown chairs are more common than three-legged ones. My own study suggests the reverse. A plausible explanation could be related to the unevenness of medieval building floors, on which a three-legged chair will stand firm wherever you put it, unlike a four-legged one. For this reason, there could have been a preference for making three-legged chairs. Rufford Old Hall has a collection of thrown chairs in a mixture of three and four-legged designs, and our chair design is an example of the former.

Construction

The general arrangement of the thrown chair is given in Fig 3.4. The construction is principally an exercise in spindle turning and fitting together of the components. Details of the spindle-turned parts are

3.2 *Thrown chair*

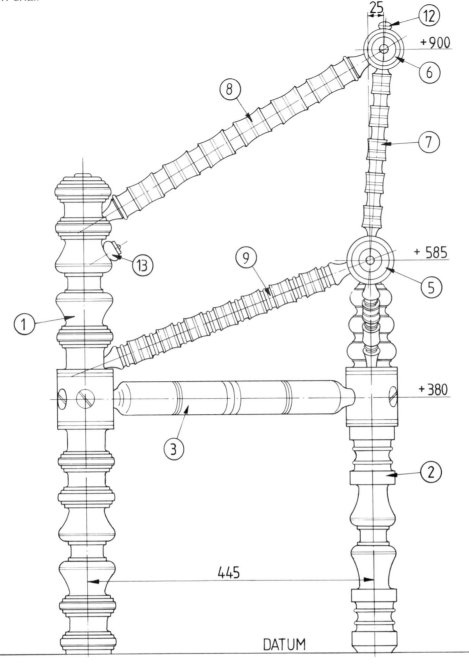

SIDE ELEVATION

3.4 *General arrangement of thrown chair*

given in Figs 3.5 and 3.6. The maximum length between centres required is approximately 750mm, which most small lathes will accommodate, and there should be no machining problems. It was somewhat difficult to ascertain the wood from which the original was made, but it may be walnut.

The order of assembly is first to fit the legs (1) and (2) to the seat rails (3). A detail of the dowel cross-connection, which is fixed by wedges, is given in Fig 3.7. Note the differing diameters of the seat rail dowel ends necessary for an assembly to be effected.

If they were the same size, one would cut the other in half. The seat (4) fits into a groove in the side rails. The remaining components are progressively added to the assembly, finishing with the crest and back bar (5), (6), intermediate spindle splates (7), armrests (8), etc.

The chair is in principle a pegged assembly, but the joints could also be glued if required. Pegging should not be done until all the components fit together satisfactorily. The spigot holes that connect the various items are best machined under a drill press with a tilting table facility. The turned item is set up

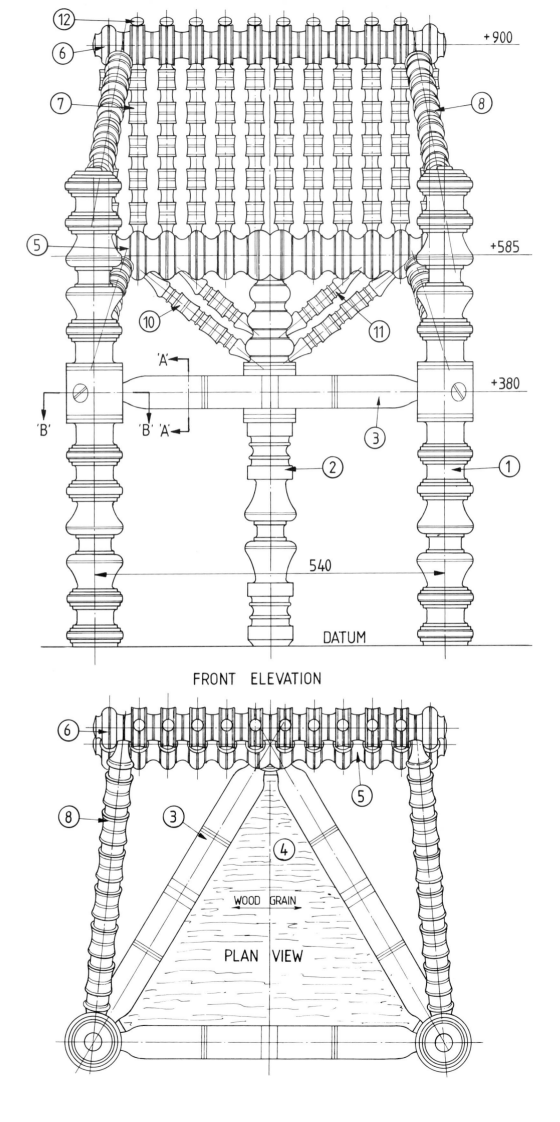

+900

+585

+380

540

DATUM

FRONT ELEVATION

WOOD GRAIN

PLAN VIEW

17

Thrown chair

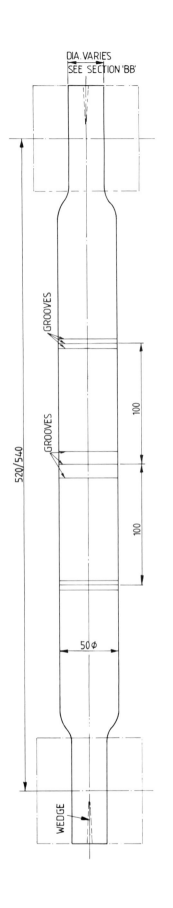

DIA. VARIES
SEE SECTION 'BB'

GROOVES

GROOVES

520/540

100

100

50⌀

WEDGE

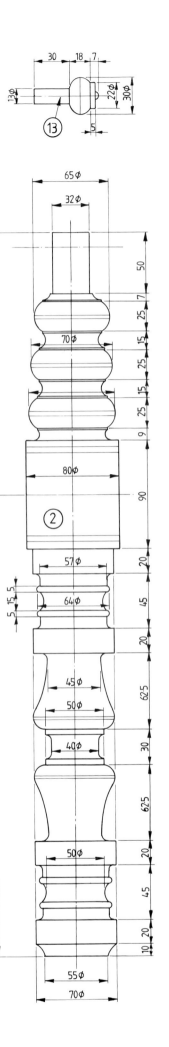

30 18 7

13⌀   22⌀ 30⌀

⑬   5

65⌀

32⌀

216

70⌀

80⌀

②

57⌀

64⌀

45⌀

50⌀

40⌀

50⌀

380

55⌀

70⌀

50

7

25

15

25

15

25

9

90

20

45

20

62.5

30

62.5

20

45

10 20

5 15 5

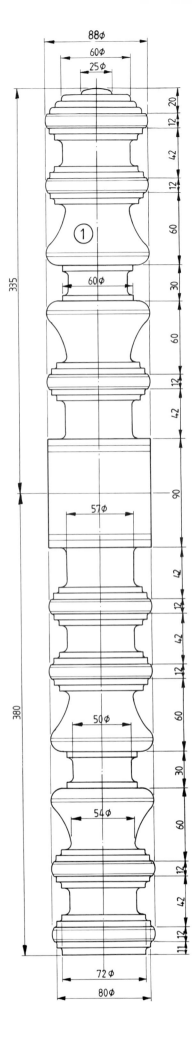

88⌀

60⌀

25⌀

①

60⌀

57⌀

50⌀

54⌀

72⌀

80⌀

335

380

20

12

42

12

60

30

60

12

42

90

42

12

42

12

60

30

60

12

42

11 12

3.5 *Details of legs and rails*

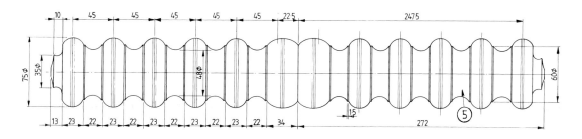

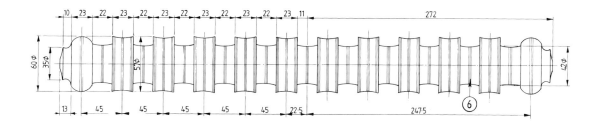

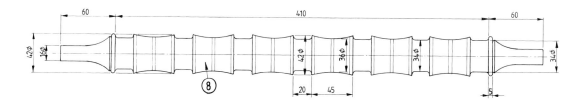

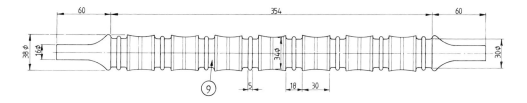

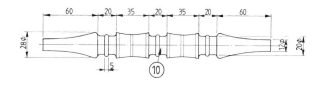

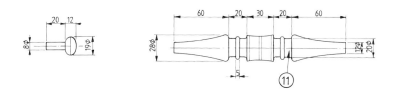

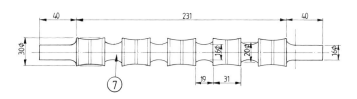

3.6 *Miscellaneous spindle-turned items*

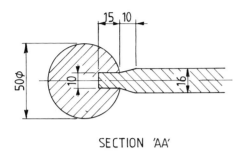

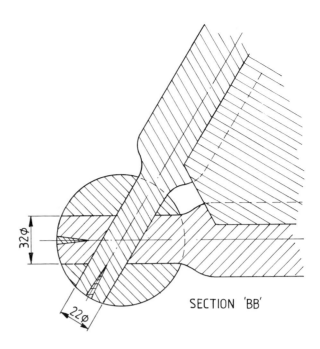

SECTION 'AA'   SECTION 'BB'

3.7 *Leg/seat rail dowel connection*

on engineer's vee blocks clamped to this, and the table tipped as necessary to obtain the correct drilling angle. Make angle templates from stiff card or hardboard, and set these against the side of a dummy 6mm diameter steel bar in the drill chuck. When the angle is correct, lock the table, and replace the dummy steel bar with the drill. The best drills are those of the saw tooth pattern, but ordinary flat bits will do if care is taken when they break through. These bits can also be adapted for special hole sizes by grinding down on the sides.

When completed the chair makes quite an attractive corner piece, and, for comfort, it may be worth making a triangular cushion to fit the seat.

Finally, if you are interested in seeing further examples of thrown chairs besides those at Rufford Old Hall, there are others in the Welsh Folk Museum (Cardiff), Cotehele, NT (Cornwall), Peover Hall (Cheshire) and Levens Hall (Cumbria). There is also an ancient four-legged turned chair in Hereford cathedral which is said to date from 1135. Because of their age,

the best places to find thrown chairs tend to be older, medieval-style manor houses.

Parts list

Item	No	Material	Dimensions (mm)
1 Front leg	2	Walnut	100sq × 770 long
2 Back leg	1	Walnut	90sq × 650 long
3 Seat rail	3	Walnut	57sq × 680 long
4 Seat	1	Oak	200 × 16 × 1000 long
5 Back bar	1	Walnut	80sq × 600 long
6 Crest bar	1	Walnut	70sq × 600 long
7 Spindle splat	11	Walnut	35sq × 350 long
8 Arm rest	2	Walnut	50sq × 570 long
9 Side stretcher	2	Walnut	45sq × 515 long
10 Support strut (1)	2	Walnut	35sq × 300 long
11 Support strut (2)	2	Walnut	35sq × 230 long
12 Finial (1)	11	Walnut	25sq × 55 long
13 Finial (2)	2	Walnut	35sq × 80 long

Chapter 4

Chippendale dining chair

Sharply contrasting with the early English thrown chairs in the Great Hall at Rufford, the adjoining Carolean wing, built in 1662, contains later seventeenth- and eighteenth-century furniture of interest to craftsmen and historians. The drawing room includes two large inlaid press cupboards, one dated 1680, a late seventeenth-century twisted leg side table and an eighteenth-century French secretaire cabinet. In the ante-room is a set of late eighteenth-century Lancashire spindle-back chairs, and in the dining room is a mid-Victorian extending dining table. Surrounding the table is a set of fine quality mahogany Chippendale style dining chairs (c. 1750).

4.1 *Chippendale dining chair*

Thomas Chippendale was pre-eminent at making high quality furniture for England's country houses. He took the earlier heavy baroque style, and developed it to give furniture a lighter, more rhythmic look. He was a master in the art of applying carving to chairs, using intricately carved cabriole legs, and splats with pierced, interlaced, and ribbon-backed figurework, etc. Some of his work is superlative.

The period between 1745 and 1780, generally known as the Chippendale era, does not infer that all high-quality furniture was made by him or his workshop. On the contrary, there were many craftsmen of this period working in this style who could turn out equally high-class furniture.

Some aspects to note on chairs of this period are design, marking, weight, and colour. As regards design, broadly speaking, Chippendale style chairs can be split into two variants: the square leg, and the cabriole. Square leg chairs always have a stretcher arrangement interconnecting the legs, whilst those with cabriole legs rarely have these. The reason for this is probably aesthetic: they simply do not look right with them. Square leg chairs without stretchers immediately raise doubt about their date of origin, and it is likely that they will not be mid-eighteenth-century at all, but rather from a later period.

Chippendale period chairs were customarily marked by the craftsman who made them with the number in the set. This was done in Roman numerals cut with a sharp chisel, usually on the back seat rail beneath the splat. The chair I measured was number four in the set. If the number is arabic, the chair is most likely to be of later date.

Chair weight and colour are also indicators of period. Mid-eighteenth-century chairs were typically made from West Indian mahoganies, such as Cuban and Jamaican varieties. These are much denser than the lighter, softer-grained Honduras mahogany, also called baywood, imported from around 1800. Chippendale chairs were never stained: the colour and acquired patina is the result of two centuries of use, polish, and exposure to the elements. Later reproductions were sometimes stained to imitate Chippendale period chairs. A quick look underneath

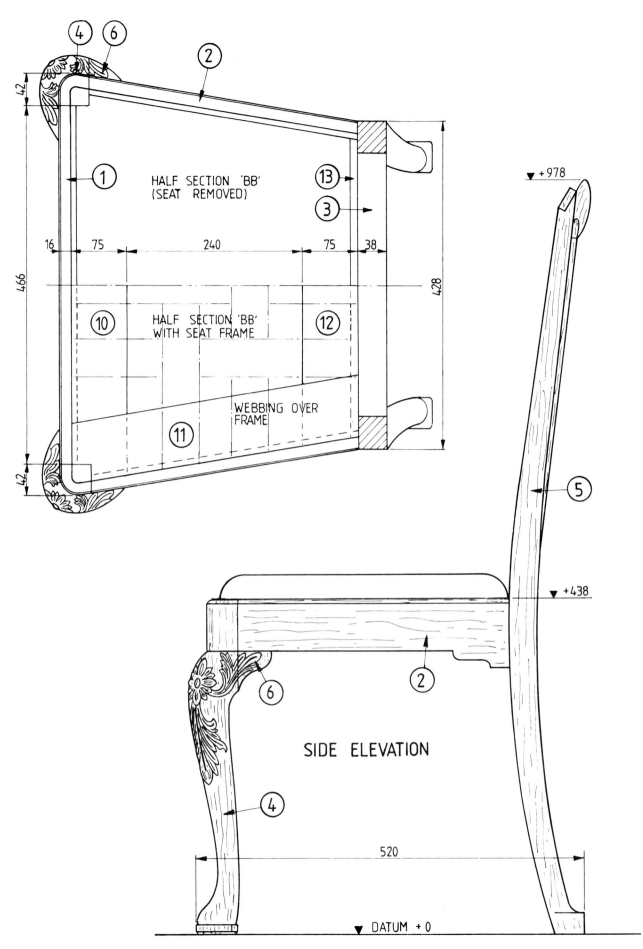

HALF SECTION 'BB'
(SEAT REMOVED)

HALF SECTION 'BB'
WITH SEAT FRAME

WEBBING OVER
FRAME

SIDE ELEVATION

DATUM + 0

4.2 *General arrangement of Chippendale dining chair*

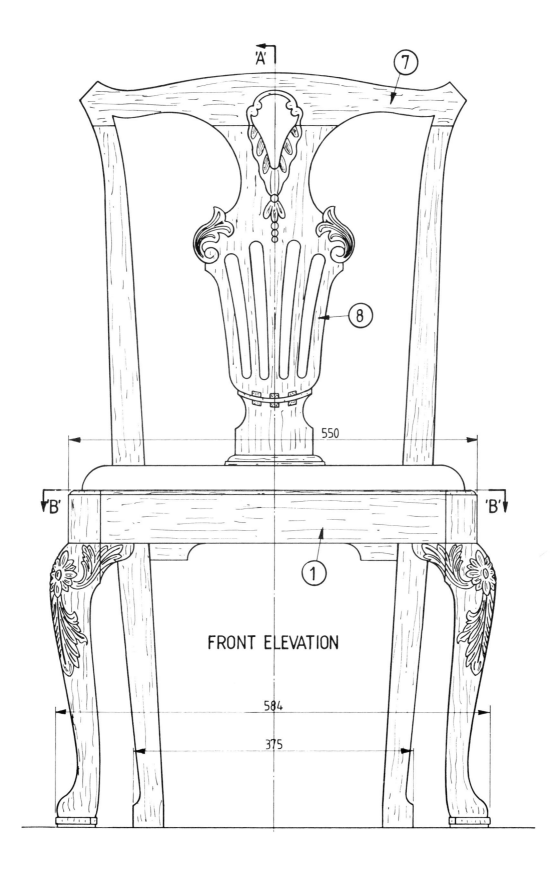

'A'

⑦

⑧

550

'B' 'B'

①

FRONT ELEVATION

584

375

4.3 *Foliate carving on front leg*

sometimes an indicator that the arm-rests were added at a later date.

The Chippendale style chairs from Rufford are of the cabriole leg form with an oval patera and foliate carving on the knee, standing on trifid feet. The back has a wavy line crest rail and a pierced vase splat with pendant carving. The seat is of the drop-in type,

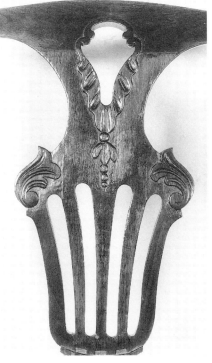

4.5 *Back splat carving*

the seat may reveal evidence that a stain has been used. Colour variations may also suggest replacement parts have been added. However, this is a common aspect generally applicable to all period furniture.

One further point about Chippendale period chair sets which include arm-chairs is the width of the front legs. Those on an arm-chair are usually 50mm or so wider than on the side chairs. If the front leg width is the same on both the arm and side chairs, this is

with stamped original leather covers which are richly painted and gilded. They are very comfortable chairs to sit in, and would complement the Gillow extending table design in Chapter 13.

Construction

The general arrangement of the Chippendale dining chair is given in Fig 4.2, and sectional details of the seat, etc, in Fig 4.6. The skills required to make it are joinery, carving of the front legs and back splat, and seat upholstery.

Front and rear legs

Details of the front and rear legs are given in Figs 4.7 and 4.8. A squared background is given to aid the transfer of the shape to the wood. When tracing the front leg pattern, allow for extra thickness in the area of the knee section for the relief carving. The middle part of the cabriole leg is circular and a number of

4.4 *Front chair leg foot detail*

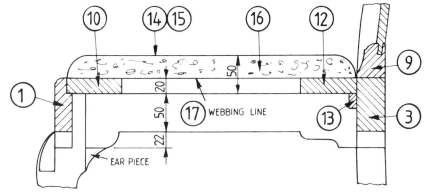

PART SECTION 'AA'

EAR PIECE

WEBBING LINE

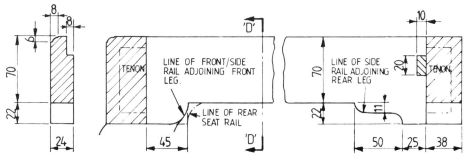

SECTION 'DD'

SEAT RAIL DETAILS

TENON

LINE OF FRONT/SIDE RAIL ADJOINING FRONT LEG.

LINE OF REAR SEAT RAIL

LINE OF SIDE RAIL ADJOINING REAR LEG

TENON

'D'

'D'

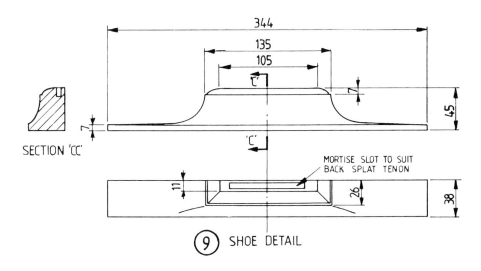

SECTION 'CC'

'C'

'C'

MORTISE SLOT TO SUIT BACK SPLAT TENON

⑨ SHOE DETAIL

4.6 *Sectional details of Chippendale dining chair*

Chippendale dining chair

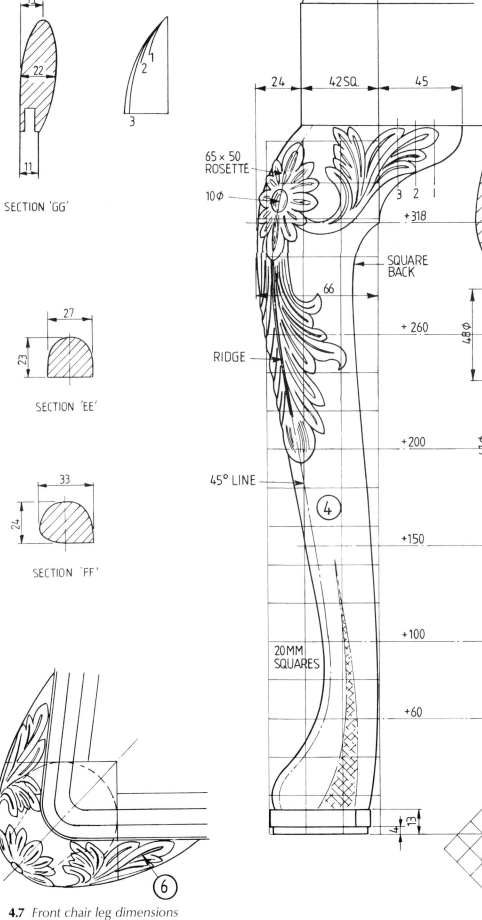

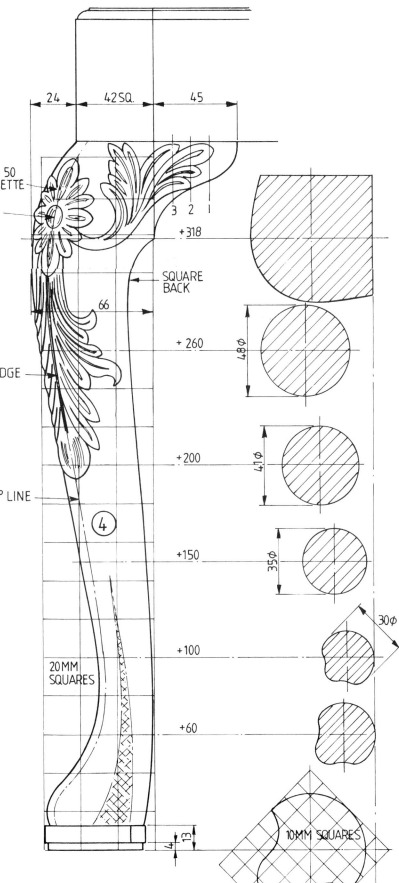

SECTION 'GG'

13
22
11

1
2
3

65 × 50 ROSETTE
10 ∅

SECTION 'EE'
27
23

SECTION 'FF'
33
24

RIDGE

45° LINE

20 MM SQUARES

24 | 42 SQ. | 45

+ 318
SQUARE BACK
66
+ 260
+ 200
④
+150
+100
+60

3 2 1

4.8 ∅
4.1 ∅
35 ∅
30 ∅

10MM SQUARES

13
4

⑥

4.7 *Front chair leg dimensions*

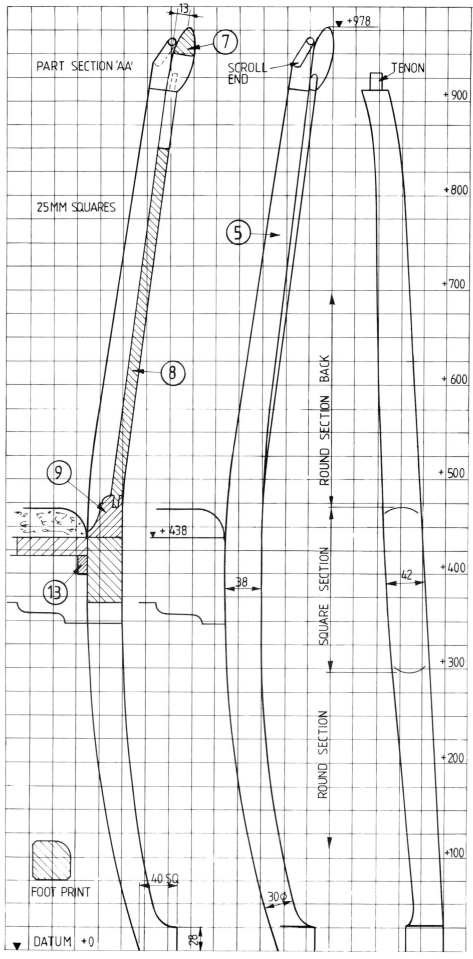

PART SECTION 'AA'

25MM SQUARES

SCROLL END

TENON

⑦

⑤

⑧

⑨

⑬

ROUND SECTION BACK

SQUARE SECTION

ROUND SECTION

FOOT PRINT

DATUM +0

13

+978

+900

+800

+700

+600

+500

+438

+400

+300

+200

+100

38

42

40 SQ

30∅

28

4.8 *Back chair leg details*

27

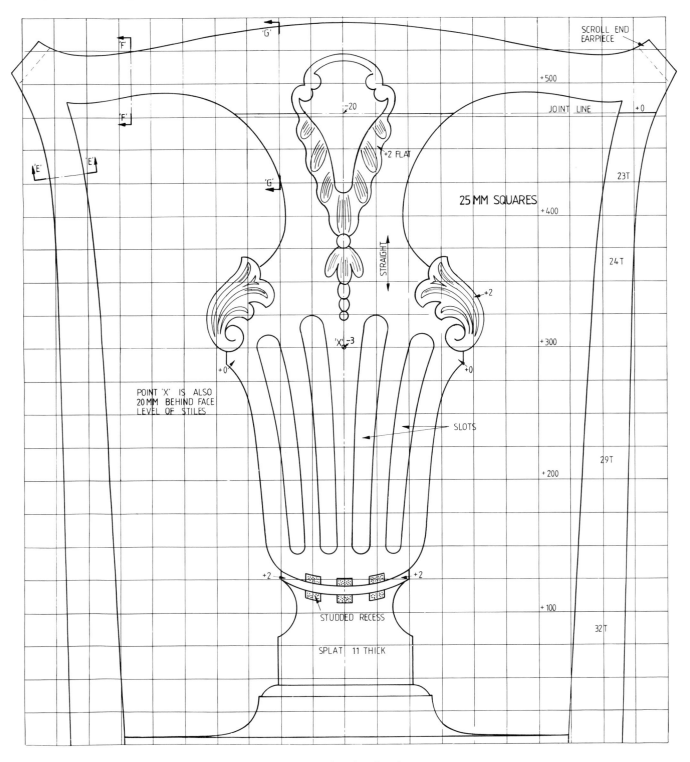

4.9 *Back splat details*

sections are given. The trifid foot shape needs careful marking and carving. For further guidance, the front leg is illustrated in Figs 4.3 and 4.4.

Framework

The framework is a mortise-and-tenon construction with the legs connected by front, side and back rails (1), (2) and (3). The front and side rails have a moulded edge, and are internally rebated to fit the drop-in seat. Routing, saw bench and scratch stock techniques can be employed to shape these. The back of the seat is supported on a wood strip (13).

Back splat

Details of the back splat are given in Fig 4.9: again, a squared background is given for transfer purposes. The splat is nominally 11mm thick, but additional thickness is required in the carved area, and also to accommodate the slightly bowed configuration. The pierced sections are cut with a fretsaw and then cleaned up. The splat carving is easier than that on the legs. The splat is tenoned into the crest rail and shoe. It is impossible to tell how the shoe is connected to the back rail (3), but it is suggested that a loose tenon strip is made acting as a bridge between the two items, rather than depending upon a glued joint alone, as this has little shear stiffness. A french polish finish is suggested for the chair.

Seat upholstery

The drop-in seat is made from a half jointed beech wood frame. This is then upholstered in the conventional manner using webbing, hessian, stuffing and a cover to personal taste. Some brief notes on upholstery tools, etc. are given in Chapter 20.

Parts list

Item	No	Material	Dimensions (mm)
1 Front rail	1	Mahogany	92 × 24 × 550 long
2 Side rail	2	Mahogany	92 × 24 × 450 long
3 Back rail	1	Mahogany	92 × 38 × 430 long
4 Front leg	2	Mahogany	66sq × 440 long
5 Back leg/stile	2	Mahogany	120 × 42 × 950 long
6 Ear piece	4	Mahogany	45 × 22 × 50 long
7 Crest rail	1	Mahogany	75 × 55 × 520 long
8 Splat	1	Mahogany	230 × 15 × 475 long
9 Shoe	1	Mahogany	45 × 38 × 350 long
10 Seat frame (front)	1	Beech	75 × 20 × 520 long
11 Seat frame (side)	2	Beech	75 × 20 × 400 long
12 Seat frame (back)	1	Beech	75 × 20 × 430 long
13 Support strip	1	Mahogany	20 × 10 × 350 long
14 Seat cover	1	Leather	Quantity to suit
15 Hessian cover	–	Hessian	Quantity to suit
16 Stuffing	–	Horsehair	Quantity to suit
17 Webbing	–	Webbing	50 wide, length to suit

Chapter 5

Oyster veneer chest

Wythenshawe Hall, on the southern perimeter of Manchester, is a brown-on-white timber-frame building. It has a wide variety of period furniture, and the designs I have selected from here are a William and Mary oyster veneer chest (*c.* 1690) and an Oak hooded rocking cradle (*c.* 1650).

The hall, possibly constructed on the site of an older medieval building, was built in about 1540 by Robert Tatton, and has been altered by subsequent generations. It was eventually acquired by Sir Ernest Simon, a local industrialist, and he gave the hall to Manchester City Corporation in 1926. It is now administered by Manchester City Art Gallery.

Wythenshawe Hall has two fine quality William and Mary oyster veneer chests in the eighteenth-century bedroom. Their similarity suggests initially that they might have been a pair, but closer inspection reveals this is not the case. One has period drawer handles of the axe-drop pattern, and the other has pear-drop handles. The overall dimensions are also slightly different, and there are variations in the oyster veneer work.

The chest design here is for the version with the pear-drop handles. It has a graduated drawer arrangement, with two short and three long drawers.

5.1 *Wythenshawe Hall*

5.2 *Oyster veneer chest*

The top, sides and drawer fronts are veneered with walnut oyster marquetry squares, with crossbanded edges separated by box or whitewood strings. A circular geometric marquetry pattern is used on the top and sides. The chest stands on typical period bun feet (see also Chapter 11, walnut side table). The drawers are lined with pale blue lining paper.

5.3 *Drawer detail*

30

5.4 *Chest top*

Construction

The general arrangement is given in Fig 5.5, and additional chest sections shown in Fig 5.6. The skills required are cabinet work, woodturning for the bun feet, and some high-quality veneer work. Problems may arise in the acquisition of the oyster veneer squares, but some suggestions for overcoming this are given below. The suggested order of construction is to start with the carcase and mount it on its bun feet, then make the drawers, and finally, add the veneer work.

Chest carcase

It is extremely difficult to check the original carcase jointing, mainly because of the veneer covering on all sides. However, it probably utilizes a dovetail construction similar to the American double chest (Chapter 18, Fig 18.4). The chest framework thus comprises the top, bottom, and sides (1), (2) and (3), with the latter jointing horizontally into the top and bottom boards. The panels should be prepared with all necessary grooving, etc, ready to accept the dust boards (5), and the back (4). The use of blockboard could be considered as an alternative in place of a pine plank carcase, although it would not of course be authentic.

The dust-boards (5) and drawer division (6) have semi-elliptic walnut lipping (10) applied to the front edges. The sides (2) also have this lipping on the faces adjacent to the drawers (Fig 5.7). This conveniently serves to conceal the dust-board grooves cut in these panels. The lipping is mitred at the interconnections. The edging around the top of the chest appears to be an applied sandwich piece stuck to the perimeter, made of thin oyster squares stuck to a triangular pinewood base, and rounded over to suit. Along the

chest bottom edge there is another decorative strip (9), with a similar sandwich construction. The latter should not be added, however, until the bun feet have been finished.

The bun feet are spindle-turned from solid walnut, and fixed with the support block (11) to the underside of the chest, thus making it free-standing.

Drawers

Details of the oak drawers, which are of standard dovetail construction, are given in Fig 5.8. A table is given with dimensions for each drawer. The direction of the drawer bottom grain is across the width. You could consider finishing the drawers internally, as in the original, with blue lining paper.

Oyster veneer work

The top and ends of the chest have a geometric veneer pattern with a crossbanded edge. Details of the design on the end panel are given in Fig 5.5, and that for the chest top in Fig 5.9.

The biggest problem in veneering the carcase will be to obtain the oyster veneer squares. These are made from small walnut branches cut transversely into thin rings, and you may have to search a bit to acquire them, or even have to make your own. A cut across the branch is not ideal from the seasoning point of view, and the risk of radial cracks will be high. The oyster squares on the original chest were not immune from this problem. To some degree, however, these cracks add character to the design, and with some skilful filling they should not be too noticeable.

The drawer fronts are veneered with oyster veneer squares as indicated in Fig 5.8, the top drawers (1) having a single row of squares, and drawers (2), (3) and (4) double rows of squares. The drawers are crossbanded around the edge with an inset box or whitewood string, to separate it from the oyster veneer centres.

Metalwork

Details of the metalwork items are given in Fig 5.7 and include the pear-drop handles and backing plates, escutcheon plates and locks. These are commercially available, with the exception of the escutcheon plate, where you may have to compromise a bit by accepting a pattern similar to the pear-drop backing plates.

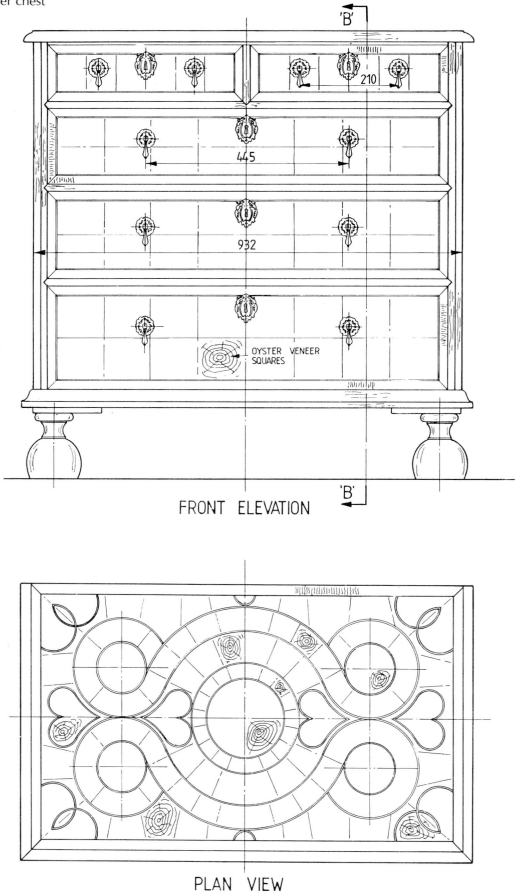

FRONT ELEVATION

PLAN VIEW

5.5 *General arrangement of oyster veneer chest*

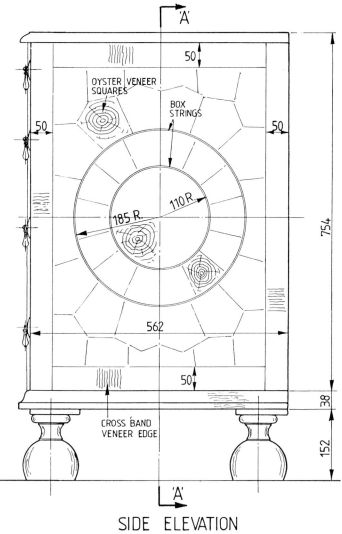

SIDE ELEVATION

Labels on drawing: 'A', 50, OYSTER VENEER SQUARES, BOX STRINGS, 50, 50, 185 R., 110 R., 754, 562, 50, 38, 152, CROSS BAND VENEER EDGE, 'A'

Parts list

Item	No	Material	Dimensions (mm)
1 Top panel	1	Pine	587 × 24 × 980 long
2 Side panel	2	Pine	562 × 30 × 778 long
3 Bottom panel	1	Pine	587 × 24 × 932 long
4 Back	1	Pine	252 × 12 × 3000 long total
5 Dustboard	5	Pine	550 × 15 × 900 long
6 Drawer partition	2	Pine	125 × 15 × 550 long
7 Spacer strip	1	Walnut	24 × 5 × 872 long

Item	No	Material	Dimensions (mm)
8 Top edging strip	–	Walnut	40 × 10 × 2200 long total
9 Bottom cover strip	1	Walnut	50 × 10 × 2200 long total on a softwood fillet piece
10 Lipping	–	Walnut	15 × 10 × 4350 long total
11 Support block	4	Pine	110 × 26 × 150 long
12 Bun foot	4	Walnut	130sq × 170 long
Drawer 1			
13 Front	2	Oak	120 × 24 × 430 long
14 Lining	2	Oak	98 × 9 × 1530 long
15 Bottom	2	Oak	185 × 7 × 1300 long
Drawer 2			
16 Front	1	Oak	160 × 24 × 875 long
17 Lining	1	Oak	138 × 9 × 2000 long
Drawer 3			
18 Front	1	Oak	185 × 24 × 875 long
19 Lining	1	Oak	163 × 9 × 2000 long
Drawer 4			
20 Front	1	Oak	215 × 24 × 875 long
21 Lining	1	Oak	193 × 9 × 2000 long
Common drawer items			
22 Bottom	3	Oak	185 × 7 × 1300 long
23 Runner	10	Oak	22 × 9 × 550 long
Metalwork items			
24 Handle pressing	10	Brass	From thin plate 42 diameter
25 Pear-drop handle	10	Brass	Make or purchase to suit
26 Escutcheon plate	5	Brass	Make or purchase to suit
27 Lock	5	Steel	Make or purchase to suit
Miscellaneous			
28 Walnut veneer	–	Walnut	Plain and oyster burr veneer obtained to suit
29 Box stringing	–	Box	Quantity to suit

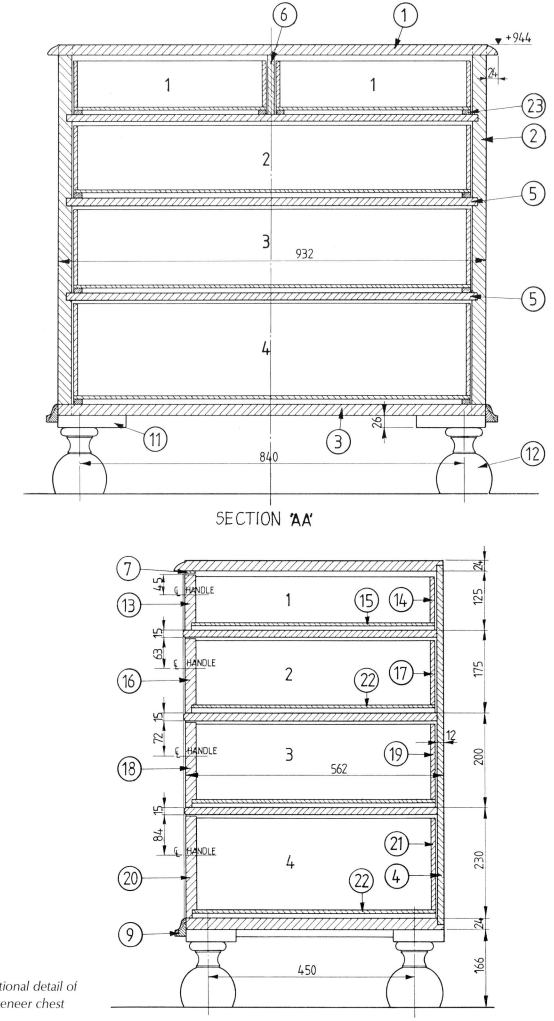

SECTION 'AA'

5.6 *Sectional detail of oyster veneer chest*

SECTION 'BB'

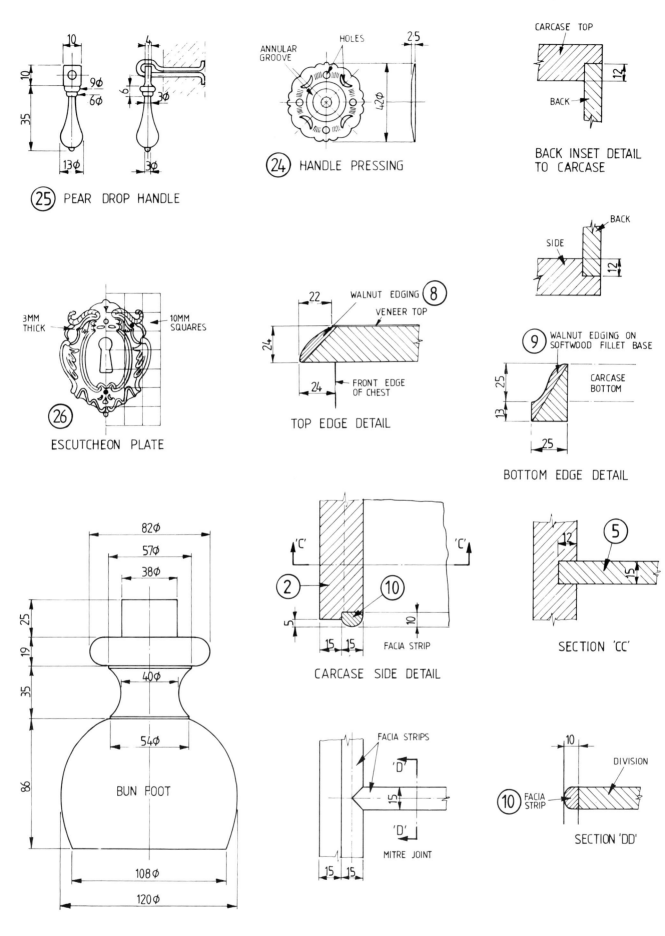

25 PEAR DROP HANDLE

24 HANDLE PRESSING

HOLES
ANNULAR GROOVE
2.5
42∅

CARCASE TOP
BACK
12

BACK INSET DETAIL
TO CARCASE

ESCUTCHEON PLATE
3MM THICK
10MM SQUARES
26

22
24
24
WALNUT EDGING
VENEER TOP
8
FRONT EDGE OF CHEST

TOP EDGE DETAIL

SIDE
BACK
12

WALNUT EDGING ON SOFTWOOD FILLET BASE
9
CARCASE BOTTOM
25
13
25

BOTTOM EDGE DETAIL

82∅
57∅
38∅
25
19
35
40∅
54∅
86
BUN FOOT
108∅
120∅

'C'   'C'
2   10
5
15   15
FACIA STRIP

CARCASE SIDE DETAIL

12
5
15

SECTION 'CC'

FACIA STRIPS
'D'
15
'D'
15   15
MITRE JOINT

10
DIVISION
10
FACIA STRIP

SECTION 'DD'

Oyster veneer chest

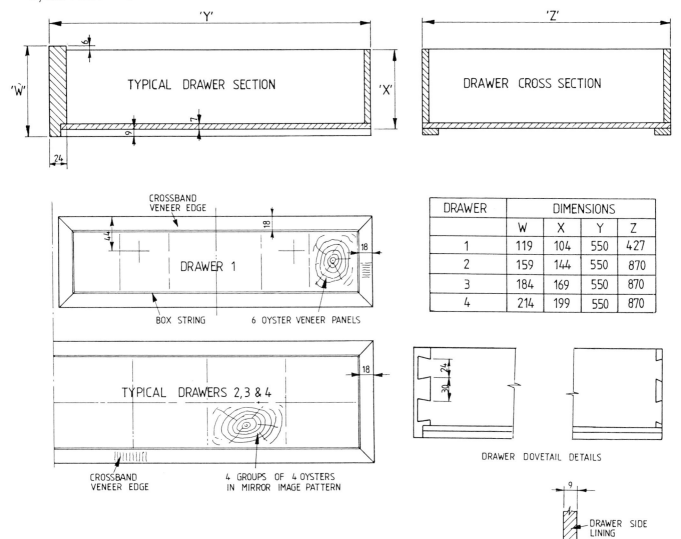

DRAWER	DIMENSIONS			
	W	X	Y	Z
1	119	104	550	427
2	159	144	550	870
3	184	169	550	870
4	214	199	550	870

5.8 *Drawer dimensions*

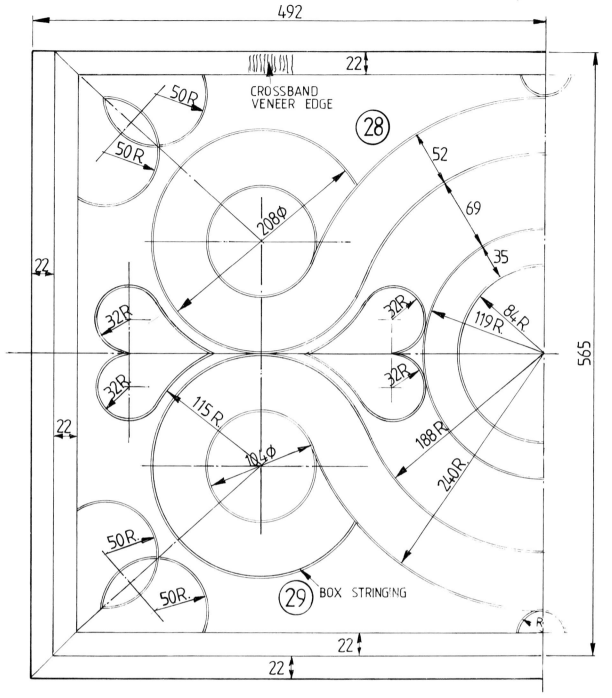

HALF PLAN VIEW

5.9 *Chest top geometric pattern*

Chapter 6

Hooded rocking cradle

Early rocking cradles are of two kinds. One swings suspended from a free-standing frame, while the other rocks back and forth on its own integral rockers. Wythenshawe Hall has both types. In the eighteenth-century bedroom there is a caned style swinging cradle, and in the Chapel bedroom there is an Oak hooded rocking cradle (c. 1650), the second furniture design featured from this hall.

The design of early rocking cradles, ie the rocker type, has similarities with chests and coffers (see Chapters 1 and 2). The simplest are of the plank type, while the more elaborate have a framed construction with fielded panels and pegged joints. The latter may be of a plain rectangular form, or can be more elaborate with a hood at one end, as in the design here. Like four poster beds, rocking cradles were in many ways status symbols; the better examples were often richly carved, and handed down from generation to generation. The rocking cradle at Wythenshawe Hall must have been a prized possession. It is carved with lozenges and flower heads on the hood, and on the sides and ends with foliate patterns amid circular pattern flute work. The hood has a carved frieze and the cradle stands on scroll end rockers.

6.1 *Hooded rocking cradle*

6.2 *Foot panel*

6.3 *Head end panels*

Construction

The general arrangement and sectional details of the cradle are given in Fig 6.4. The skills required to make it are joinery, carving on the panels, and some minor spindle turning. The suggested order of construction is to assemble the cradle framework complete with its panels first, then complete the carving work. If, however, you feel that the carving aspect is too difficult to attempt, the cradle could be left plain.

38

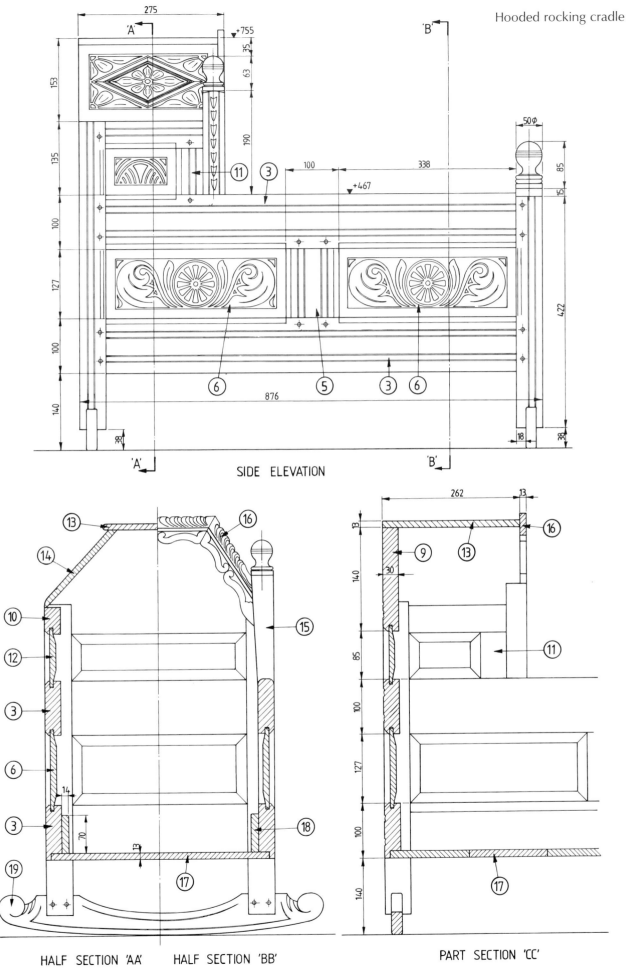

SIDE ELEVATION

HALF SECTION 'AA'   HALF SECTION 'BB'   PART SECTION 'CC'

6.4 *General arrangement of rocking cradle (cont. overleaf)*

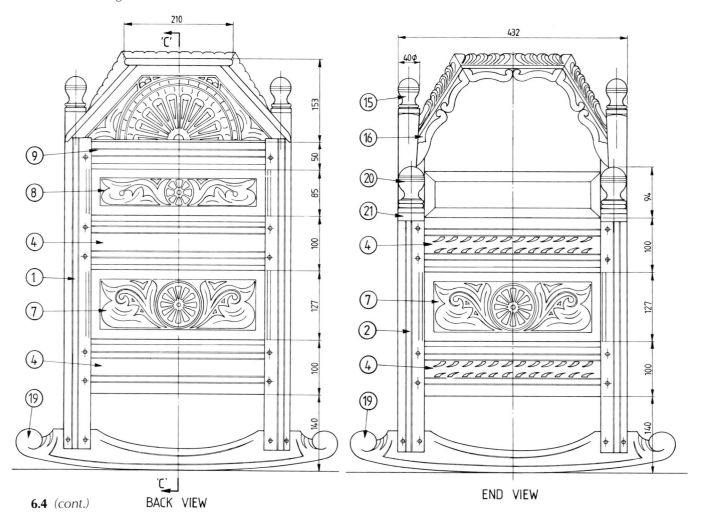

6.4 *(cont.)*   BACK VIEW

END VIEW

6.5 *Hood panel*

Framework

First build the two side frames. These consist of upper and lower rails (3) connected at either end by corner posts (1), (2), and in the centre by a muntin (5). Also fitted at this point are the hood rail (10), muntin (11),

and the hood post (15). All jointing is by pegged mortise and tenons, but no pegging is carried out at this preliminary stage, while the fielded panels have yet to be added. The rails and corner posts, etc, should be finished with all necessary grooving ready for the fielded panels, and also the floor boarding.

The side frames are joined at either end by rails (4) and the hood panel (9) tenoned into the corner posts. These rails are grooved ready for the fielded panels, etc. After this preliminary assembly, the frame is dismantled to finish other miscellaneous work. This includes preparation of the corner post bottom ends ready to take the rockers, and these can now be made. The rocker pattern is given in Fig 6.6. The ornamental beadwork on the rails is also completed using a scratch stock. The knob finials on the hood and foot posts are turned and added.

Carved panels

Details of the panels fitting in between the rails and posts are given in Figs 6.7, 6.8 and 6.9. These panels

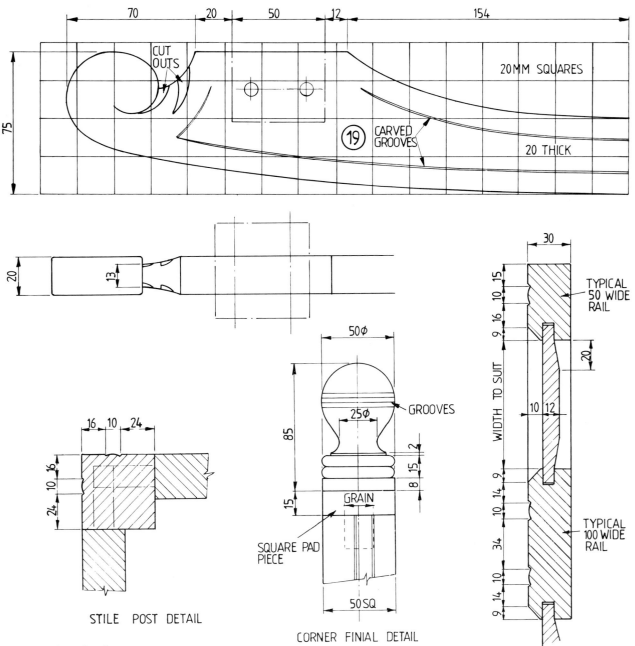

6.6 Rocker details

are flat on the carved face, and fielded on the inside, as shown in Fig 6.6. They should be prepared initially as plain panels without carving. A preliminary assembly of the whole cradle is then carried out, including fitting the panels into the grooved rails. When this is satisfactory, dismantle, and remove the panels ready for carving, as it is easier to carve these individually as loose items.

The panel patterns are given on a squared background to aid transfer to the wood. A number of sections are also given to assist in the carving aspect, together with the illustrations in Figs 6.2, 6.3 and 6.5. These should be sufficient to complete the work, but

if you are still uncertain about some aspect, a visit to Wythenshawe Hall may be useful. The groundwork within the pattern is not cut away very deeply, but needs to be of uniform profile. A simple depth gauge can be made from a flat piece of wood with a matchstick stuck through it in a tightly fitting hole.

Final assembly

Having finished all the major joinery and carcase work, final assembly can now be completed. In the original, of course, no glue was used on the framework, which was held together by pegs through

41

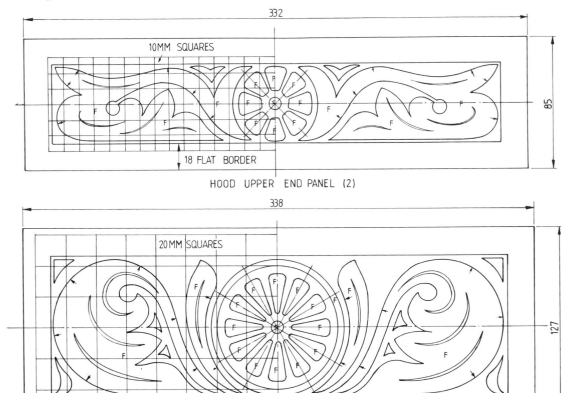

HOOD UPPER END PANEL (2)

SIDE PANEL (1)

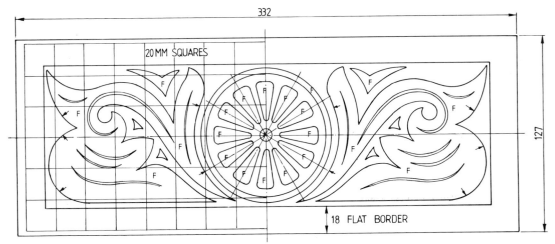

END PANEL (1)

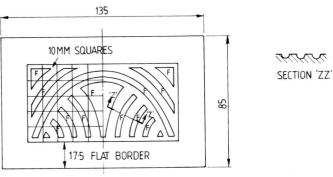

SECTION 'ZZ'

6.7 *Side and end panel details*

SIDE PANEL (2)

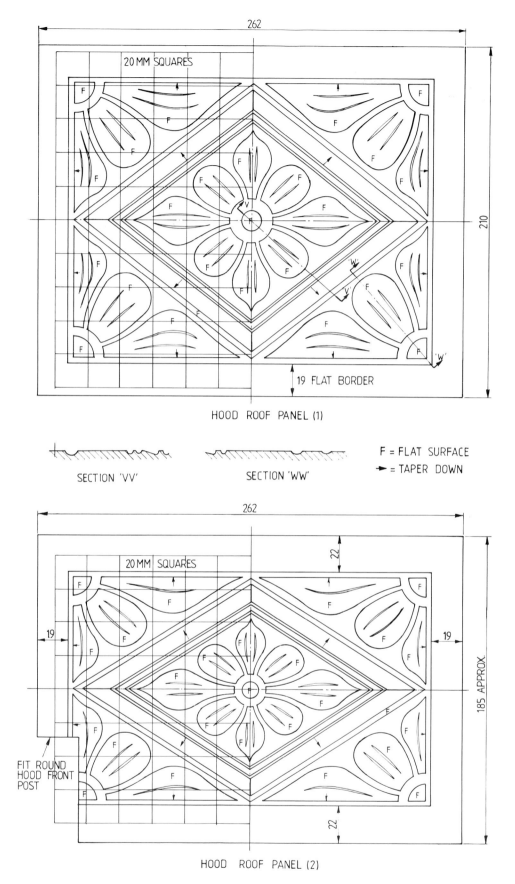

HOOD ROOF PANEL (1)

SECTION 'VV'   SECTION 'WW'   F = FLAT SURFACE
                                    ➤ = TAPER DOWN

HOOD ROOF PANEL (2)

6.8 *Hood panel details (1)*

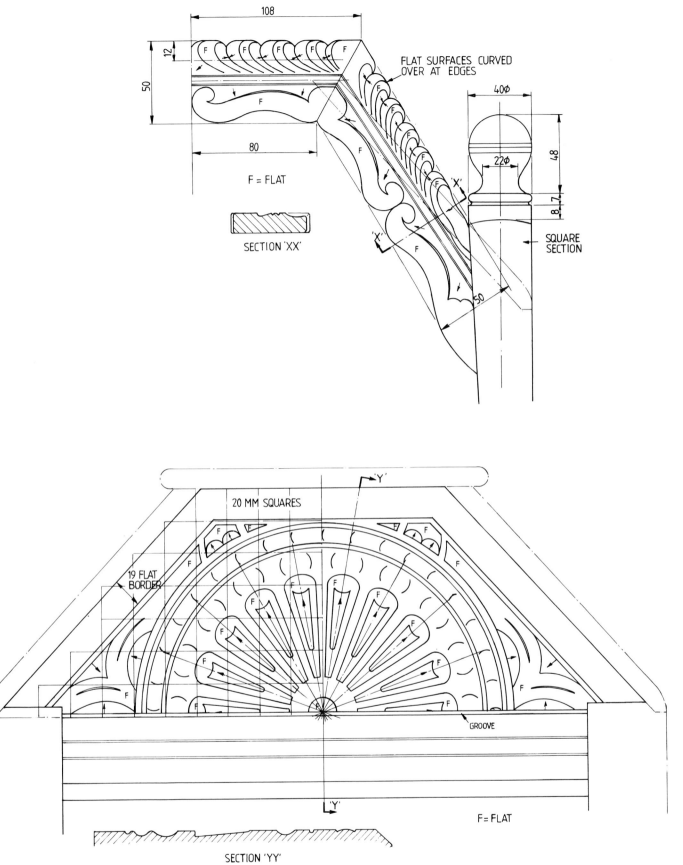

108

12

50

80

F = FLAT

SECTION 'XX'

FLAT SURFACES CURVED
OVER AT EDGES

F

F

F

F

F

F

F

'X'

'X'

F

40∅

22∅

48

8.7

SQUARE
SECTION

50

'Y'

20 MM SQUARES

19 FLAT
BORDER

F

F

F

F

F

F

F

F

F

F

F

F

F

F

F

GROOVE

'Y'

F = FLAT

SECTION 'YY'

6.9 *Hood panel details (2)*

the mortise and tenons. Today the framework can be glued, but the fielded panels within should remain free to take account of any wood movement which may occur later. A dark oak stain with a wax finish is recommended.

Parts list

Item	No	Material	Dimensions (mm)
1 Corner post (1)	2	Oak	50sq × 600 long
2 Corner post (2)	2	Oak	50sq × 440 long
3 Side rail	4	Oak	100 × 30 × 870 long
4 End rail	4	Oak	100 × 30 × 430 long
5 Frame muntin	2	Oak	105 × 30 × 230 long
6 Side panel (1)	4	Oak	150 × 12 × 370 long
7 End panel (1)	2	Oak	150 × 12 × 360 long
8 End panel (2)	1	Oak	110 × 12 × 360 long

Item	No	Material	Dimensions (mm)
9 End panel (hood)	1	Oak	200 × 30 × 430 long
10 Side rail (hood)	2	Oak	50 × 30 × 270 long
11 Hood muntin	2	Oak	50 × 30 × 180 long
12 Side panel (2)	2	Oak	105 × 12 × 155 long
13 Roof panel (1)	1	Oak	210 × 13 × 262 long
14 Roof panel (2)	2	Oak	210 × 13 × 262 long
15 Hood stile	2	Oak	40sq × 340 long
16 Hood fascia	—	Oak	50 × 13 × 650 long total
17 Floor	—	Oak	150 × 13 × 2600 total
18 Support strip	2	Oak	70 × 14 × 780 long
19 Rocker	2	Oak	75 × 20 × 620 long
20 Finial	2	Oak	50sq × 160 long
21 Pad piece	2	Oak	50sq × 15 thick

Chapter 7

Sausage chair

In the search for fine period furniture designs, The American Museum in Britain at Claverton Manor near Bath offers a new dimension together with furniture with a totally different emphasis to interest the craftsman. If you want to learn something about the early colonization of America in a short space of time, you will not regret a visit to Claverton Manor. The museum, on the outskirts of the city, and the only one of its kind in Britain, was founded in 1959 by two enterprising Americans, Dallas Pratt and John Rudky. The house, in Bath stone with a classical south façade, was designed in 1820 by the architect Sir Jeffrey Wyatville. Sir Winston Churchill made his first political speech there in 1897.

The interior rooms are set out in historical order showing various facets of domestic life in the United States of America. Each setting is furnished to portray a different period. Many are lined with panelling brought over from the USA, along with furniture from houses in a number of American States. From these I have picked two traditional chair designs, a late-seventeenth-century Sausage-turned spindle-back chair and a Shaker rocking chair (c. 1820). These illustrate two different aspects of early American life; the beginnings of colonization, and the Shaker religious movement.

7.1 *Claverton Manor*

7.2 *Sausage chair*

The first furniture design is in the Keeping Room which is furnished in seventeenth-century colonial style with a typical low-beamed ceiling, and is set for a Bible reading. The beams and floorboards come from a house in Wrentham, Massachusetts (c. 1690). The furniture includes a New England ladder back chair (seventeenth century), a Connecticut carved oak chest decorated with split spindles (c. 1680), a pedestal table, and a New Jersey sausage-turned spindle back chair (late seventeenth century).

The sausage chair, with its vernacular form and beaded turnings, may possibly have associations with earlier 'thrown' chairs (c. 1600–50) (see Chapter 3). We could speculate that the craftsman who made it, having noted the ornate turnings on these bobbin-style chairs, considered incorporating similar beaded features into his more simple colonial side chair. The attractive sausage turnings on the spindle splats and front stretchers combine with the beaded legs and rush seating to make a harmonious arrangement. The chair back is characteristically straight, as the practice of bending it above the seat by steaming, to make it more accommodating to the human form, had not yet been perfected.

Construction

The general arrangement of the sausage chair is given in Fig 7.3, and details of the individual components in Figs 7.4 and 7.5. Its construction is principally a spindle-turning exercise, followed by fitting the items together, and adding the rush seating. The length between centres required for the spindle-turning work is just under 1000mm. In machining, take some care to match the beadwork and make it with a well-formed profile. The original chair is made in red mulberry, which may be difficult to obtain, particularly in England, and it is suggested that ash is used as an alternative. This timber was commonly used on eighteenth- and nineteenth-century English country furniture, such as the spindle back and ladder back chairs of Lancashire and Cheshire. The rush seating is not difficult to apply, and Fig 7.6 shows the basic procedure for doing this. It can be hard work. The rushes should be wetted overnight to ensure they are in a pliable state for weaving. A wax finish for the chair is suggested.

Parts list

Item	No	Material	Dimensions (mm)
1 Front leg	2	Red mulberry	54sq × 510 long
2 Back leg/stile	2	Red mulberry	54sq × 940 long
3 Spindle rail	2	Red mulberry	30sq × 370 long
4 Spindle splat	4	Red mulberry	30sq × 310 long
5 Seat rail (front)	1	Red mulberry	22 dia × 440 long
6 Seat rail (side/back)	3	Red mulberry	22 dia × 370 long
7 Front stretcher	2	Red mulberry	30sq × 440 long
8 Side/back stretcher	6	Red mulberry	25sq × 370 long
9 Rush seating	–	Rush	Purchase to suit
10 Brass cap	4	Brass	13 diameter dome shape

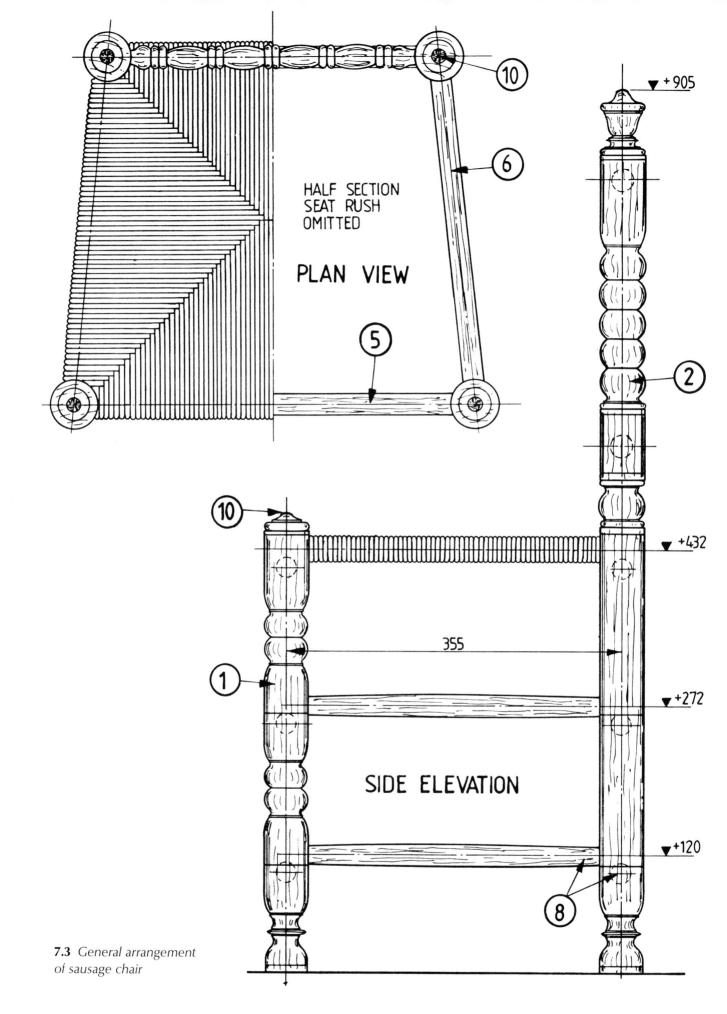

HALF SECTION
SEAT RUSH
OMITTED

PLAN VIEW

⑩

⑥

⑤

▼ +905

②

▼ +432

355

①

▼ +272

SIDE ELEVATION

⑩

▼ +120

⑧

7.3 *General arrangement
of sausage chair*

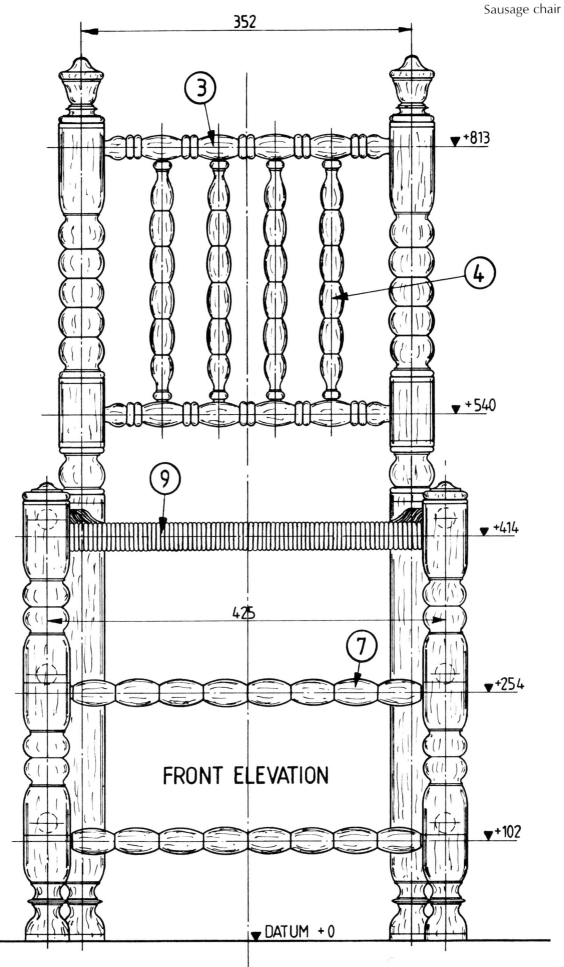

352

③

④

⑨

425

⑦

+813

+540

+414

+254

+102

FRONT ELEVATION

DATUM + 0

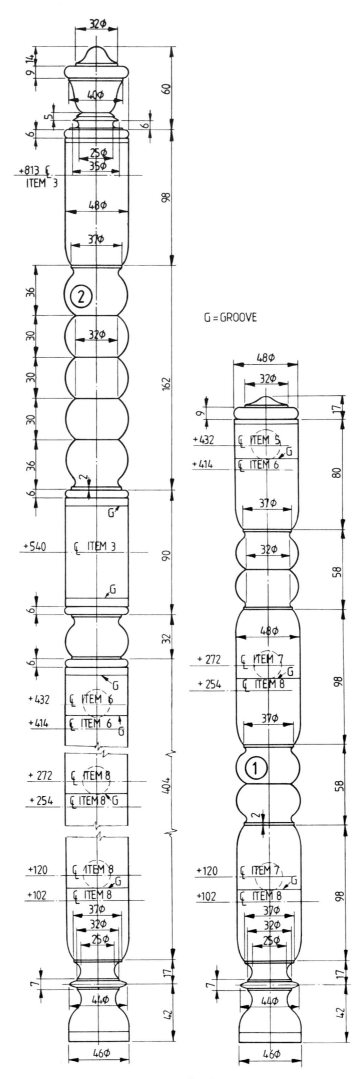

G = GROOVE

50

7.4 Leg details

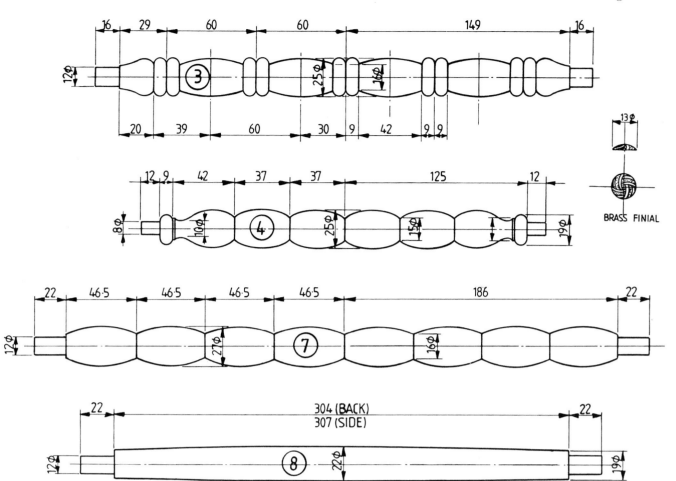

7.5 *Spindle splat and stretcher details*

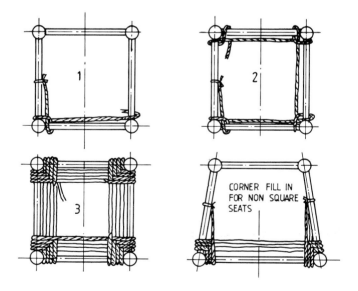

7.6 *Rush seating*

Chapter 8

Shaker rocking chair

The second furniture design from the American Museum in Britain is from the Shaker collection, and is a Shaker rocking chair (c. 1820) from Hancock, Massachusetts. A simple, austere piece, utilitarian but beautifully made, it is unquestionably Shaker, and is a fine example of the unique style of furniture that evolved with the movement started by Mother Ann Lee in 1774. She became associated with the 'Quaking Shakers' in her early 30s. After her release from prison, where she was held because of her preachings, she left England with a number of others, and formed the Shaker movement in Watervliet, Albany, USA. Shakers were a religious Utopian sect who believed in celibacy and called themselves the 'United Society of Believers of Christ's Second Appearing'. They became known as Shakers because of their early prayer meetings, during which the participants exhibited erratic dancing and shaking movements.

Shaker lives were based on the principles of order, harmony and utility. They had a number of maxims, including, 'Put your hands to work and your hearts to God', and, 'Do your work as though you had a thousand years to live and as if you were to die tomorrow'. At its peak in the 1840s the Shakers had over 6000 members living in self-sufficient communities. It was an empty sort of life, where meals were taken in silence and conversation not encouraged, which probably explains why today only one Shaker village remains, at Sabathday Lake in Maine.

Shaker furniture

Shaker furniture is uniquely simple, totally functional and instantly recognizable. It was built to harmonize with Shaker living rooms, traditionally painted white with pale blue window surrounds. Shaker designs decried the use of expensive woods such as mahogany and rosewood, and veneer inlays and complicated carvings were never employed. Instead, they preferred to work with woods like cherry, pine and maple, and the furniture was made for a specific purpose, with a classical, uncluttered form.

When not in use, chairs were hung up on a peg rail surrounding the room, leaving a clean and empty floor space for the Shakers to perform their prayer recitations and rhythmic dances. The Shaker rocking chair, as in Fig 8.1, with its rockers stopped at the front, thus presents the minimum of interference when hung up for these activities.

Shaker rocking chair

The general arrangement of the Shaker rocking chair is given in Fig 8.2. Details of the armrest and back slat are shown in Fig 8.3 and of the back stile and rocker, etc, in Fig 8.4. The construction is principally a turning exercise, followed by fitting together of the parts, and then completion of the seat weaving. The longest turned component is the back stile, which requires a length between centres of approximately 1400mm, and use of a lathe steady is recommended. Note that each front leg is a one-piece turning complete with its mushroom top. By careful timber selection, it should be possible to economize on hardwood usage, though if necessary these could be machined as separate parts and carefully spigotted together. The shape of the armrest and rocker are given on a squared background to aid transfer to the wood.

Back slats

The profile of the curved back splat is given in Fig 8.3. Steam bending techniques (see D. Bryant, 'Bending hoop rims for spinning wheels', *Practical Woodworking*, January 1988 p 794–6) are required to shape these to the curvature indicated. Cherry is suitable for steam bending, and as the slats are only 6mm thick, no problems should be experienced. For safety reasons, steam bending should be undertaken outdoors. The timber must be of top quality, without shakes or knots.

The equipment needed is a steaming chamber together with a strong timber mould of the required profile, round which to clamp the wood strip after it has been made suitably plastic. The mould shape should be equal to or slightly tighter than the inside curvature of the slat. This will allow for possible

8.1 *Shaker chair*

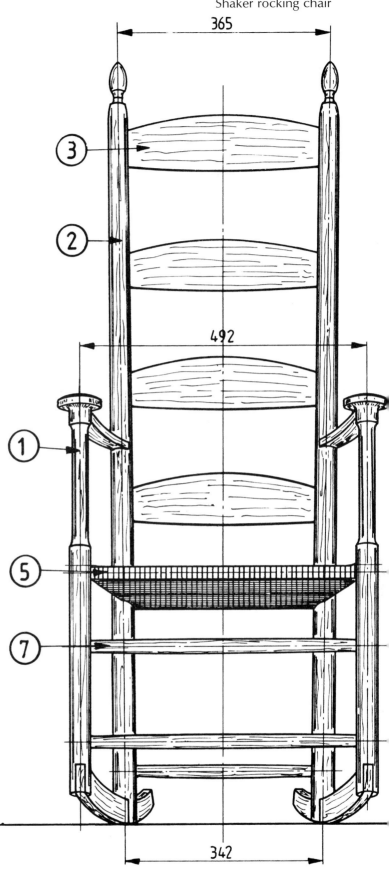

365

③

②

492

①

⑤

⑦

342

FRONT ELEVATION

8.2 *General arrangement of Shaker chair*

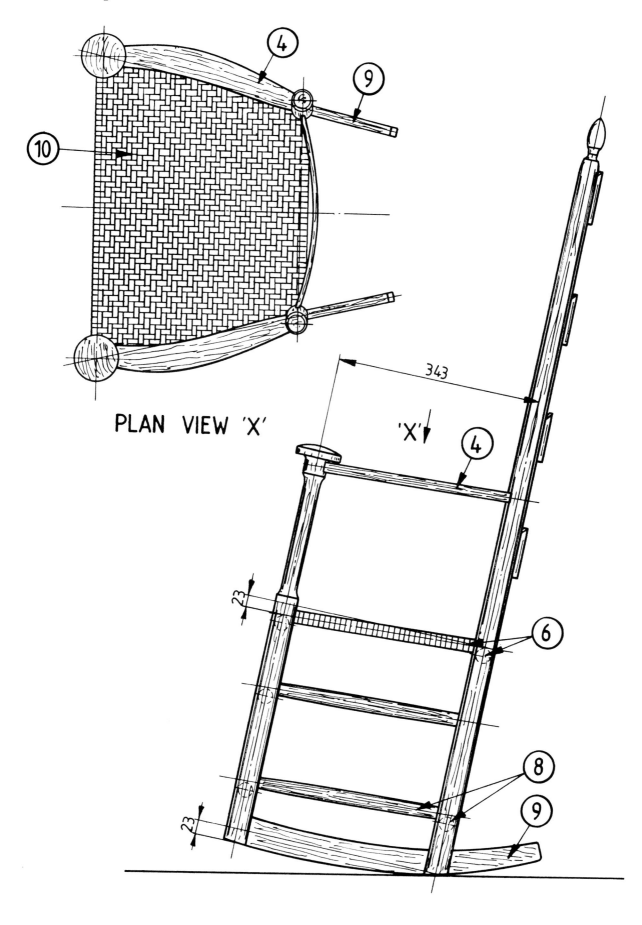

PLAN VIEW 'X'

SIDE ELEVATION

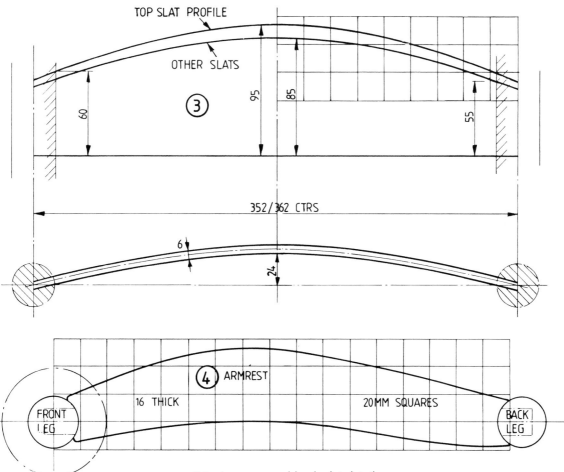

8.3 *Arm rest and back slat details*

spring-back after bending and drying out. The steaming time is roughly one hour per 25mm of thickness, so the back slats will only require about twenty minutes' steaming.

When removing the slat from the steamer, you only have about one minute to fix it round the mould before it looses its plasticity, so all necessary clamps should be ready to hand for this operation. If you do not succeed the first time, put the slat back in the steamer, reheat it and try again. Always handle the heated timber strip with leather gloves to protect against scalding.

Assembly and seat weaving

When the turned parts, slats, armrests and rockers are finished, with all necessary spigot holes and cut-outs, etc, a preliminary assembly can be carried out, and when this is satisfactory it can be glued together. The chair finishing and polishing is carried out before the addition of the woven seat.

In the original the seat is made from wood splint, which may be difficult to obtain. An alternative is a strong fabric tape, which was also used on original

Shaker chairs. Cane and rush were other seat materials used by the Shakers, but these are not so appropriate here. The seat pattern shown in Fig 8.4 is a 2 + 2 regular twill weave. This is done by weaving two plaits over and two plaits under, as compared to an ordinary one over and under tabby weave.

Parts list

Item	No	Material	Dimensions (mm)
1 Front leg	2	Cherry	80sq × 700 long
2 Back leg/stile	2	Cherry	45sq × 1330 long
3 Back splat	4	Cherry	95 × 6 × 400 long
4 Arm rest	2	Cherry	80 × 16 × 380 long
5 Seat rail (front)	1	Cherry	22 dia × 520 long
6 Seat rail (side/back)	3	Cherry	22 dia × 370 long
7 Front stretcher	2	Cherry	25sq × 520 long
8 Side/back stretcher	5	Cherry	25sq × 370 long
9 Rocker	2	Cherry	80 × 16 × 560 long
10 Seat	—	Wood splint	9 wide × 1 thick

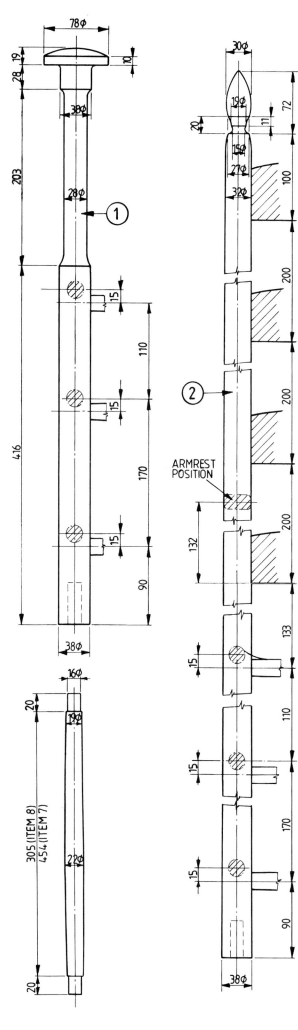

78⌀

28 · 19

10

38⌀

203

28⌀

①

416

15

110

15

170

15

90

38⌀

30⌀

19⌀

72

20

11

15⌀

27⌀

32⌀

100

200

②

ARMREST
POSITION

200

200

132

133

15

110

15

170

15

90

38⌀

16⌀

20

19⌀

305 (ITEM 8)
454 (ITEM 7)

22⌀

20

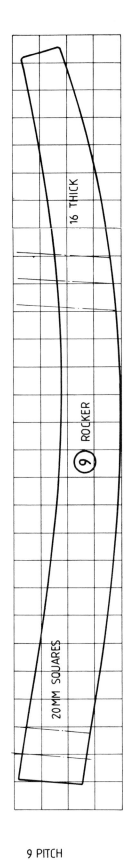

16 THICK

⑨ ROCKER

20MM SQUARES

16

ROCKER
SECTION

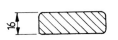

16

ARMREST SECTION

9 PITCH

SEAT WEAVE PATTERN

8.4 *Back stile and rocker details*

Chapter 9

Whatnot

The next two furniture designs are taken from Erddig (NT) near Wrexham, Clywd. This architecturally undramatic, long, stone-faced brick building was built by Joshua Edisbury between 1684 and 1687. In the process he overstretched himself financially and subsequently fled to London, owing money to many creditors. John Mellor, a wealthy London lawyer, was involved in the bankruptcy case that followed, and eventually made a successful offer to the principal mortgagee. He was responsible for adding new wings to the house between 1720 and 1724. His nephew, Simon Yorke, was closely connected in overseeing the purchase of furniture for Erddig during this time, much of which was supplied by London cabinet makers. John Mellor died unmarried and Simon Yorke inherited Erddig in 1733.

Erddig was owned by the Yorke family in an unbroken descent through the male line until 1973. The last custodians, Simon Yorke IV in 1922, and his brother Philip Yorke III in 1966, were confronted with a formidable task of restoring a house in a dangerously decaying state aggravated by the effects of two World Wars, and by coal mining subsidence

directly under the house. After a heroic effort, in 1973 Philip finally donated Erddig to the National Trust, who have patiently restored the house to its original condition.

Erddig has a good collection of mahogany and walnut furniture and from this I have selected a design for a George III mahogany whatnot and a foldover walnut tea table (c. 1720).

The whatnot evolved as a distinctive piece of furniture in the period 1800–1900. Its development stems from the smaller mid-eighteenth-century stands and the later Regency/Victorian period canterburies. Many whatnots of the 1790 to 1840 period feature a music canterbury at the bottom, with a tiered arrangement above. Some also have a drawer in the frieze below one or more of the tiers. Their design commonly consists of a three- or four-tier arrangement supported on four spindle-turned corner balusters. The tiers may have a gallery surround. Varied use in the library, music room, lounge or salon necessitated their being mounted on casters.

Whatnot styles changed somewhat after 1850, when they evolved more as display stands for the

9.1 *Erddig Hall*

9.2 *Whatnot*

9.3 *Corner post*

miscellaneous ornaments and knick-knacks which all Victorians collected. Hence their form is quite variable after this time. No longer necessarily square, they may be rectangular or triangular with graduated tier platforms, and perhaps also highly ornamented.

The whatnot design detailed is of the late George III period with a three-tier arrangement and baluster turned uprights. It is measured from an original in Erddig adjacent to the entrance hall.

Construction

The general arrangement of the whatnot is given in Fig 9.4, and dimensional details of the baluster columns and casters are shown in Fig 9.5. Construction is an exercise in spindle turning and

fitting together of the components. The length between centres required is 1100mm and a lathe steady will be needed. If length is a problem, an alternative approach is to make the corner posts in two halves spigotted together at some inconspicuous point. The corner posts (1) are linked by rails (3) at three levels, connected by mortise-and-tenon joints as shown in section 'BB'. The tier platforms (2) fit between the corner posts resting on these rails. Support blocks (4) give additional reinforcement. The brass casters are available from commercial sources. A french polish finish is suggested.

Parts list

Item	No	Material	Dimensions (mm)
1 Corner post	4	Mahogany	34sq × 1100 long
2 Tier platform	3	Mahogany	355 × 11 × 355 long
3 Rail	12	Mahogany	32 × 10 × 350 long
4 Support block	36	Mahogany	15sq × 1500 total length
5 Castor	4	Brass	Purchase to suit

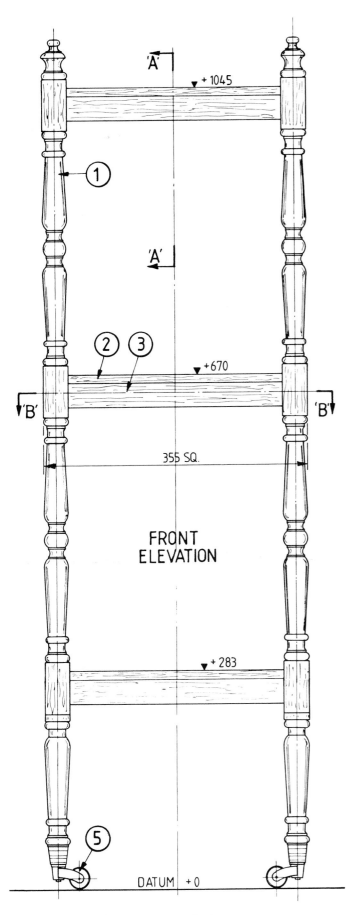

'A'
▽ + 1045

①

'A'

② ③
▽ +670

'B'◀   ▶'B'

355 SQ.

FRONT
ELEVATION

▽ + 283

⑤

DATUM + 0

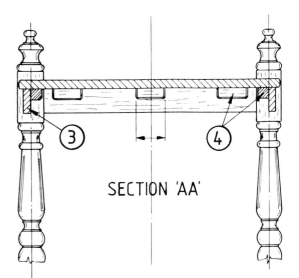

③   ④

SECTION 'AA'

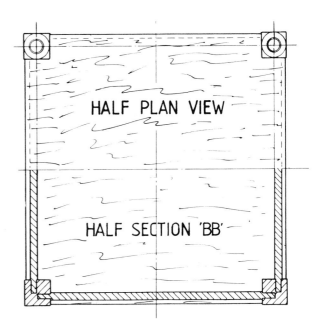

HALF PLAN VIEW

HALF SECTION 'BB'

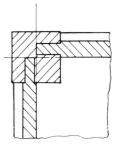

SHELF CORNER
DETAIL

9.4 *General arrangement of whatnot*

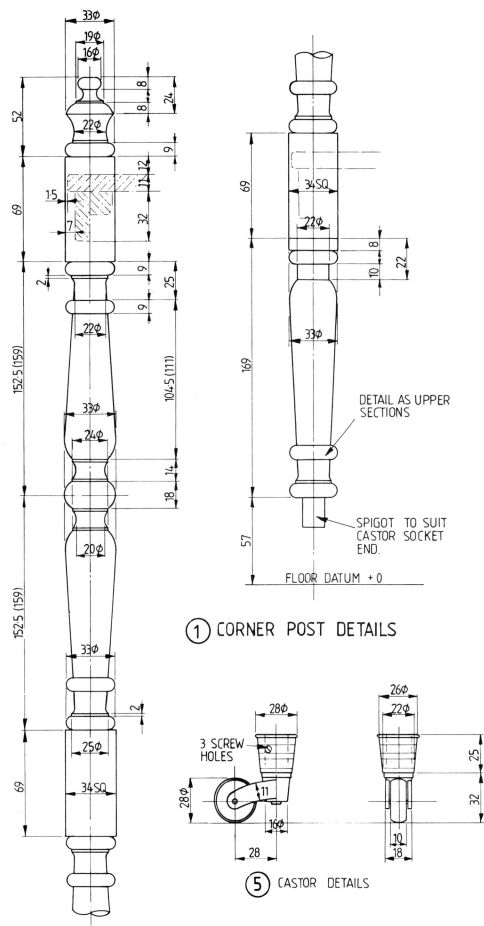

① CORNER POST DETAILS

DETAIL AS UPPER SECTIONS

SPIGOT TO SUIT CASTOR SOCKET END.

FLOOR DATUM + 0

3 SCREW HOLES

⑤ CASTOR DETAILS

9.5 *Corner post and castor details*

Chapter 10

Walnut tea table

The early- eighteenth-century walnut furniture at Erddig (NT) includes a set of eight caffoy walnut-tree chairs, walnut pier glasses acquired by Mellor, a walnut veneered tallboy chest, and blanket chest, all dating from the 1720s. In the library is a fine quality English walnut tea table (c. 1720) which is the second furniture design I have selected from this country house. The table has a foldover top with re-entrant style corners, and is inlaid with cross and feather bandings typical of the period. The frieze is veneered in a similar manner. The table opens with a double concertina action, and stands on turned Queen Anne-style cabriole legs with pad feet and foliated angles at the intersection with the frieze.

When extended the concertina sides are held open by a pair of latches, one each side. An alternative method of holding the sides, sometimes employed on tables of this form, was to fit internally a horizontal board sliding in grooves in the inside faces of the side/concertina rails. When the table was extended this board was pushed back across the face of the concertina rails, thus holding the assembly rigid. If the item was a card table then the slide might also be fitted with a tray to store cards, etc.

A mystery regarding the intended use of the

10.1 *Walnut tea table*

10.2 *Concertina mechanism*

original table becomes apparent when you open the foldover top. This reveals that the inner faces are unfinished. They are not veneered as one would expect, and this raises the question whether the craftsman intended the item to be a tea table or a card table, and why it was never completed. (See Martin Drury, 'Early eighteenth-century furniture at Erddig', *Apollo magazine*, July 1978, pp 46–55.)

Construction

The general arrangement of the tea table is given in Fig 10.4, and sectional details with the concertina mechanism are shown in Fig 10.5. The skills required

10.3 *Leg end*

Walnut tea table

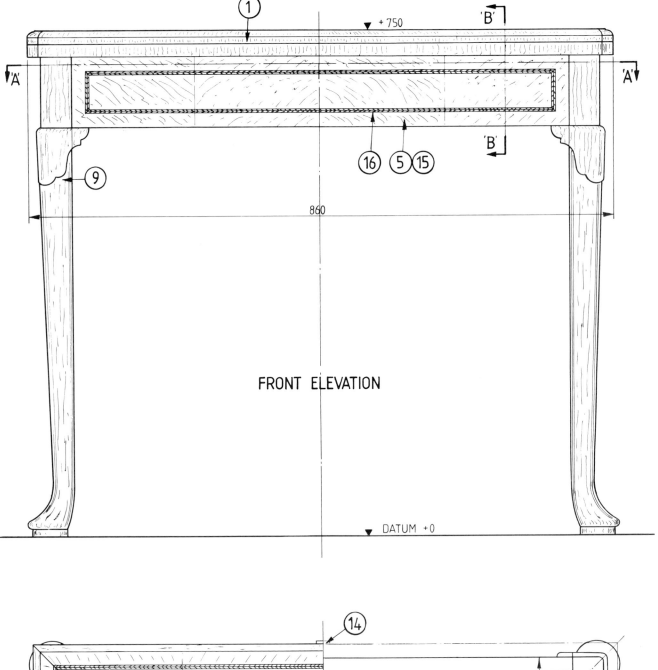

FRONT ELEVATION

+750

860

DATUM +0

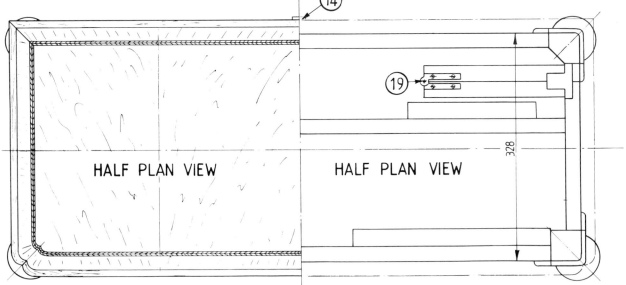

HALF PLAN VIEW   HALF PLAN VIEW

328

10.4 *General arrangement of tea table*

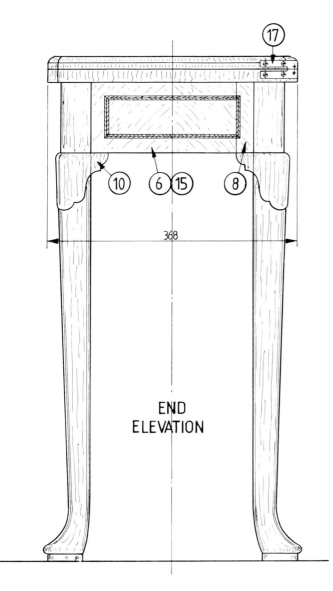

END
ELEVATION

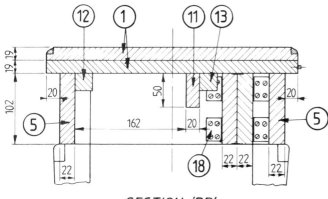

SECTION 'BB'

are joinery, spindle turning for the legs, and veneer work on the table top and frieze. Some minor carving is also necessary at the top of the legs where they join the frieze. Construction can be split into three aspects: the legs, the framework, and the table top.

Legs

Enlarged details of the cabriole legs are shown in Fig 10.6. It should be noted that while spindle turning is used in part to make the legs, the shape does not permit the whole of it to be turned. This is limited to machining of the taper length, which is of straight circular section, and the 52mm diameter foot pad at the end. The cabriole leg end between these then has to be completed by hand. The length between centres required for turning is 750mm.

The suggested order of machining is as follows. First mark out the cabriole shape on to the rectangular section timber. Before spindle-turning, consider bandsawing off surplus material. Next, set the leg up between lathe centres, suitably aligned to turn the tapered section of the leg. Machine this, taking care to avoid the cabriole foot end which will gyrate wildly and may give some unbalance if the lathe is run too fast. Now adjust the leg centre at either end to align with the middle of the pad foot, and carefully proceed to turn the footprint end. This is as far as you can go with lathe work, and the cabriole end form then has to be completed by hand, together with the simple carving at the top of the leg. To avoid a disaster using the hardwood, it may be worth trying this out on a length of softwood first.

Table framework

The oak framework consists of items (5), (6), (8) and (11) joined to the legs (9) with mortise and tenons. Make the concertina pieces (7) with lap joints and mount these with hinges (18) and (19). Carry out a preliminary assembly of the framework but, before gluing together, consider applying the walnut veneer and feather banding to the frieze rails. You may find it easier to complete this work while the rails are still loose.

Table top

The table top construction is set out in Fig 10.7. Each half consists of an oak centrepiece with a 48mm wide border strip. The jointing is probably a tongue connection, but this is difficult to tell. The fold-over

Walnut tea table

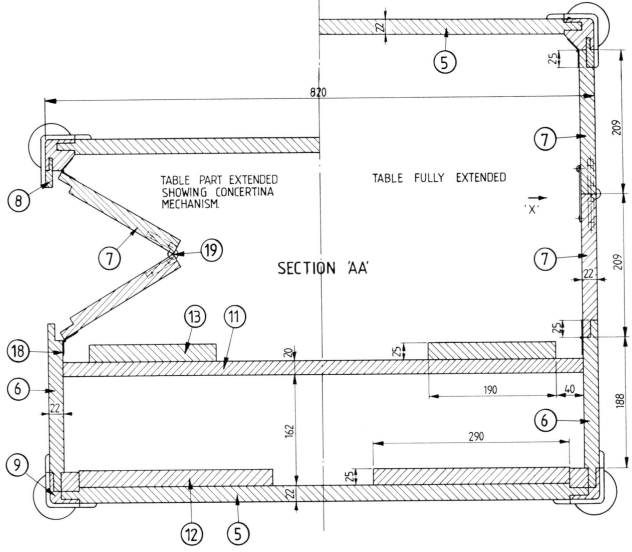

The image contains the following labels and dimensions:

22
5
25
820
7
209
TABLE PART EXTENDED
SHOWING CONCERTINA
MECHANISM.
TABLE FULLY EXTENDED
8
'X'
7
19
SECTION 'AA'
209
7
7
22
13
11
25
18
20
25
6
190
40
22
162
188
290
9
25
6
22
12
5

10.5 *Sectional details of tea table*

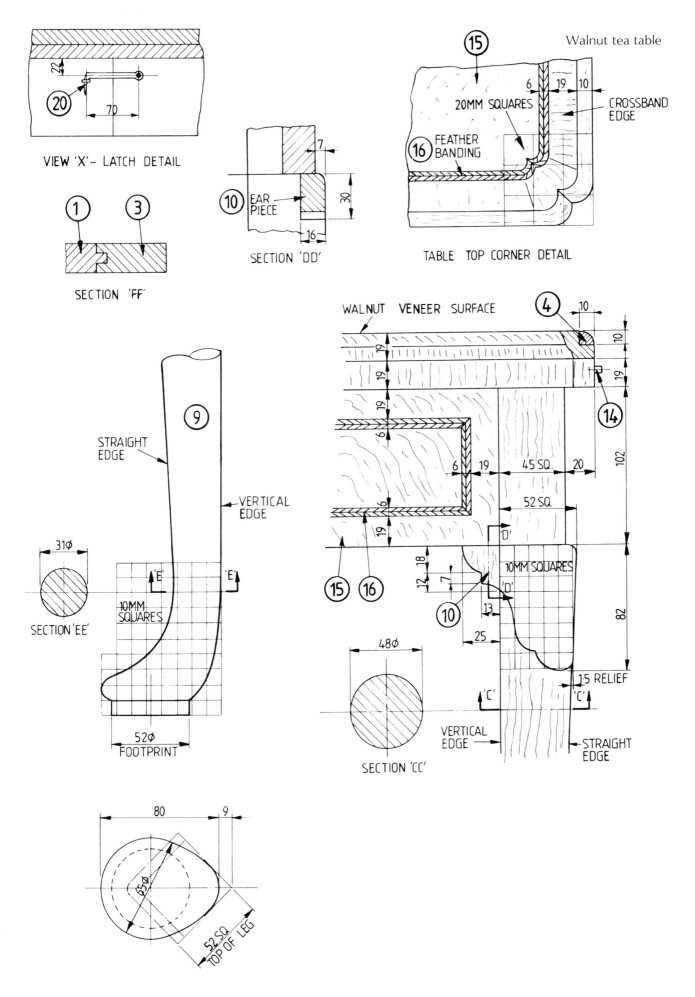

VIEW 'X'– LATCH DETAIL

22
70
20

SECTION 'FF'
1 3

SECTION 'DD'
10 EAR PIECE
7
30
16

Walnut tea table

TABLE TOP CORNER DETAIL
15
6 19 10
20MM SQUARES
CROSSBAND EDGE
16 FEATHER BANDING

WALNUT VENEER SURFACE
4
10
10
19
19
19
19
6
14
102
6 19 45 SQ. 20
52 SQ.
15 16
12 18
7
'D'
10
13
25
10MM SQUARES
82
1·5 RELIEF
VERTICAL EDGE
'C' 'C'
STRAIGHT EDGE

9
STRAIGHT EDGE
VERTICAL EDGE

SECTION 'EE'
31∅
'E' 'E'
10MM SQUARES
52∅
FOOTPRINT

SECTION 'CC'
48∅

80 9
∅50
52 SQ.
TOP OF LEG

10.6 *Miscellaneous details of tea table*

65

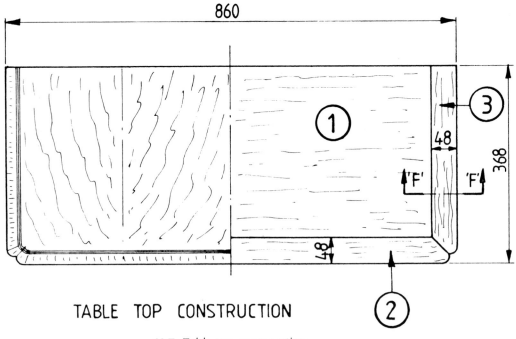

TABLE TOP CONSTRUCTION

10.7 *Table top construction*

top leaf has an applied walnut edging strip, and walnut veneer and feather banding as per details in Figs 10.4 and 10.6. Assuming the table is to be finished as a tea table, the inside faces of the table top could then be veneered in a similar fashion. Alternatively, it could be completed as a card table by applying a baize centrepiece and a crossbanded walnut veneer perimeter. Instructions on fixing baize are given in Chapter 24. The bottom half table top is glued to the frame, and no screws are used (see comments in Chapter 11). The table top uses side pattern card table hinges, which are commercially available.

Parts list

Item	No	Material	Dimensions (mm)
1 Table top	2	Oak	327 × 19 × 778 long
2 Front strip	2	Oak	48 × 19 × 860 long
3 Side strip	4	Oak	48 × 19 × 370 long
4 Edge beading		Walnut	10sq × 2600 long total

Item	No	Material	Dimensions (mm)
5 Front/back tail	2	Oak	102 × 22 × 820 long
6 Side rail	2	Oak	102 × 22 × 250 long
7 Concertina rail	4	Oak	102 × 22 × 209 long
8 End piece	2	Oak	102 × 11 × 40 long
9 Leg	4	Walnut	90 × 75 × 712 long
10 Ear piece	8	Walnut	25 × 16 × 30 long
11 Centre rail	1	Oak	50 × 20 × 820 long
12 Support block (1)	2	Oak	25sq × 290 long
13 Support block (2)	2	Oak	25sq × 190 long
14 Tongue piece	1	Walnut	8 × 4 × 20 long
15 Walnut veneer	–	Walnut	Quantity to suit
16 Feather banding	–	Walnut	Purchase to suit
17 Card table hinge	2	Brass	End pattern
18 Hinge	8	Brass	35 × 25 wide
19 Swivel hinge	4	Brass	Purchase to suit
20 Latch/eye	2	Brass	Purchase to suit

Chapter 11

Walnut side table

Levens Hall, a white stone Elizabethan building in south Cumbria, stand majestically at the crossroads into the Lake District. This house, with its imposing Pele Tower, is a welcome break for a visitor with an hour or two to spare and who is willing to divert from the nearby motorway. The hall is renowned for its topiary in the adjoining gardens, while its interior, features magnificently carved overmantles, cordova lined walls, and a wealth of period walnut furniture.

The building of Levens Hall extended over many centuries. The oldest part, the Pele Tower and adjoining hall was built by the de Redman family (c. 1250–1300). In the sixteenth century the house was sold to the Bellingtons, who added a new wing and completely refurbished it as a gentleman's residence. A later member of this family gambled and lost the estate in 1688, and Levens was eventually acquired by a kinsman, Colonel James Grahme. In the nineteenth century Levens Hall was inherited by the Bagot family, and succeeding generations have striven to preserve the house as it is seen today.

The house is particularly rich in walnut furniture. A magnificent set of Charles II walnut hand-carved dining chairs, among the finest in the country, is worth noting, as is a set of four William and Mary walnut torchères. There is also furniture by Gillow, and a gilded candelabra by Thomas Chippendale. In the drawing room is a Charles II walnut side table with double spiral twisted legs.

The variety of side tables is wide and their evolution and changing style extends over a long period from 1650 through to Victorian times. The side table design here is typical of the Charles II/William and Mary period (1660–1700). It is unusual in having five twisted legs with bun feet, the fifth being in the centre. An X-stretcher arrangement with further double spiral twist work interconnects these legs. The table has a single drawer in the frieze, with a milled moulding below this, repeated on the stretcher ends.

Construction

The general arrangement is given in Fig 11.3, and sectional information in Fig 11.6. The skills needed to

11.1 *Levens Hall*

11.2 *Levens Hall topiary*

make it are joinery, woodturning, veneer work on the table top, and carving of the double spiral twisted legs. Construction can be split into three aspects: the framework, the leg twist work, and the table top and drawer.

Framework

The framework consists of the legs (4) connected to the front, side and back rails (8), (9) and (10) using mortise-and-tenon joints. A cross beam (15) supports the fifth centre leg. Spindle-turn the legs (4), and X-

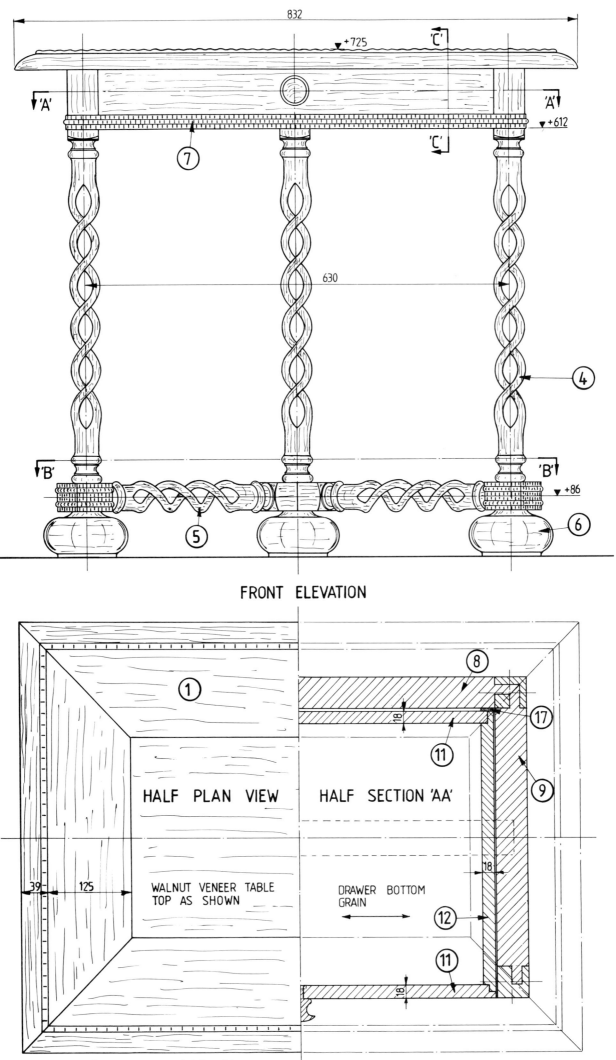

FRONT ELEVATION

HALF PLAN VIEW   HALF SECTION 'AA'

WALNUT VENEER TABLE
TOP AS SHOWN

DRAWER BOTTOM
GRAIN

11.3 *General arrangement of side table*

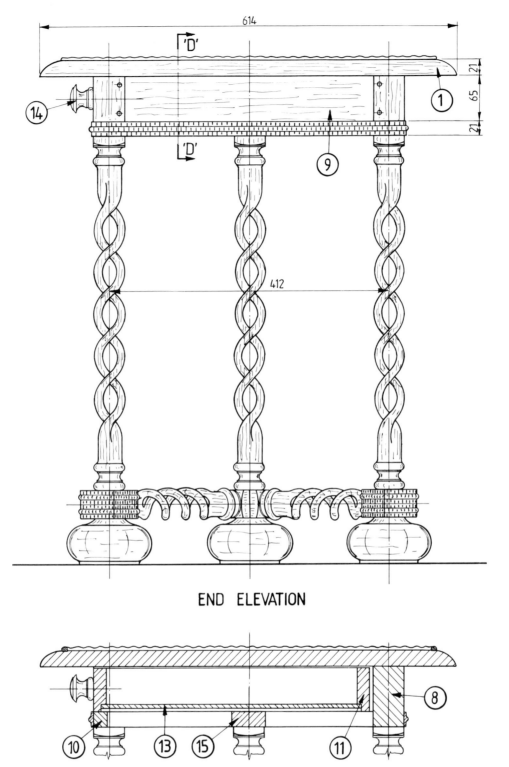

614

'D'

'D'

14

1

21

65

21

9

412

END ELEVATION

8

10   13   15   11

SECTION 'CC'

69

11.4 *Dutch side table*

stretchers (5) in readiness for the twist carving. Next, carry out a trial assembly of the table framework complete with legs, stretchers, bun feet, etc. When this is satisfactory, dismantle, and proceed to finish the leg twist work as follows.

Leg/stretcher twist carving

The most challenging part of the project is unquestionably the carving of the open double twist legs. If you have never carved one before, perhaps you should try making a single barley sugar twist form

11.5 *Bun foot detail*

first, before attempting the more ambitious double twist bine legs for the side table.

A twisted leg is like a screw thread. A barley sugar twist is usually either a one or two start, carved out of the solid. The side table twisted leg is a double start one, but with two separate bines. The twist pitch is twice the axial distance between the crown of an adjacent pair of bines. Assuming the leg/stretcher has been spindle turned over the required length, it is convenient to leave it mounted on the lathe between centres for marking out.

Marking out

First mark the spindle with rings every quarter pitch, (ie approximately every 26–30mm) along its length, and divide it circumferentially into four, with axial lines along the twist length. The horizontal marking can be conveniently done with a scribbing block, fitted with a pencil set at the lathe centreline height. Slide the scribbing block along the bed rails with the pencil held against the edge of the timber to mark a line. Turn the work 90° to mark the next line. If the lathe has a dividing head this will make accurate quartering much easier.

Next prepare a cardboard template as in Fig 11.9. Use this wrapped around the leg/stretcher, as a guide to mark the twist centreline. This line should run through the intersections of the rings/axial lines previously marked. The thickness of the bine twist is approximately one third of the leg diameter (ie 16mm), and the cardboard template can be used again to mark the width either side of each twist centreline. Scribble on the waste material to be removed in between.

Carving

Carving an open double twist is commenced by gouging out the wood as in Fig 11.9(A) in a hollow section on either side of the bines. This is then gradually refined by cleaning up as in Fig 11.9(B), using a rasp and appropriate carving chisels. Finally, the twisted leg is drilled through the centre and the internal form is completed. An ordinary knife blade may prove easier for removing the internal waste material. It is suggested that you drill through the centre in short sections initially, leaving the two bines attached at intermittent points for a while. Clean up the open bine sections between these, and then finally break through the remaining connections. Finish the twists off with knife work and glasspaper.

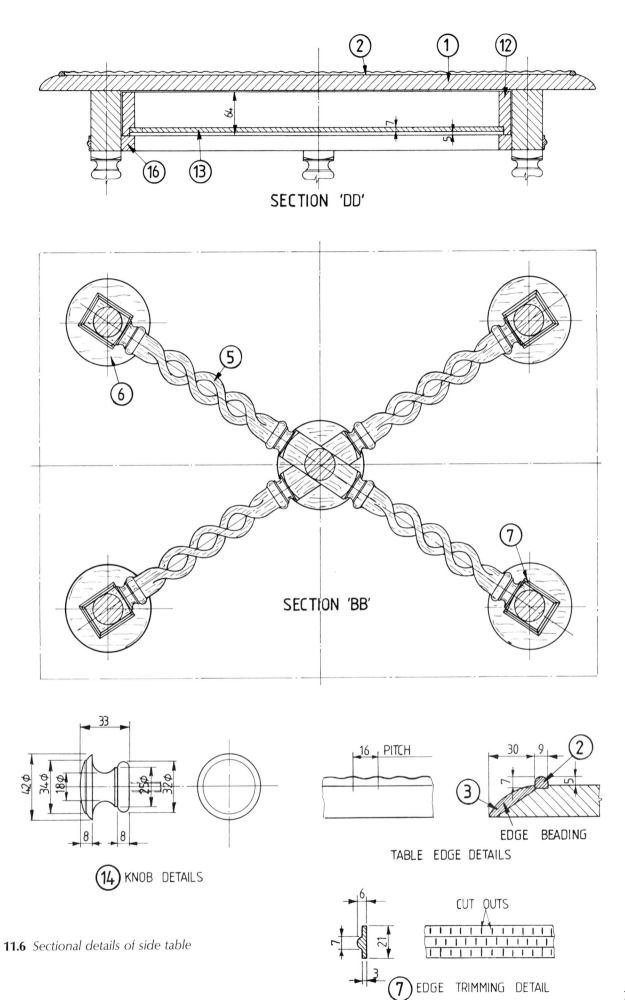

SECTION 'DD'

SECTION 'BB'

33

42∅

34∅

18∅

25∅

32∅

8

8

⑭ KNOB DETAILS

16 PITCH

TABLE EDGE DETAILS

30   9   ②

7   5

③

EDGE BEADING

6

7   21

3

CUT OUTS

⑦ EDGE TRIMMING DETAIL

11.6 *Sectional details of side table*

71

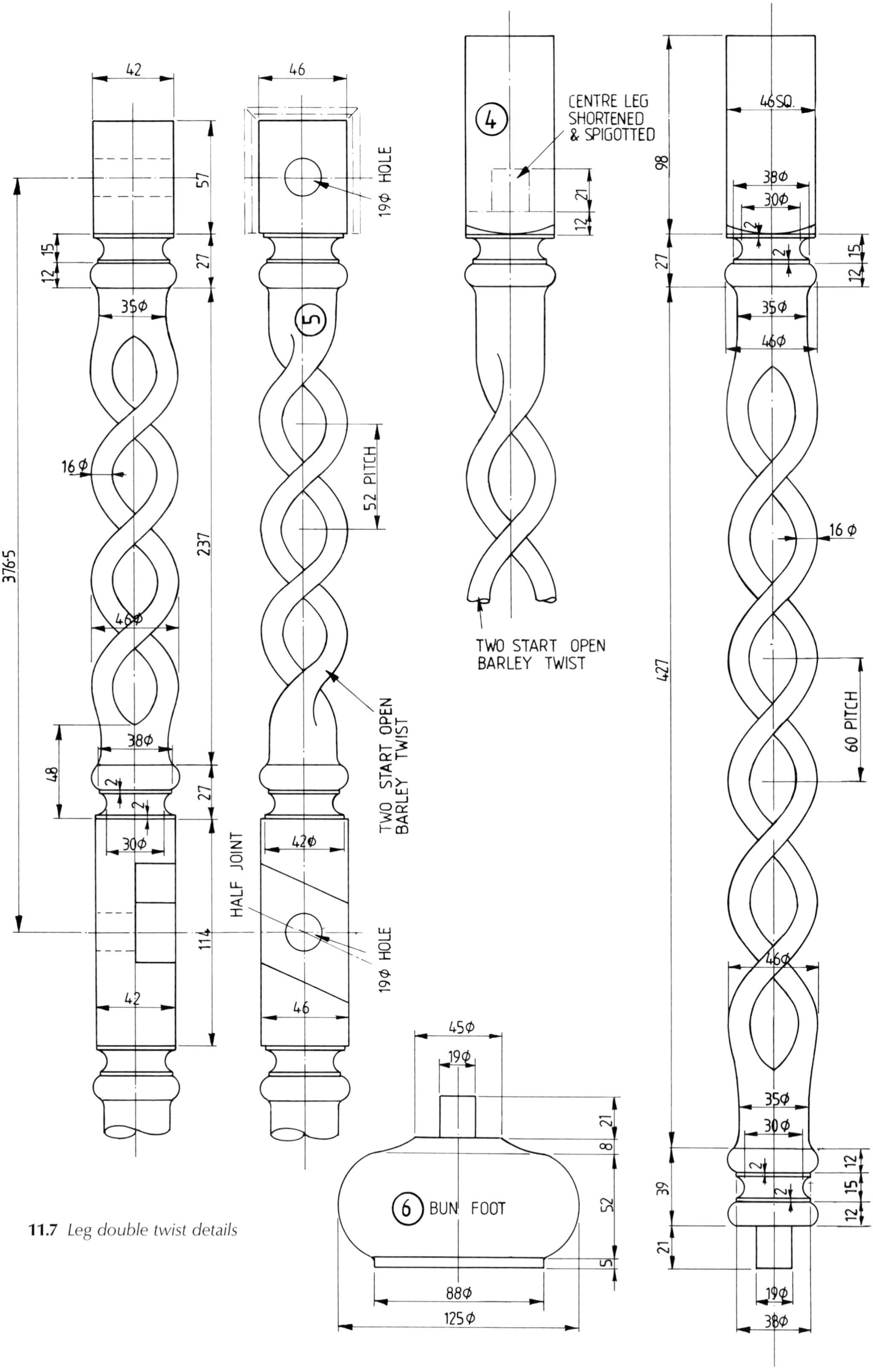

42
57
27
12 15
35ϕ
16ϕ
237
376·5
46ϕ
38ϕ
48
2
27
30ϕ
114
42
46
19ϕ HOLE
5
52 PITCH
TWO START OPEN BARLEY TWIST
42ϕ
HALF JOINT
19ϕ HOLE
46
4
CENTRE LEG SHORTENED & SPIGOTTED
21
12
TWO START OPEN BARLEY TWIST
98
46SQ.
38ϕ
30ϕ
2
12 15
27
35ϕ
46ϕ
16 ϕ
427
60 PITCH
46ϕ
35ϕ
30ϕ
39
12
15
12
21
19ϕ
38ϕ
45ϕ
19ϕ
21
8
52
5
6 BUN FOOT
88ϕ
125ϕ

11.7 *Leg double twist details*

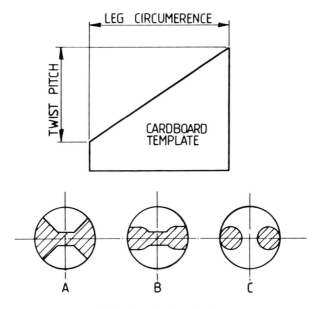

11.8 *Carving leg twist*

Parts list

Item	No	Material	Dimensions (mm)
1 Table top	1	Block-board	614 × 832 × 20 thick
2 Wavy-line bead edge	1	Walnut	9 × 7 × 2800 long total
3 Table edging	1	Walnut	40 × 10 × 3000 long total
4 Leg	5	Walnut	46sq × 630 long
5 Stretcher	2	Walnut	46sq × 850 long
6 Bun foot	5	Walnut	130sq × 100 long
7 Milled edge moulding	1	Walnut	21 × 6 × 4000 long total
8 Back rail	1	Walnut	86 × 46 × 675 long
9 Side rail	2	Walnut	86 × 46 × 460 long
10 Front rail	1	Walnut	21 × 20 × 675 long
11 Drawer front/back	2	Walnut	64 × 18 × 584 long
12 Drawer side	2	Walnut	64 × 18 × 406 long
13 Drawer bottom	1	Walnut	392 × 7 × 570 long
14 Knob	1	Walnut	45sq × 50 long
15 Cross beam	1	Walnut	50 × 21 × 675 long
16 Runner	1	Walnut	21 × 20 × 840 long total; fit in short pieces
17 Back stop	2	Oak	20 × 6 × 65 long
18 Veneer	–	Walnut	Quantity to suit table top

Reassembly

With the legs completed and reassembly work in progress, this is an appropriate point to add the milled edge moulding (7) around the bottom of the frieze and on the stretcher ends. As these are a little laborious to make by hand, it might be worth setting up some sort of routing jig.

Table top

The original table top is made from a number of pieces of softwood. Whether you construct it in this manner or settle for an easier option such as using plywood or blockboard is up to you. The latter will be much more stable, but it will not be authentic. The table centre veneer plan is shown in Fig 11.5, and the inset walnut wavy line edge beading in Fig 11.6. The original table top is glued to the framework, and no screws are used. Note that although screws were beginning to be introduced about this time, they were not regularly used for securing table tops until about 1740. The underside of the table perimeter external to the framework is walnut stained to match the top.

Drawer

The original drawer has a simple half-jointed construction with pinned ends as shown in half section 'AA' (Fig 11.3). You may, however, prefer to use dovetails. Set the drawer flush with the frieze by adjusting the back stops (17) as necessary. It is suggested that the table is french polished.

Chapter 12

Mahogany tray

The second furniture design chosen from Levens Hall, Cumbria, was one I stumbled on quite by chance in the Great Hall: a George III mahogany tray. This is probably the simplest item of furniture in this book to make, but nevertheless quite a desirable little piece. If you are hesitant about trying some of the other items this is not a bad one to start with, as it will give you confidence to try one of the others.

With regard to trays in general, these tend to be two varieties: large and small. The larger ones are known as butler's trays and usually rested on a small four-legged stand. Sometimes, through the passage of time, the two items became separated. Smaller trays tend not to be fitted to a stand. The two most common forms are rectangular and, as here, oval, with a galleried edge to stop things falling off. The provision of handles varies according to the style. The Levens Hall design is a mahogany oval tray with a wavy line gallery, satinwood crossbanding and carrying handles.

Construction

The general arrangement drawing is given in Fig 12.2, and Fig 12.3 shows a quarter section of the tray set out on a squared background to aid transfer of the shape to the wood. The tray is made from a single

12.1 *Mahogany tray*

sheet of mahogany 13mm thick. The wavy line edging is set into a rebated edge round the perimeter. This edging is not added until the crossband edge veneer work is complete.

Crossbanding and fan inlay motif

The groundwork is prepared for the perimeter satinwood crossbanding and the centre fan motif by reducing the thickness locally as necessary.

Ready-made fan inlay motifs are commercially available, though you may have difficulty in getting one of the right size. However, it is not difficult to make your own motif, using the pattern details in Fig 12.3. Note that the radial satinwood fan pieces are sand-shadowed on one edge to create a three dimensional effect. The method of sand-shadowing veneer is as follows:

Prepare a small bed of silver sand about 25mm deep in a tin tray, and heat this over a gas or electric ring. Using tweezers to hold the veneer strips, place them edge on into the sand surface, and leave for a number of seconds allowing the veneer to tone gently under the heat. You will need to experiment a bit with the temperature, the period of time the veneer strip is embedded in the sand, and maybe with the sand depth, to achieve the required degree of shading. The veneer should not be allowed to touch the tray bottom, otherwise it will scorch. When the shading is completed, damp down the veneer with a sponge to replace the water which evaporated during the shading process. Then place the veneer under a caul to keep it flat.

Wavy line edging and handles

The wavy line edging detailed in Fig 12.3 is best prepared in short sections. Steam bending techniques should be used to shape the pieces to the required curvature: see Chapter 8 for notes on this subject. Tray handles are commercially available if required. The tray has a french polished finish, and the bottom has a baize underfelt applied with flour or rice paste: details of this are given in Chapter 24.

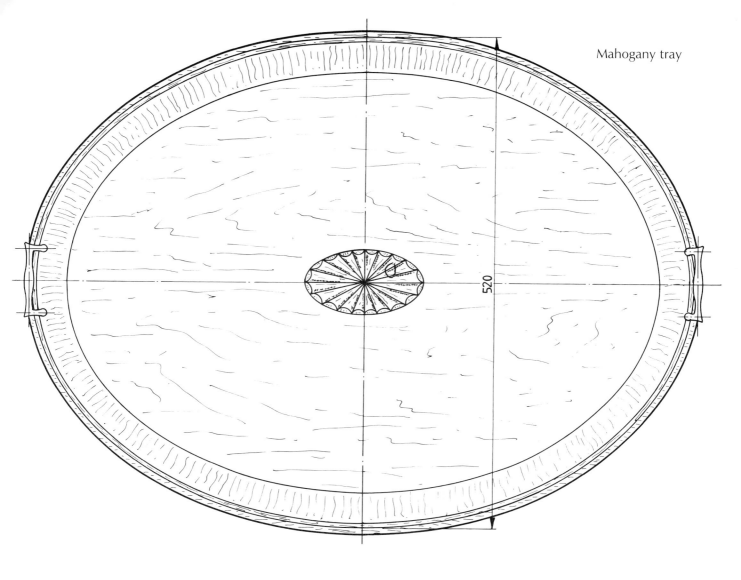

Mahogany tray

520

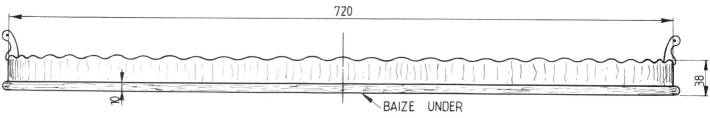

720

38

10

BAIZE UNDER

12.2 *General arrangement of tray*

Parts list

Item	No	Material	Dimensions (mm)
1 Base	1	Mahogany	534 × 10 × 734 long
2 Wavy-line edging	20	Mahogany	100 × 5 × 28 long
3 Handle	2	Brass	Purchase to suit
4 Fan motif inlay	1	Veneer	Purchase or make to suit
5 Edge crossbanding	1	Satinwood	Quantity of veneer to suit
6 Underfelt	1	Baize	750 × 550

Mahogany tray

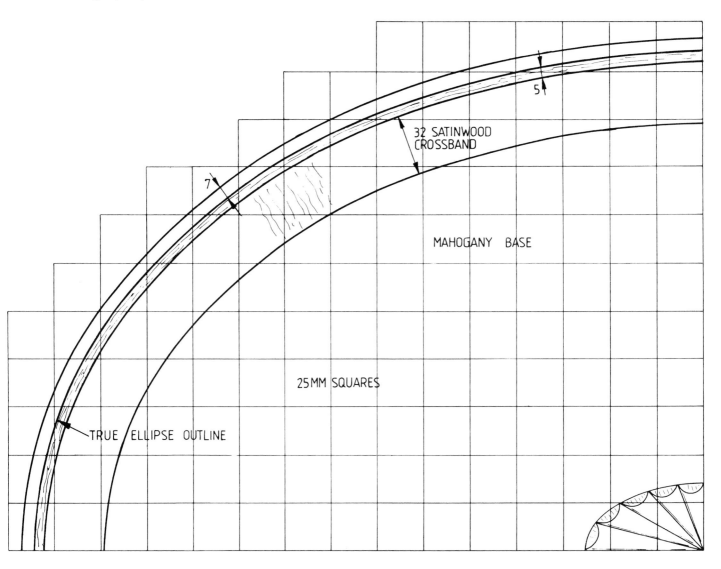

5

32 SATINWOOD CROSSBAND

MAHOGANY BASE

7

25 MM SQUARES

TRUE ELLIPSE OUTLINE

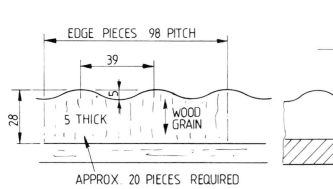

EDGE PIECES 98 PITCH

39

5

28

5 THICK

WOOD GRAIN

APPROX. 20 PIECES REQUIRED

15

'A'

'A'

5

28

10

12

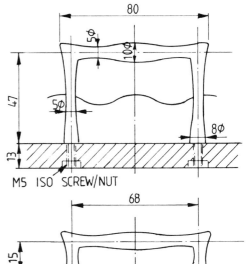

80

5ø

10ø

47

5ø

8ø

13

M5 ISO SCREW/NUT

68

15

5

6

'A-A'

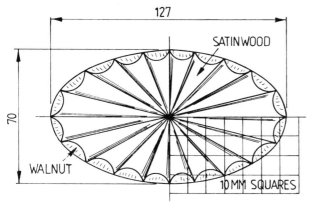

127

SATINWOOD

70

WALNUT

10 MM SQUARES

CENTRE FAN VENEER MOTIF

12.3 *Miscellaneous details*

Chapter 13

Gillow dining table

Leighton Hall is the historic seat of the Gillow furniture family, so it is appropriate that the designs selected from this house reflect the importance of this firm, which made high quality furniture during the eighteenth and nineteenth centuries. The two items I have selected are a Gillow dining table and the complementary set of Queen Anne chairs which surround it. I could, however, have picked several other notable Gillow items, I was so spoilt for choice. This chapter discusses the extending table, but first gives some brief notes on the house and Gillow ancestry.

Leighton Hall is just south of the Lake District near Carnforth. It dates from 1245, when it is thought that there was a fortified manor on the site. It has had an eventful ownership, but in 1763 the wealthy George Townley rebuilt the hall in the Adam style on earlier ruins. A later resident, Alexander Worswick, subsequently restyled the front with a Gothic façade (c. 1800).

The house came into Gillow's ownership in 1822 when Richard Gillow purchased the hall from a cousin. He was a grandson of Robert Gillow, the founder of the furniture business of Gillow & Co. of Lancaster, originally started in about 1728. This firm was prolific in the nineteenth century, and you will find their furnishings in many of Britain's country houses. The family connection remains to this day, and there is a homely atmosphere in the house. The dining room (originally a snooker room) contains a particularly impressive Gillow dining table of the extending type as shown in Figs 13.2 and 13.3.

The principle of the dining table extension is based on a series of rectangular frames which slide one within the other on runners, as shown in Figs 13.4 and 13.5. There are two sets of five frames, and each group stows away within the respective table end. The table is lengthened by withdrawing the two ends on their castor-end legs to reveal these inner sliding frames. Table support is provided as it is extended by further legs on castors fitted to the intermediate table frames. Additional loose table leaves are then added on top of the framework between the table ends, to suit the required length. The leaves and table ends

13.1 *Leighton Hall*

locate with one another on a series of tongue pieces, fitting into matching grooves in the adjacent member. The leaves are held together by table forks fitted at each intersection into brass connectors on either side.

This table extension principle is thought to have been patented by the Gillow furniture company in about 1800. However, as Richard Gillow did not move into Leighton Hall until 1822, it is possible that this particular extending table may have been made at or about this time.

In its fully extended configuration, the table length is 4420mm, so you might well be forgiven for thinking that it is not suited to a modern house. Closed up,

13.2 *Gillow extending table*

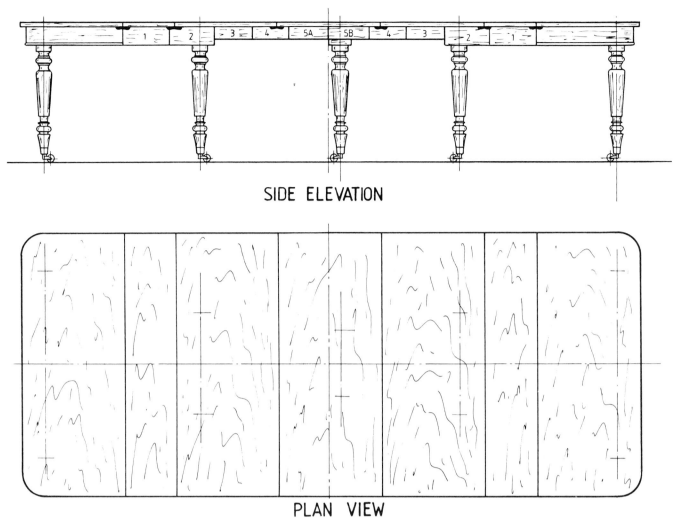

SIDE ELEVATION

PLAN VIEW

13.3 *Table elevation and plan*

however, it measures an amazingly compact 1120mm overall, which would compare favourably with the average household dining table. The beauty is that with its variable number of leaves, you can adjust its length to suit virtually any room size. It has another valuable attribute: wherever around it you sit, and however the table is extended, the legs never interfere with your sitting position.

Construction

The construction divides into four aspects: the table ends; the extending framework; the legs; and the additional table leaves. It is suggested you begin with the table ends, details of which are given in Fig 13.5. Check the spacing of the inner frame rails (5), to see that these are accurately gauged to suit the extending frame packs, and that the table tops match together. Use dummy runners (9) to align the two ends during this exercise. The table has a triple beaded edge which is probably best shaped with a router. There is also a small amount of external mahogany veneer work to hide the joins in the carcase side frame.

13.4 *Extending rails*

Frames

The table requires two sets of extending frame packs, details of which are given in Figs 13.6 and 13.7. When these are complete and slide together satisfactorily, fit each pack into the respective table end.

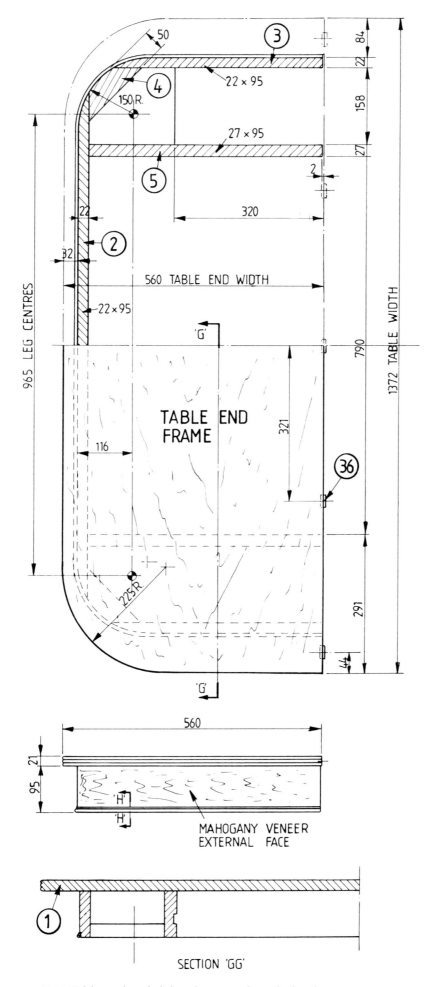

50

③

22 × 95

④

150 R.

27 × 95

⑤

2

22

②

320

32

560 TABLE END WIDTH

22 × 95

'G'

TABLE END
FRAME

116

321

㊱

965 LEG CENTRES

225 R

'G'

84

22

158

27

790

1372 TABLE WIDTH

291

560

21

95

'H'

'H'

MAHOGANY VENEER
EXTERNAL FACE

①

SECTION 'GG'

13.5 *Table end and sliding framework pack details
(cont. overleaf)*

79

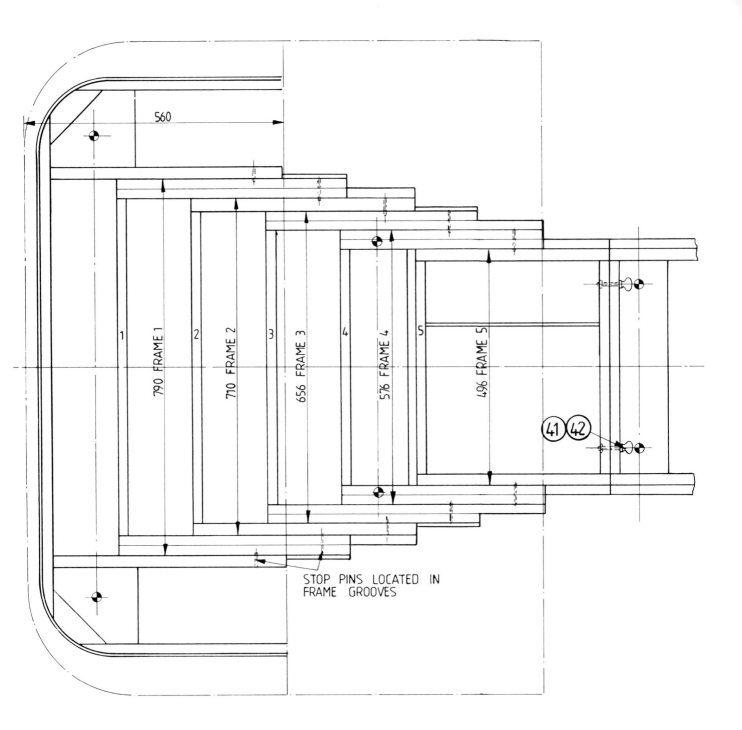

560

1 790 FRAME 1
2 710 FRAME 2
3 656 FRAME 3
4 576 FRAME 4
5 496 FRAME 5

41 42

STOP PINS LOCATED IN
FRAME GROOVES

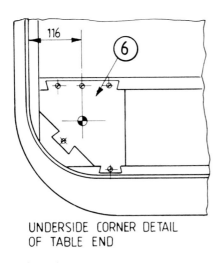

116

6

UNDERSIDE CORNER DETAIL
OF TABLE END

21

TABLE EDGE SECTION

7   6

4

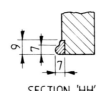

9
7

7

SECTION 'HH'

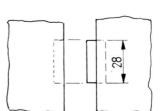

28

36 TONGUE CONNECTION
DETAIL

13.5 (cont.)

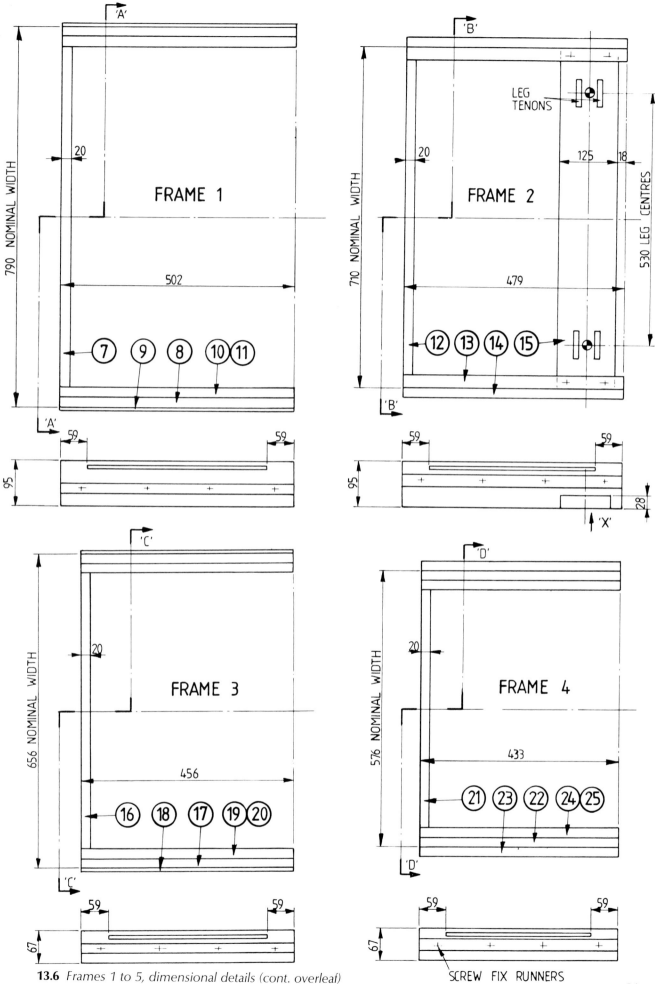

13.6 *Frames 1 to 5, dimensional details (cont. overleaf)*

81

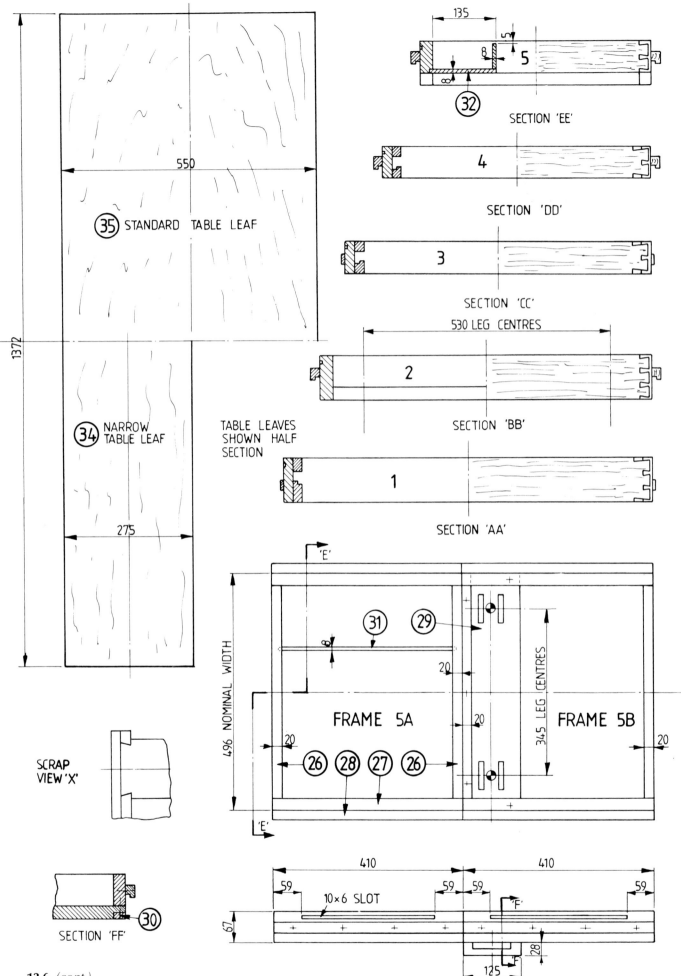

550

(35) STANDARD TABLE LEAF

1372

(34) NARROW
TABLE LEAF

275

TABLE LEAVES
SHOWN HALF
SECTION

135

5

(32)

SECTION 'EE'

4

SECTION 'DD'

3

SECTION 'CC'

530 LEG CENTRES

2

SECTION 'BB'

1

SECTION 'AA'

'E'

(31)   (29)

20

FRAME 5A   345 LEG CENTRES   FRAME 5B

20

20   20

8

(26) (28) (27) (26)

'E'

496 NOMINAL WIDTH

SCRAP
VIEW 'X'

SECTION 'FF'   (30)

67

410   410

59   59 59   59

10×6 SLOT   'F'

28

125

13.6 *(cont.)*

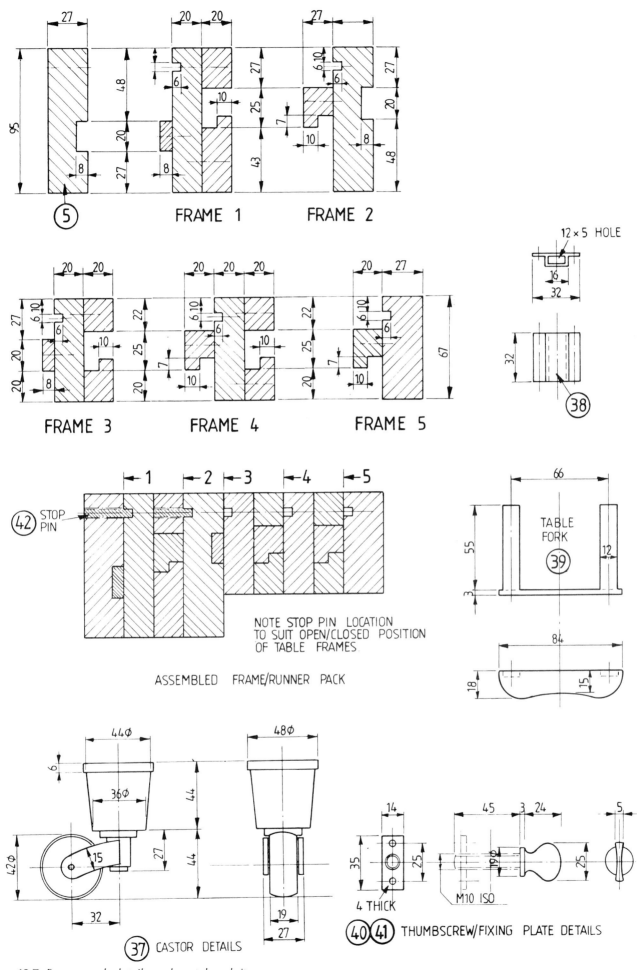

13.7 *Frame pack details and metalwork items*

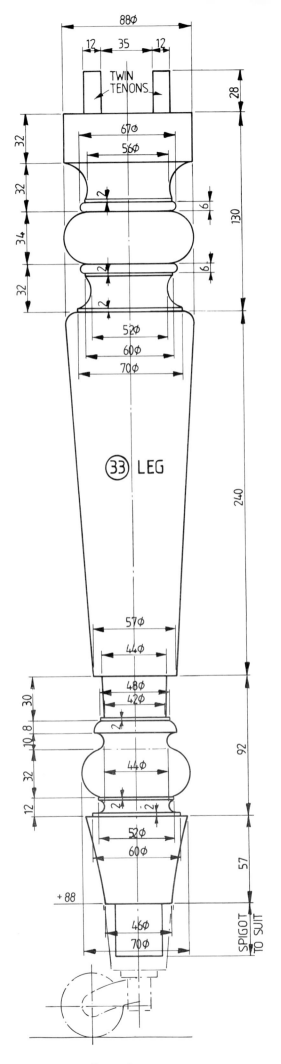

88⌀
12 35 12

TWIN
TENONS

28

67⌀
56⌀

32
32
34
32

2
2
2

6
6

130

52⌀
60⌀
70⌀

33 LEG

240

57⌀
44⌀

48⌀
42⌀

30
10 8
32
12

2

92

44⌀

2 2

52⌀
60⌀

57

+ 88

46⌀
70⌀

SPIGOT TO SUIT

13.8 *Leg dimensions*

Legs

The table has ten legs, which require woodturning and fitting to the underside of the table ends, and frames 2 and 5, and the addition of castors. Leg dimensions are given in Fig 13.8, and there is detail of the assembly to the frame pack in Fig 13.9. Invert the table ends during the leg fitting exercise, with the top suitably protected against damage on the bench face. When you know the extending frame packs need not be dismantled for any further constructional reason, fit the stop pins so that they cannot come apart. It should now be possible to upturn each table end complete with frame pack and legs. These free-standing half units will be more stable if the frame packs are slightly extended for the moment. Align the ends of the middle frames 5A and 5B, and connect these with the tablescrew and fixing plate details (40) and (41). After the two table ends are linked there should be full stability, and a check can be made that the extending mechanism works correctly.

13.9 *Leg and framework detail*

Table leaves

Additional table leaves are made as required, and table fork connectors added to link them. Details of these are given in Figs 13.6 and 13.7. You will probably not need all the table leaves, but if you are making a table of this capacity which will extend to over 4m, it seems a shame not to make them all.

Note that this project requires a substantial amount of hardwood. The table tops in the Leighton Hall original are made of heavy West Indian Sea Island mahogany. You are unlikely to obtain such quality mahogany hardwood today, so a compromise might be to face the table top with matching mahogany curl veneers.

Parts list

Item	No	Material	Dimensions (mm)
Table end frame (× 2)			
1 Table top	1	Mahogany	560 × 21 × 1372 long
2 End rail	1	Mahogany	95 × 22 × 1000 long
3 Side rail	2	Mahogany	95 × 22 × 440 long
4 Corner block	2	Mahogany	95 × 50 × 280 long
5 Inner frame rail	2	Mahogany	95 × 27 × 505 long
6 Leg support block	2	Mahogany	200 × 28 × 200 long
Frame 1 (× 2)			
7 End rail	1	Mahogany	95 × 20 × 790 long
8 Side rail	2	Mahogany	95 × 20 × 502 long
9 Runner	2	Mahogany	20 × 8 × 502 long
10 Bearer	2	Mahogany	50 × 20 × 502 long
11 Cover strip	2	Mahogany	27 × 20 × 502 long
Frame 2 (× 2)			
12 End rail	1	Mahogany	95 × 20 × 710 long
13 Side rail	2	Mahogany	95 × 20 × 479 long
14 Runner	2	Mahogany	25 × 20 × 479 long
15 Crossbeam	1	Mahogany	125 × 28 × 710 long
Frame 3 (× 2)			
16 End rail	1	Mahogany	67 × 20 × 656 long
17 Side rail	2	Mahogany	67 × 20 × 456 long
18 Runner	2	Mahogany	20 × 8 × 456 long
19 Bearer	2	Mahogany	27 × 20 × 456 long
20 Cover strip	2	Mahogany	22 × 20 × 456 long
Frame 4 (× 2)			
21 End rail	1	Mahogany	67 × 20 × 576 long
22 Side rail	2	Mahogany	67 × 20 × 433 long
23 Runner	2	Mahogany	25 × 20 × 433 long
24 Bearer	2	Mahogany	27 × 20 × 433 long
25 Cover strip	2	Mahogany	22 × 20 × 433 long
Frame 5 (× 2)			
26 End rail	2	Mahogany	67 × 20 × 496 long
27 Side rail	2	Mahogany	67 × 27 × 410 long

Item	No	Material	Dimensions (mm)
Frame 5 continued			
28 Runner	2	Mahogany	25 × 20 × 410 long
29 Crossbeam	1	Mahogany	125 × 28 × 496 long: on frame 5B only
30 End cap	2	Mahogany	28 × 27 × 125 long
31 Clip box side	1	Mahogany	54 × 8 × 410 long: on frame 5A only
32 Clip box bottom	1	Mahogany	142 × 8 × 410 long on frame 5A only
Common items			
33 Leg	10	Mahogany	95sq × 600 long
34 Table leaf (1)	2	Mahogany	275 × 21 × 1372 long
35 Table leaf (2)	5	Mahogany	550 × 21 × 1372 long
36 Tongue piece	30	Mahogany	12 × 4 × 28 long: 5 required per table leaf
Metalwork items			
37 Castor	10	Brass	Purchase to suit
38 Table connector	32	Brass	From 1.5 thick plate or purchase to suit
39 Table fork	16	Brass	Fabricate or purchase to suit
40 Thumbscrew	2	Brass	Purchase to suit
41 Screw plate	2	Brass	35 × 14 × 4 thick
42 Stop pin	10	Brass	8 dia × length to suit; two required per frame
43 Screws	–	Brass	To secure end table tops to frame, frame runners, etc.

Chapter 14

Queen Anne dining chair

The abundance of Gillow furniture at Leighton Hall put me in a quandary over what to choose for the second furniture design. There are a number of notable pieces which I could have picked, such as the 'Daisy Table', so called because of its petal-shaped perimeter, and believed to be the only one if its kind, or a lady's work box, made about 1820, probably for Mrs Richard Gillow. There is also a fine eighteenth-century games table on serpentine legs, with impressive crossband veneer work; and a satinwood writing table. These are all pieces characteristic of the sort of furniture Gillow was making about the end of the eighteenth century. However, I felt that if readers were going to attempt the extending dining table featured in Chapter 13, they would appreciate the design for the matching set of Queen Anne dining chairs.

14.1 *Queen Anne chair*

The Queen Anne chairs in Virginia walnut were made by Robert Gillow's father *c.* 1740. Although the material differs from the dining table, the items are well suited. Virginia walnut has a much darker colour than the paler English variety, which makes the material difference not significantly noticeable. Indeed, it is sometimes difficult to distinguish between them without closer inspection. There are eighteen chairs altogether, in three sets of six with slightly different back splat designs.

If you prefer the use of mahogany to match the table, an alternative is to consider another chair design in this book, such as Chippendale, Hepplewhite or Sheraton, to which this material is more suited.

Construction

The chair construction is basically a joinery exercise with some carving work on the front legs, and steam-bending for the back splats. The general arrangement of the chair is given in Fig 14.3, and sectional details through the drop in seat, etc, in Fig 14.2.

Back stile

The chair back form, with its undulating curvature, illustrates how eighteenth-century furniture makers fully developed the profile to suit the human posture. The legs at the back have also been nicely tapered in at the bottom to make them less obtrusive, yet still fully functional. This is quite the most comfortable dining chair I have ever sat on.

Details of the chair back stile are given in Fig 14.4 on a squared background as a transfer aid. If you choose your hardwood carefully it should be possible to make the two stiles from one piece of timber, bandsawing the curved form down the middle in between. About 50mm or so extra width will be required compared to the size given in the parts list. With the spare material you may be able to make other parts, such as the stretcher (6), and the shoe detail (12).

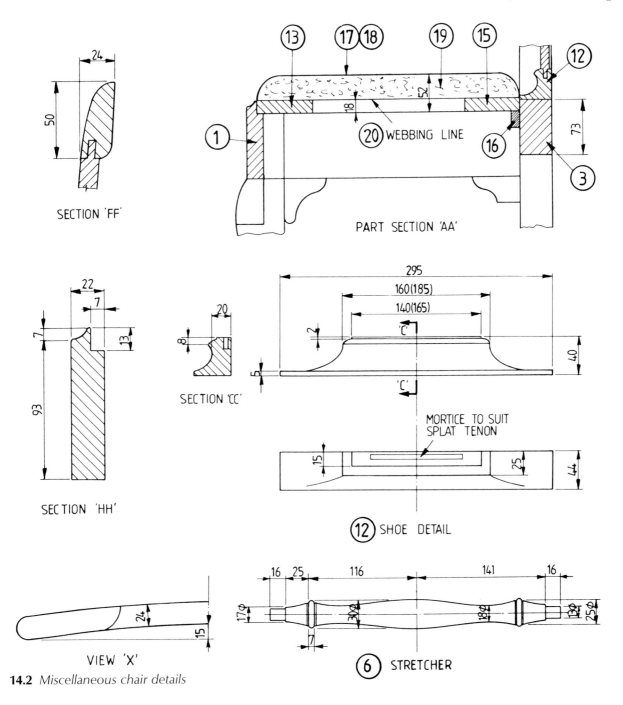

SECTION 'FF'

PART SECTION 'AA'

WEBBING LINE

SECTION 'HH'

SECTION 'CC'

MORTICE TO SUIT
SPLAT TENON

(12) SHOE DETAIL

VIEW 'X'

(6) STRETCHER

14.2 *Miscellaneous chair details*

Front leg

The front legs are of the cabriole form with small ear pieces added at the top where they meet the seat rails. Detailed dimensions and sections are given in Fig 14.5. A Queen Anne cabriole leg of the proper form is a beautiful shape when carved with skill, but can be horribly bulbous and ugly if the proportions are incorrect. The profile is set out on a squared background to assist in achieving a good result.

The lower leg sections are circular. The most critical point is in the knee section, and in the formation of the scroll pieces. The ear pieces should be securely fixed, if necessary with additional dowelling. It was noted that on a number of the original chairs these pieces had become detached.

Framework

The framework is a mortise-and-tenon construction with the front, back and side rails tenoned into the legs. The front and side rails have a moulded edge,

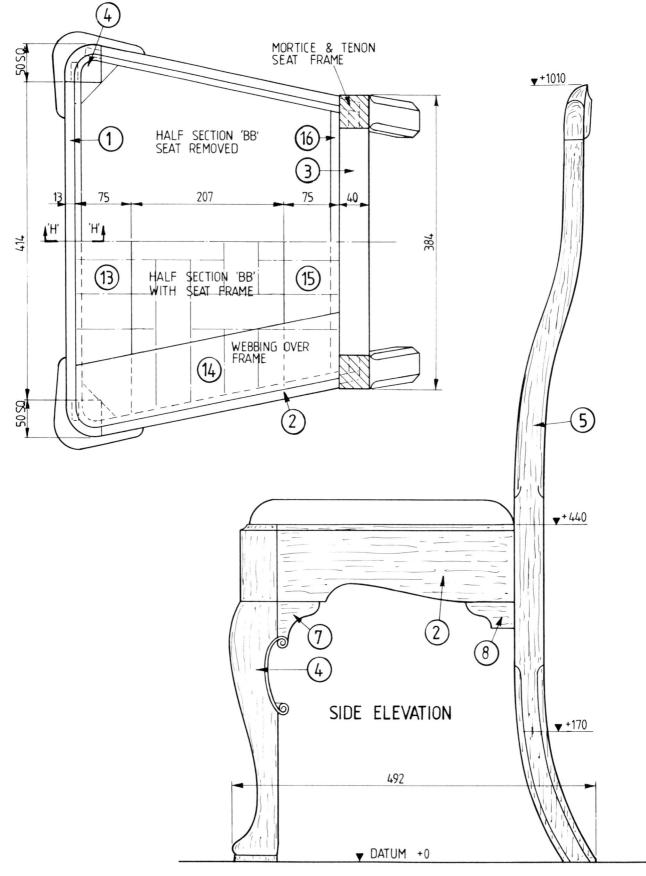

MORTICE & TENON
SEAT FRAME

HALF SECTION 'BB'
SEAT REMOVED

HALF SECTION 'BB'
WITH SEAT FRAME

WEBBING OVER
FRAME

SIDE ELEVATION

DATUM +0

14.3 *Chair elevations and plan*

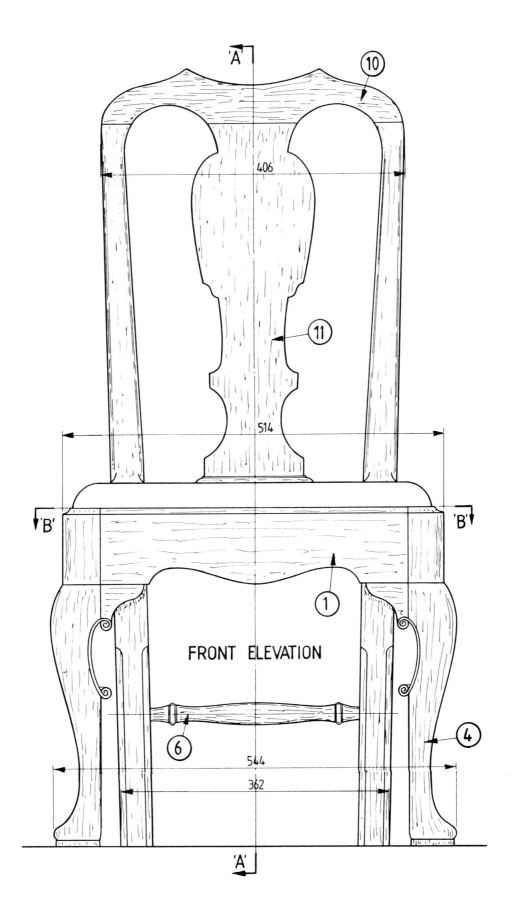

FRONT ELEVATION

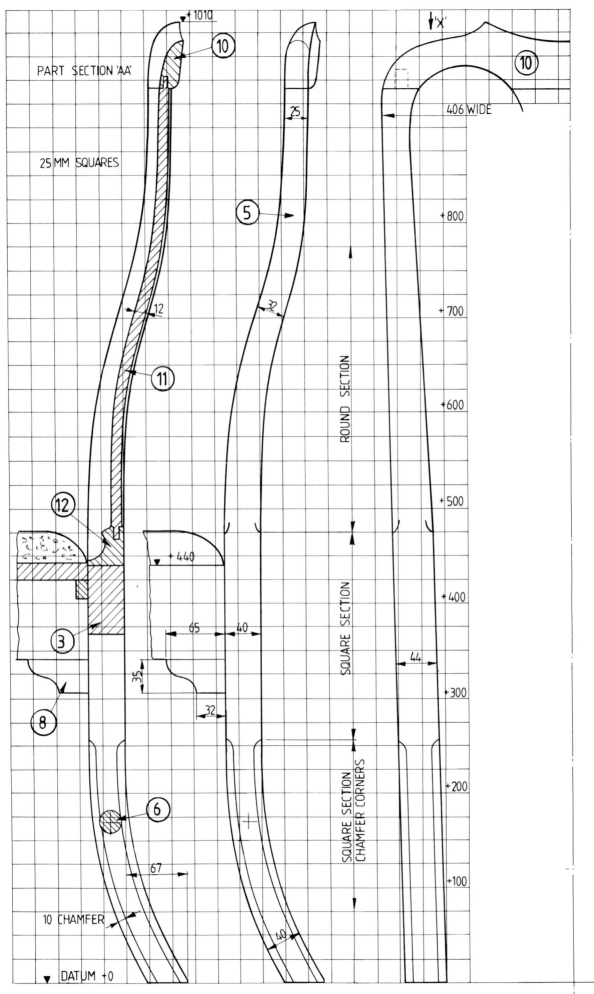

14.4 *Dimensions of back stile*

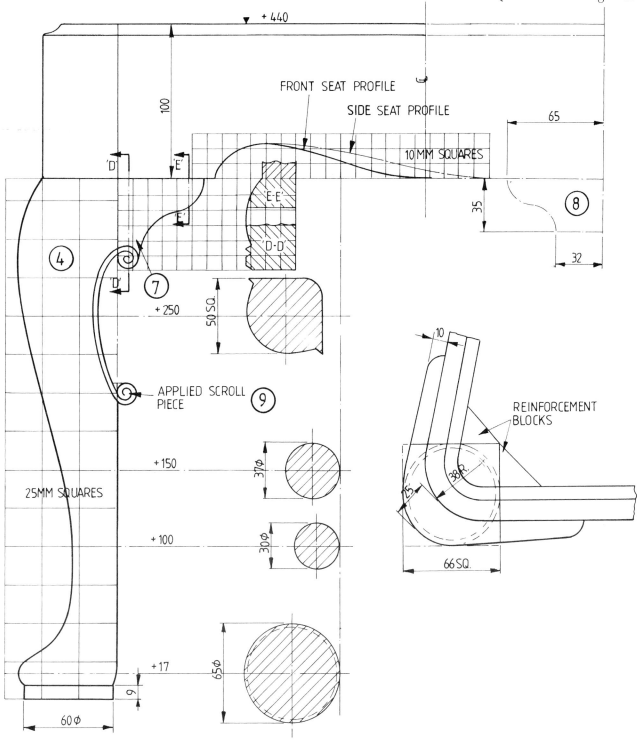

14.5 *Chair leg details*

and are rebated internally to take the drop seat (section HH). Routing and scraping techniques should be used to form these.

There are three variations in the back splat design, and the profiles for these are given in Fig 14.6. Outline 2 is the vase profile, so called because of its shape. Walnut has a reasonable affinity to being bent so it should be possible to successfully steam-bend the

splats without much trouble. You may have to experiment a bit with the moulded shape, and make the profile slightly tighter than required to allow for spring back. Make sure you select straight-grained wood without shakes or knots as these will cause defects in the final shape: chapter 8 gives further information on steam-bending.

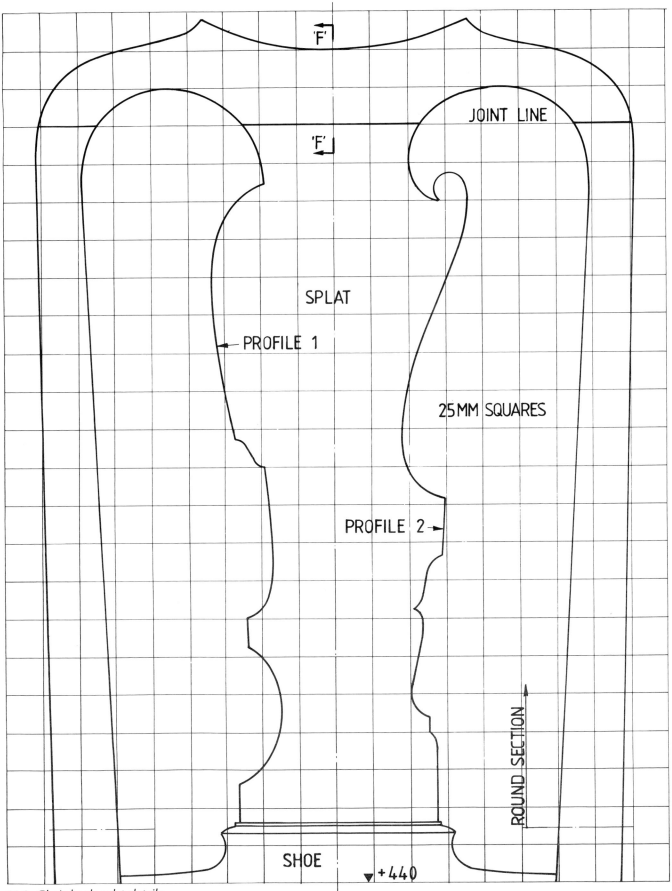

'F'

'F'

JOINT LINE

SPLAT

PROFILE 1

25 MM SQUARES

PROFILE 2

ROUND SECTION

SHOE

▼ +440

14.6 *Chair back splat details*

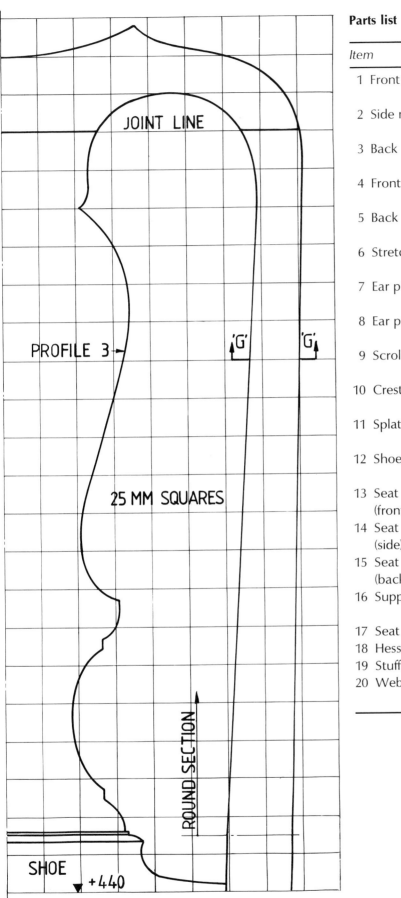

JOINT LINE

PROFILE 3

'G'　'G'

25 MM SQUARES

ROUND SECTION

SHOE ▼ +440

Parts list

Item	No	Material	Dimensions (mm)
1 Front rail	1	Virginia walnut	100 × 22 × 500 long
2 Side rail	2	Virginia walnut	100 × 22 × 400 long
3 Back rail	1	Virginia walnut	73 × 40 × 380 long
4 Front leg	2	Virginia walnut	66sq × 440 long
5 Back leg/stile	2	Virginia walnut	107 × 44 × 970 long
6 Stretcher	1	Virginia walnut	35sq × 360 long
7 Ear piece (1)	4	Virginia walnut	60 × 35 × 60 long
8 Ear piece (2)	2	Virginia walnut	35 × 22 × 65 long
9 Scroll piece	4	Virginia walnut	15sq × 50 long
10 Crest rail	1	Virginia walnut	70 × 40 × 420 long
11 Splat	1	Virginia walnut	180 × 12 × 520 long
12 Shoe	1	Virginia walnut	44 × 40 × 300 long
13 Seat frame (front)	1	Beech	75 × 20 × 500 long
14 Seat frame (side)	2	Beech	75 × 20 × 370 long
15 Seat frame (back)	1	Beech	75 × 20 × 400 long
16 Support strip	1	Virginia walnut	20 × 12 × 350 long
17 Seat cover	1	Leather	Quantity to suit
18 Hessian cover	–	Hessian	Quantity to suit
19 Stuffing	–	Horsehair	Quantity to suit
20 Webbing	–	Webbing	50 wide, length to suit

Chapter 15

Quartetto tables

The next two designs are from Dunham Massey in Cheshire, the seat of the Booths and Greys for many centuries, now owned by the National Trust. This red brick quadrangular building with an inner courtyard is referred to in the Domesday Book as belonging to a Saxon freeman, Eluard, and in 1070 to Hamo-de-Massey. In 1453 it was inherited by Robert Bothe (or Booth), and a later member of this family, Lord George Booth, 2nd Earl of Warrington, carried out major development work during 1720–50, enlarging the building to what it is today. He also laid out the formal parkland and gardens, and collected the outstanding walnut furniture and Huguenot silver.

In 1736 Lord George's daughter Mary married Henry Grey, 4th Earl of Stamford. The Greys were an extremely wealthy family, already owning land at Enville (Staffs) and Bradgate (Leics), and Dunham Massey became a third principal seat. The house was under tenancy for most of the nineteenth century. In 1905 the 9th Earl decided to reoccupy Dunham Massey, and carried out extensive repairs, engaging furniture historian Percy Macquoid to carry out interior redecoration. Roger Grey, 10th Earl of Stamford, painstakingly preserved Dunham Massey and its treasures, and when he died in 1976 the

15.2 *Quartetto tables*

custodianship passed to the National Trust.

One of the rooms restored in 1905 is the Green Saloon, where the set of mahogany quartetto tables (*c.* 1815) is found.

15.1 *Dunham Massey*

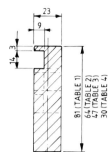

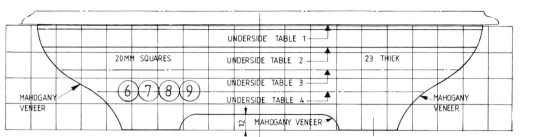

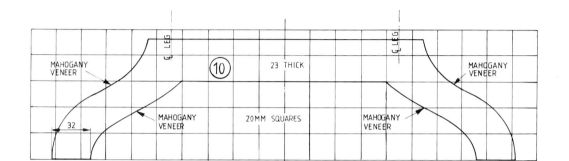

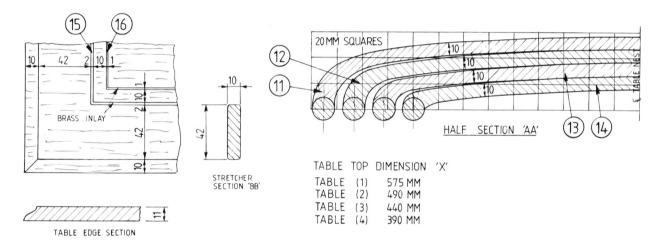

TABLE TOP DIMENSION 'X'

TABLE (1)   575 MM
TABLE (2)   490 MM
TABLE (3)   440 MM
TABLE (4)   390 MM

STRETCHER SECTION 'BB'

TABLE EDGE SECTION

15.3 *Miscellaneous table details*

Quartetto tables are a graduated set of four small tables that stow neatly within one another. They may be separated as required to serve as occasional tables for miscellaneous use. Typically, they stand on four finely-turned spindle legs, paired at each end. Each pair is joined at the top by the table rail, and at the bottom by a foot piece which, crudely, looks rather like a coat hanger. The spindle legs are linked at the back by semi-curved stretchers to stiffen the arrangement. Occasionally these tables are found supported on a pair of bar-form end standards, and sometimes one of the table tops may be inlaid chessboard style to serve as a games board. The finest are made of mahogany, rosewood or satinwood. They date mainly from the George III era to the early Victorian period. The quartetto tables here are inlaid with Regency brass banding.

Construction

The general arrangement drawings are given in Fig 15.4, and construction is an exercise in joinery, spindle turning and brass inlay work. Details of the end spindles (5) are given in Fig 15.5. These are long and slender, and therefore require the use of a lathe steady in turning. They are spigotted ready for connecting into the adjoining members. The support rails and foot pieces should present no difficulties, the only point to note about them is the external mahogany veneer added to conceal the end grain.

95

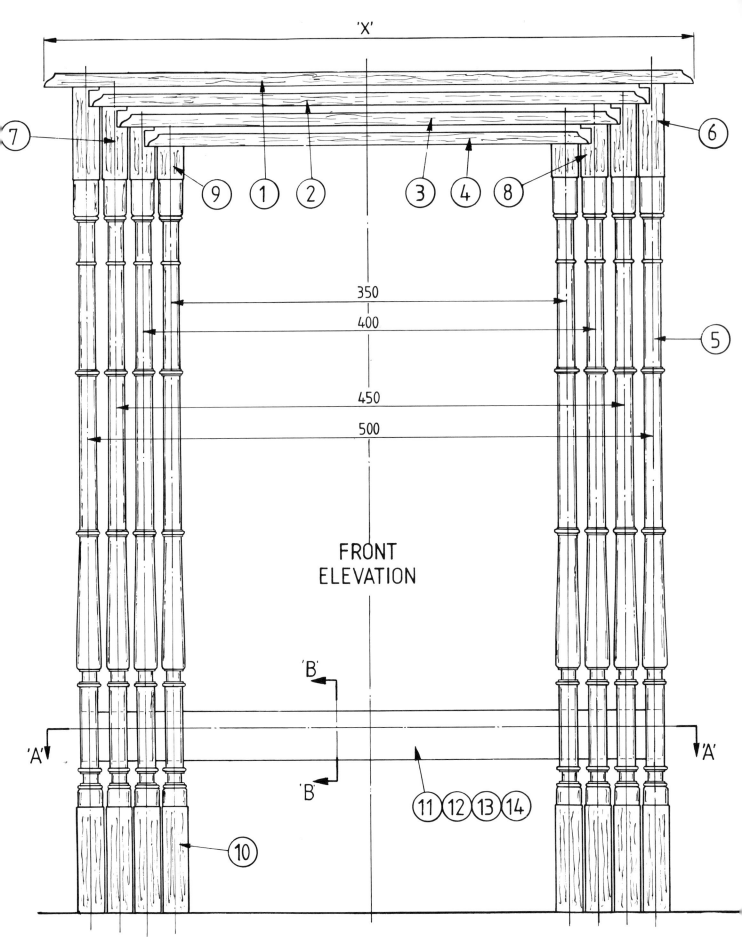

'X'

⑦

⑨ ① ② ③ ④ ⑧

⑥

350

400

⑤

450

500

FRONT
ELEVATION

'B'

'A'

'A'

'B'

⑪ ⑫ ⑬ ⑭

⑩

15.4 *General arrangement of quartetto tables*

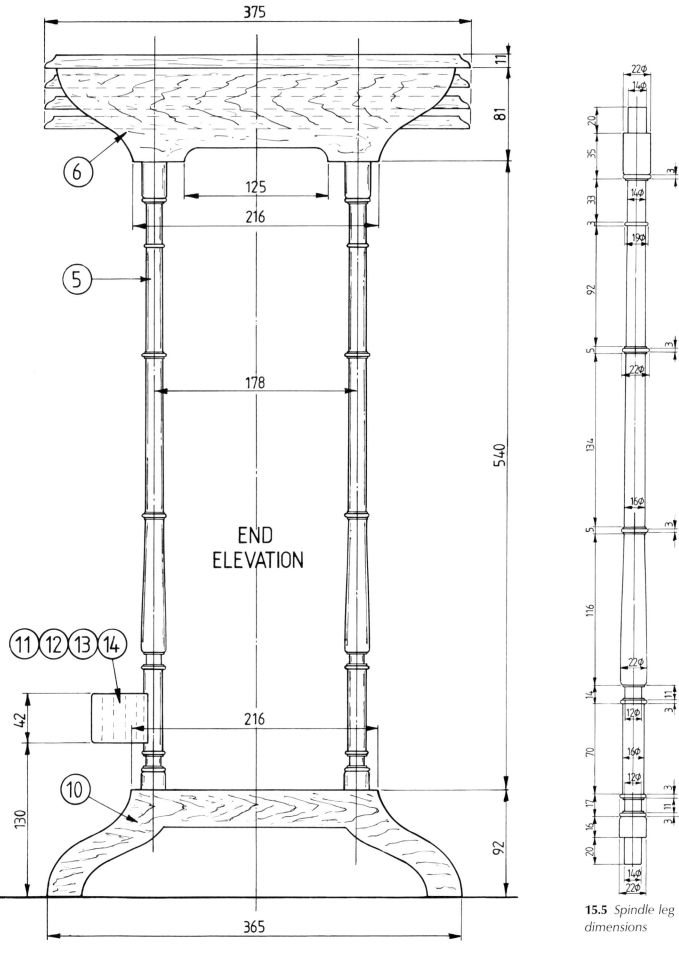

375

11

81

6

125

216

5

178

540

END
ELEVATION

11 12 13 14

42

216

130

10

365

92

22φ
14φ

20

35

3

33

14φ

3

19φ

92

5

3

22φ

134

16φ

5

3

116

22φ

14

3 11

12φ

70

16φ

17

12φ

3

3 11

16

20

14φ

22φ

15.5 Spindle leg
dimensions

Each table top is made from a single piece of mahogany. Since today it is difficult to obtain fine, high-quality, close grained mahogany, you might consider the application of a curl veneer for better effect. The table edge profile is formed using routing techniques. In the original the table tops are glued to the support rails, but it might be wise to consider additional screw fixing in some way from the underside. The profile of the semi-curved stretchers is given in Fig 15.5. These are screw-fixed, as well as glued to the spindle legs, and the holes filled to conceal the screw heads. The table is french polished.

Brass inlay

One of the problems with brass inlay is that if it is not properly fixed flush with the surface of the wood, when the item is polished it has a habit of being caught on the duster. This lifts it further, generally making things worse. It is therefore important to

15.6 *Table top brass inlay*

ensure that the brass strips are well fitted and glued in flush with the surface of the wood. The brass inlay is illustrated in Fig 15.6. In Regency furniture, the shrinkage of the wood in which the brass strip is fitted sometimes forces the strip out of its groove. It then has to be relaid.

Parts list

Item	No	Material	Dimensions (mm)
1 Table top (1)	1	Mahogany	375 × 11 × 575 long
2 Table top (2)	1	Mahogany	375 × 11 × 490 long
3 Table top (3)	1	Mahogany	375 × 11 × 440 long
4 Table top (4)	1	Mahogany	375 × 11 × 390 long
5 Spindle leg	16	Mahogany	30sq × 600 long
6 Support rail (1)	2	Mahogany	81 × 23 × 360 long
7 Support rail (2)	2	Mahogany	64 × 23 × 360 long
8 Support rail (3)	2	Mahogany	47 × 23 × 360 long
9 Support rail (4)	2	Mahogany	30 × 23 × 360 long
10 Foot piece	8	Mahogany	92 × 23 × 370 long
11 Stretcher (1)	1	Mahogany	75 × 45 × 450 long
12 Stretcher (2)	1	Mahogany	Bandsawn from wood for item 11
13 Stretcher (3)	1	Mahogany	Bandsawn from wood for item 11
14 Stretcher (4)	1	Mahogany	Bandsawn from wood for item 11
15 Inlay (1)	1	Brass	2 wide × 6200 long total
16 Inlay (2)	1	Brass	1 wide × 6200 long total

Chapter 16

Satinwood Pembroke table

The second furniture design from Dunham Massey, is, like the Quartetto tables, selected from the Green Saloon. Originally a dining room, the saloon was so distant from the kitchens that the 9th Earl of Stamford changed it into a comfortable sitting room. Furniture here includes a William and Mary walnut oyster veneer side table c. 1690, satinwood bookcases (c. 1790), a small marquetry bonheur de jour, and three fine quality George III Pembroke tables, two in mahogany with marquetry inlay, and a third, in Satinwood (c. 1815).

Pembroke tables are closely associated with the Sheraton period. They are small rectangular or oval tables, standing typically on square tapered legs, with a single drawer in the frieze, and a small table flap either side. Their name originates from the Countess of Pembroke and Montgomery, who is said to have been the first to commission one. Their period dates from about 1765 to 1820.

16.1 *Pembroke table*

16.2 *Drawer front*

Pembroke tables adapt particularly well to the oval form top, and the more ornate rectangular ones sometimes have a wavy or serpentine outline. Extended, their size varies between 900–1100mm in length, and the small table flaps pivot on a rule joint supported on knuckle hinged brackets. The frieze on the opposite side to the drawer is usually simulated as a false drawer front to match the sliding one. Although the square, tapered leg form is predominant, other variants include designs with turned and fluted style legs. Less frequently, one may come across Pembroke tables mounted on a centre pedestal. In the main they do not have stretchers, but if these are present, they will be of fine proportions to match the delicate table form. They always stand on petite castors.

16.3 *Table top centre detail*

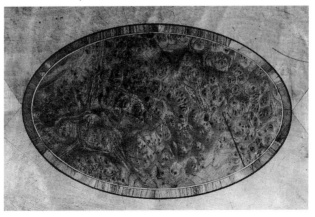

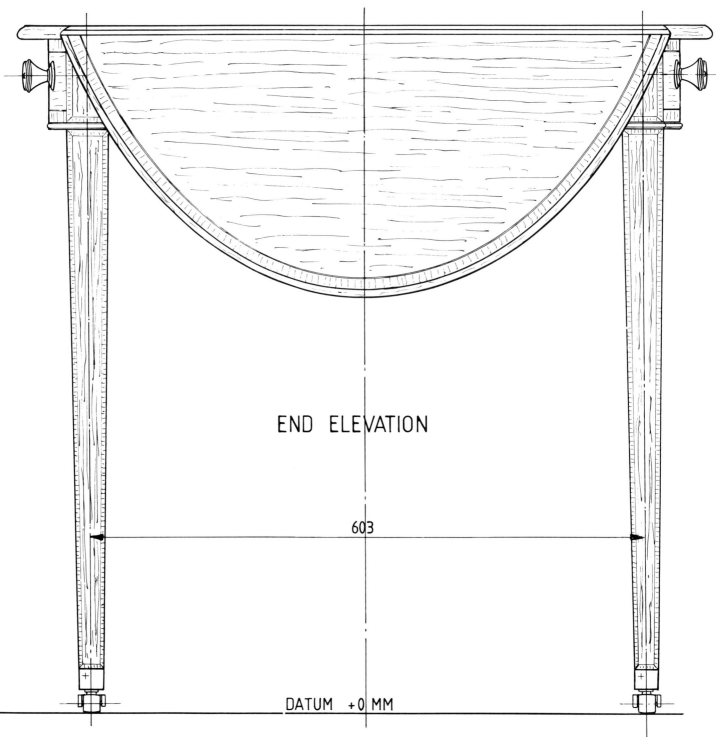

END ELEVATION

603

DATUM +0 MM

16.4 *General arrangement of Pembroke table*

Construction

The general arrangement is shown in Fig 16.4, with additional sectional details in Figs 16.5 and 16.8. The work can be divided into two aspects: first, the preparation of the table framework, complete with legs; and second, the table top. The table is of fine quality and requires the craftsman to work with some degree of accuracy. The marquetry work covers not only the table top, but also the drawer fronts and legs.

Legs and framework

Commence construction with the preparation of the legs (1) and adjoining rails (5), (6), (7) and (8). Details of these are given in Figs 16.5 and 16.7. Complete these components with all necessary mortise-and-tenon

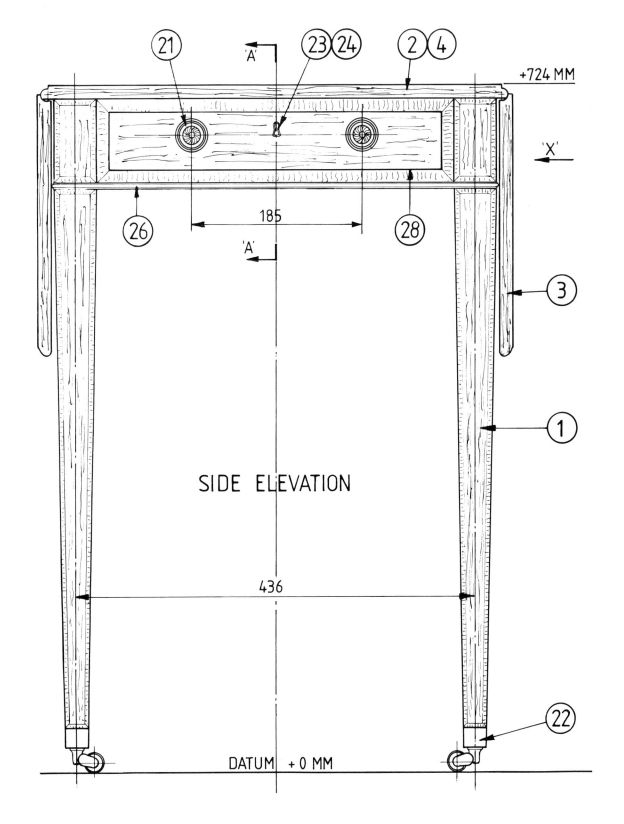

'A'

+724 MM

'X'

185

'A'

SIDE ELEVATION

436

DATUM + 0 MM

jointing, castor end tenons, beading rebates, etc, and then carry out a trial assembly. When this is acceptable, dismantle the frame and finish the external veneer work, which is much easier done on the loose parts. This includes the satinwood marquetry on the legs and the simulated false drawer veneer work on the end rail (8). Note that while the legs are veneered on all sides, the edge crossbanding

only extends to the two external faces. Finally, add the swivel flap and side linings (10), (11) and (12).

Drawer

The workmanship on the drawer reflects the skill of the craftsman who carried out the original commission. The oak linings, in the finest English tradition, are only 6mm thick, and the dovetails

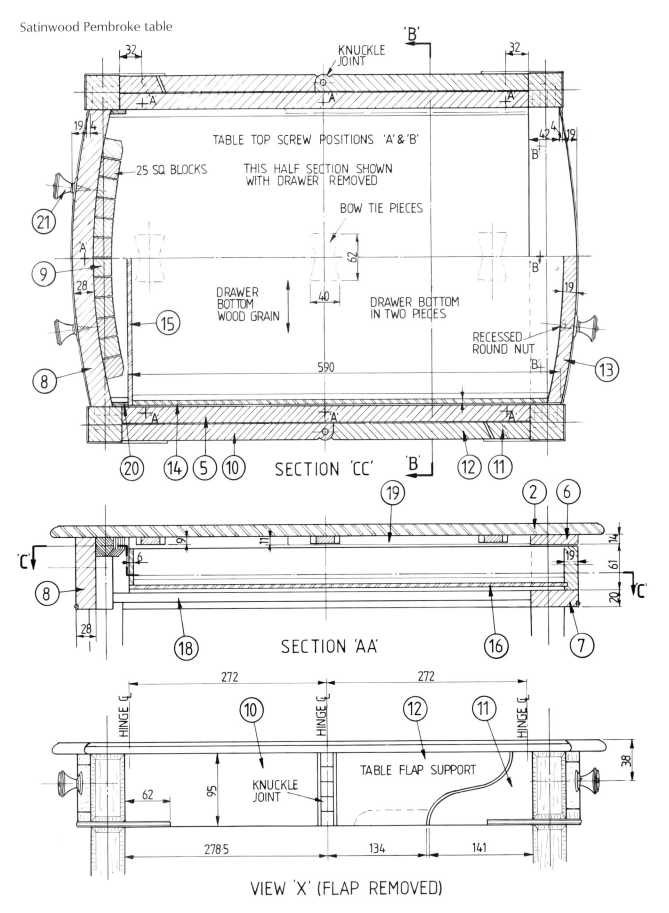

'B'

KNUCKLE
JOINT

32

32

'B'

19 4

TABLE TOP SCREW POSITIONS 'A' & 'B'

42 4 19

'B'

25 SQ BLOCKS

THIS HALF SECTION SHOWN
WITH DRAWER REMOVED

21

BOW TIE PIECES

'B'

9

62

'B'

28

A

15

DRAWER
BOTTOM
WOOD GRAIN

40

DRAWER BOTTOM
IN TWO PIECES

19

8

590

RECESSED
ROUND NUT

'B'

13

20 14 5 10

SECTION 'CC'

'B'

12 11

19

2 6

'C'

9

11

14

8

6

19

61

'C'

18

SECTION 'AA'

16

20

7

272

272

HINGE ℄

10

HINGE ℄

12

11

HINGE ℄

38

62

95

KNUCKLE
JOINT

TABLE FLAP SUPPORT

278·5

134

141

VIEW 'X' (FLAP REMOVED)

16.5 *Sectional details of Pembroke table*

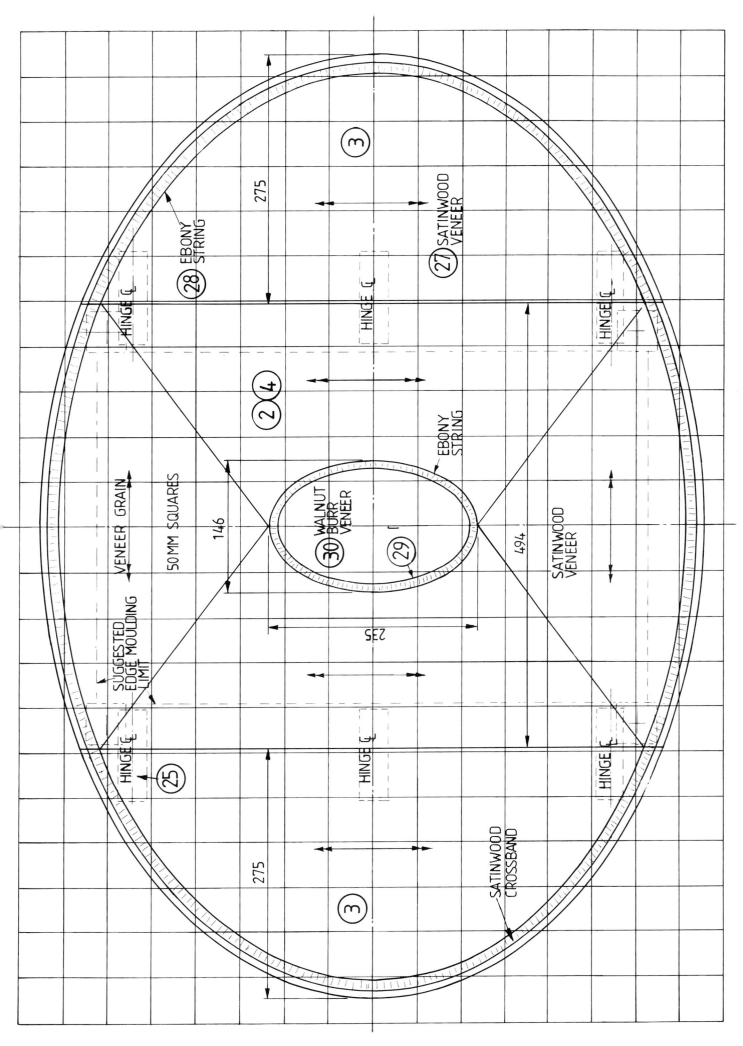

16.6 *Table top details*

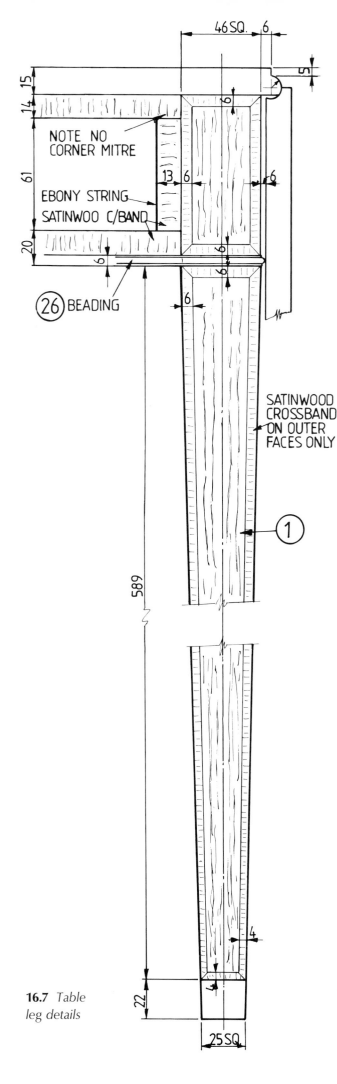

46 SQ. **6**

15
14
61
NOTE NO
CORNER MITRE
13 6
6
6
EBONY STRING
SATINWOO C/BAND
20
6
6
6
6

26 BEADING

SATINWOOD
CROSSBAND
ON OUTER
FACES ONLY

1

589

4

16.7 *Table leg details*

22

25 SQ.

connecting the drawer front are finely cut. The grain direction of the drawer bottom is across the drawer, typical of the period. Whether the drawer front veneer work is completed prior to drawer assembly is optional. When the drawer is completed and satisfactorily fitted, set the thickness of the back stop (20) so that the front is flush with rails (6) and (7).

Table top

The table top is constructed separately, then added to the supporting framework. Fig 16.6 shows this on a squared background to aid marking out on the hardwood. In the original, the centre table section (2) appears to be made of oak, possibly in two pieces, with mahogany edging outside the table frame where it can be seen, and the end flaps (3) are made in mahogany. The rule joints also appear to be in mahogany. The bow tie pieces on the underneath (section CC) are puzzling, and I believe they may be further evidence of the craftsman's skill: He probably foresaw that this joint could open due to seasoning contraction at some later date, and incorporated three transverse dovetail pieces to counteract this.

When the table top assembly is complete, add the satinwood veneer, centre elliptic motif, and box and the ebony string work. The table top is screw-fixed to the frame as detailed in Fig 16.8. The row of 25mm square blocks fixed to the edge of the back rail (8) suggests that the original was also glued.

Brasswork

The drawer and its opposing false front are fitted with rosette pattern knobs, and the table stands on tiny brass castors typical of the period. Details of these are given in Fig 16.9, and are available commercially.

Finish

The suggested finish is a french polish. In the original the swivel flap and side linings (10), (11) and (12) are made of beech, but have a simulated dull mahogany finish to tone in with other visible mahogany work. Both the satinwood Pembroke table and the Quartetto table design in Chapter 15 were stamped 'P.S.', indicating they were made by the same person.

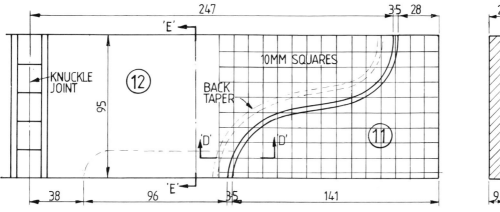

247

'E'

35 28

12

95

KNUCKLE
JOINT

10MM SQUARES

BACK
TAPER

11

'D' 'D'

38

96 'E'

35

141

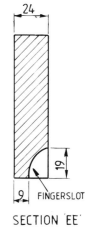

24

19

9 FINGERSLOT

SECTION 'EE'

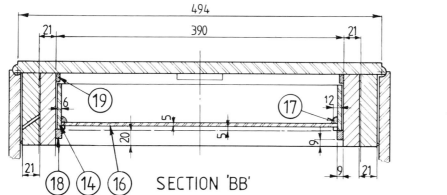

494

21

390

21

19

6

17

12

5

20

5

9

18 14 16

SECTION 'BB'

21

9 21

SECTION 'DD'

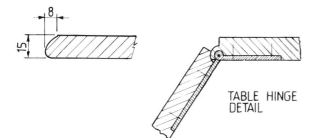

8

15

TABLE HINGE
DETAIL

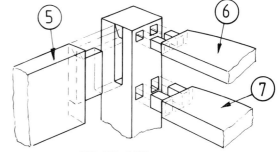

5

6

7

CORNER DETAIL

SATINWOOD
CROSSBAND

MAHOGANY
BASE

EBONY
STRING

13

TABLE EDGE DETAIL

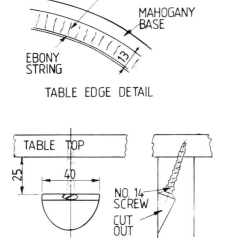

TABLE TOP

25

40

NO. 14
SCREW

CUT
OUT

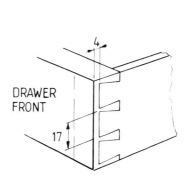

4

DRAWER
FRONT

17

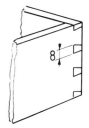

8

16.8 *Miscellaneous table details*

Satinwood Pembroke table

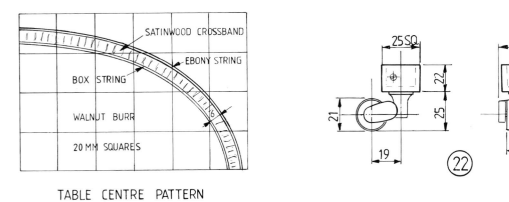

TABLE CENTRE PATTERN

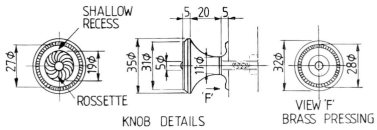

16.9 *Brasswork details*

ROSSETTE

KNOB DETAILS

VIEW 'F'
BRASS PRESSING

Parts list

Item	No	Material	Dimensions (mm)	Item	No	Material	Dimensions (mm)
1 Leg	4	Mahogany	48sq × 700 long	17 Beading	2	Oak	8 × 600 long
2 Table top	1	Oak	800 × 520 × 15 thick	18 Runner	2	Softwood	12 × 9 × 600 long
				19 Tip stop	2	Softwood	11 × 5 × 330 long
3 Table flap	2	Mahogany	300 × 15 × 700 long	20 Back stop	2	Softwood	30 × 9 × 90 long
4 Table edging	1	Mahogany	15 thick section to suit	21 Knob	4	Brass	Regency style, purchase to suit
5 Side rail	2	Softwood	95 × 24 × 650 long	22 Castor	4	Brass	Regency style, purchase to suit
6 Top rail	1	Oak	70 × 14 × 480 long				
7 Bottom rail	1	Oak	70 × 20 × 480 long	23 Lock	1	Brass	Purchase to suit
8 End rail	1	Mahogany	95 × 50 × 480 long	24 Escutcheon	2	Brass	Purchase to suit
9 Support block	12	Mahogany	25sq × 350 total length	25 Table top hinge	6	Steel	Purchase to suit, see script
10 Side piece	2	Beech	95 × 20 × 320 long	26 Veneer, burr walnut	–	Walnut	160 × 260
11 End piece	2	Beech	95 × 20 × 170 long				
12 Table flap	2	Beech	95 × 20 × 290 long	27 Veneer, satinwood	–	Satinwood	Quantity to suit table top
13 Drawer front	1	Oak	65 × 45 × 420 long				
14 Side lining	2	Oak	65 × 6 × 600 long	28 Ebony string	–	Ebony	5200 approx. length
15 Back lining	1	Oak	65 × 6 × 420 long	29 Box string	–	Box	4000 approx. length
16 Drawer bottom	1	Oak	310 × 5 × 840 total length	30 Screws	–	Steel	Miscellaneous

Chapter 17

Hepplewhite chair

The pinnacled building of Capesthorne Hall in Cheshire is about three miles from the Jodrell Bank radio telescope, and is the home of the Bromley-Davenport family. The next two furniture designs are from this house: a Hepplewhite dining chair (*c.* 1780) and an American double chest (*c.* 1775).

Historical references quote Ranuf de Capesthorne as the last owner bearing the name of the estate during the late fourteenth century. His daughter Sarah brought it to John Le Warde as her marriage dowry, and descendants of this family were Capesthorne's custodians for more than 300 years. In 1722, John Ward demolished the old manor on the site, and built a new Jacobean style brick building. His heiress daughter Penelope married Davies Davenport, and the ownership of Capesthorne has since remained with this family in an unbroken descent through the male line.

Capesthorne Hall and its two adjoining wings were substantially altered by Edward Blore in 1837. In 1861, the south façade was destroyed by a disastrous fire, and was later rebuilt by Anthony Salvin. It was he who changed the main entrance from the centre to the side where visitors now enter.

Furniture of note at Capesthorne includes an unusual set of Ceylonese (Sri Lankan) settees and chairs in the saloon, and the drawing room and the state bedroom feature several impressive pieces of Boulle work, the latter including a gilt commode and a serpentine table. In the Yellow Room are part of a set of four Hepplewhite dining chairs. These I thought would suit the Gillow or the 'D-end' dining table designs featured in his book, as an alternative to the Chippendale and Queen Anne dining chairs.

The chair which the cabinetmaker George Hepplewhite is probably most closely associated with is the Hepplewhite shield-back. Another style attributed to him has an arched moulded crest rail, as in Fig 17.2, sometimes referred to as a 'camel's back' chair, for obvious reasons. This arch is cleverly repeated in the form of the seat front. The back has a pierced splat, with a wheel back centre carved with a radial wheat ear motif. The front legs are of the reeded, square taper form. These features are all typical Hepplewhite. If you are interested in viewing other chairs of this type, there are some in the corridors of Dunham Massey, which have plain pierced splats but not the wheel back centrepiece.

Construction

The general arrangement of the Hepplewhite chair is given in Fig 17.2, and sectional details of the seat, etc,

17.1 *Capesthorne Hall*

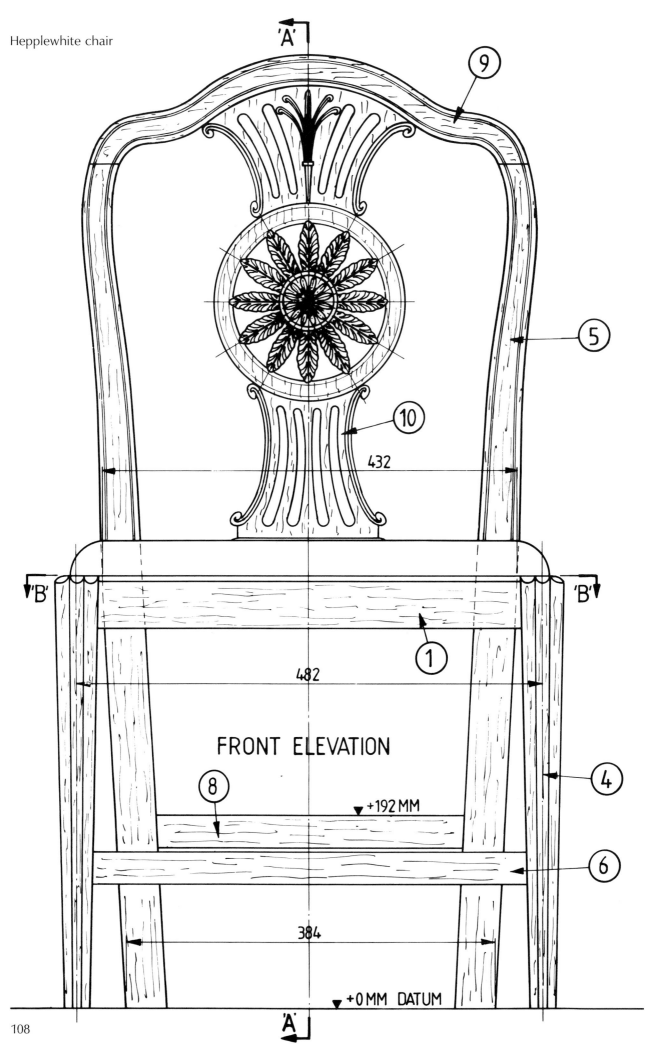

Hepplewhite chair

'A'

⑨

⑤

432

⑩

'B'   'B'

482

①

FRONT ELEVATION

⑧

▽ +192 MM

④

⑥

384

▽ +0 MM DATUM

'A'

17.2 *General arrangement of chair*

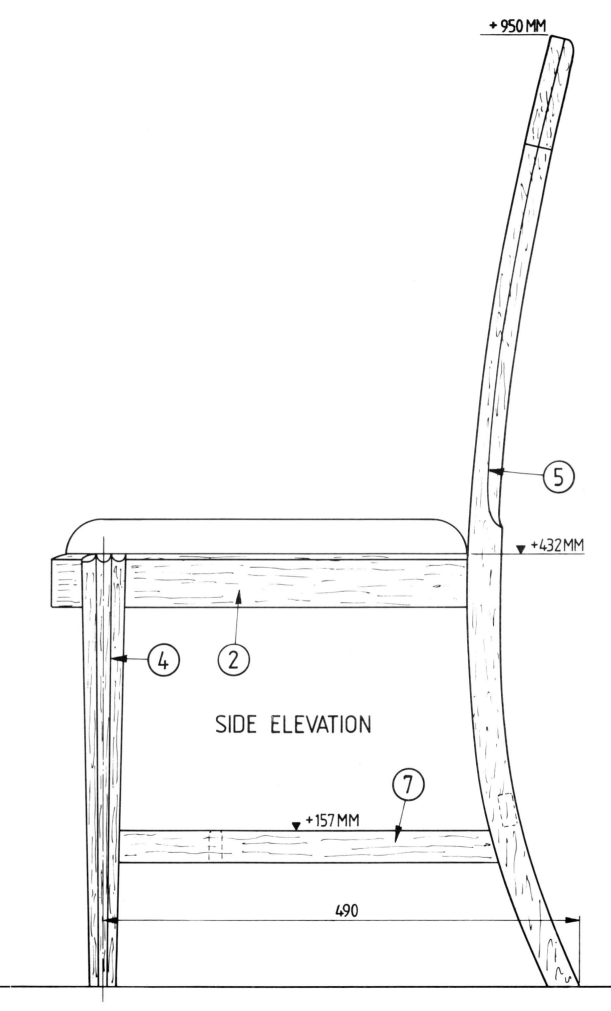

+ 950 MM

⑤

▼ +432MM

④

②

SIDE ELEVATION

⑦

▼ +157 MM

490

17.3 *Hepplewhite dining chair*

in Fig 17.4. The chair is principally an exercise in joinery, a small amount of carving on the splat, and some seat upholstery work.

Front legs

Dimensions of the front legs, seat rails, stretchers and other miscellaneous details are given in Fig 17.5. The seat rails are connected to the legs using mortise-and tenon-joints. A problem may be experienced in cutting the leg taper reeds. Referring to Fig 17.6, a suggested method of doing this is as follows. Prepare a leg section 45mm square, and on to this mark out the vein lines of the tapered reeds, ie lines 'B' and 'C'.

Mark another pair of tapered lines 'A' one either side, from the top of the leg and parallel to lines 'C'. Now plane the leg down to the outer taper lines 'A'. Prepare a scratch stock with a cutter to profile 'X', and using the side of the half-tapered leg as a fence, cut one of the centre veins 'C'. Repeat this procedure down the opposite side of the leg to form the second vein. This will complete the centre reed. Now plane the leg down further and taper it to lines 'B', ie to the final leg taper. Prepare the scratch stock again, only this time for cutting the corner beads using a cutter as 'Y'. Using the leg side again as a fence, finish scratch-cutting the outer two reeds. This procedure should then be repeated at 90° to cut the reeds on the second external face.

Legs and splat

Details of the chair back stile are given in Fig 17.7. These are drawn out on a squared background to aid transfer to the wood. It should be possible to cut two stiles from one piece of wood. The chair back profile is given in Fig 17.8, along with miscellaneous sections through the splat and stile. The pierced back splat sections can be cut with a fretsaw.

To produce the beaded edging of the annular section surrounding the wheat ears (section 'JJ'), set up a scratch stock with a suitable cutter fixed to a radial bar arranged to pivot about the splat centre. Finally, complete the wheat ears and feather motif carving. The back splat is tenoned into the crest rail (9) and the shoe (11). The splat centre is illustrated in Fig 17.9. The scratch stock used for forming the moulding on the splat centre piece can also be used for those on the back stile and crest rail.

Seat

The seat is of the drop-in type, and the upholstery follows the usual pattern with webbing, hessian lining, stuffing and cover. Recommendations for an upholstery took kit are given in Chapter 20, and the choice of cover is left to you. I found these chairs very comfortable to sit on.

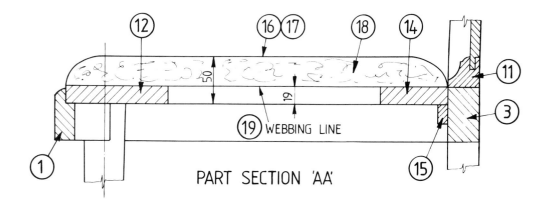

PART SECTION 'AA'

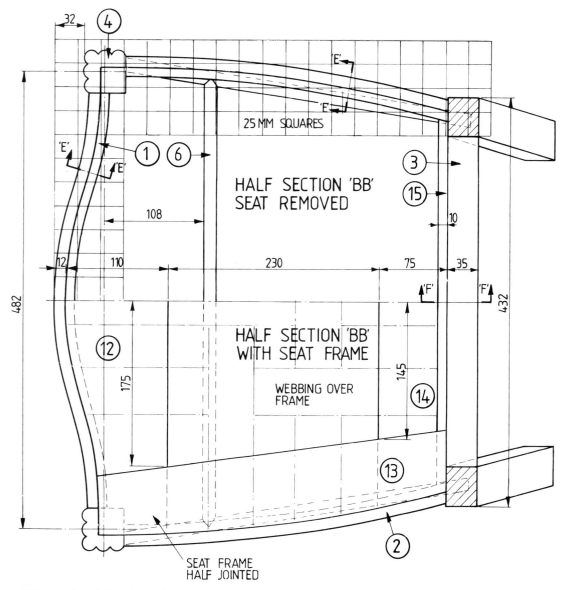

25 MM SQUARES

HALF SECTION 'BB'
SEAT REMOVED

HALF SECTION 'BB'
WITH SEAT FRAME

WEBBING OVER
FRAME

SEAT FRAME
HALF JOINTED

17.4 *Sectional details of chair*

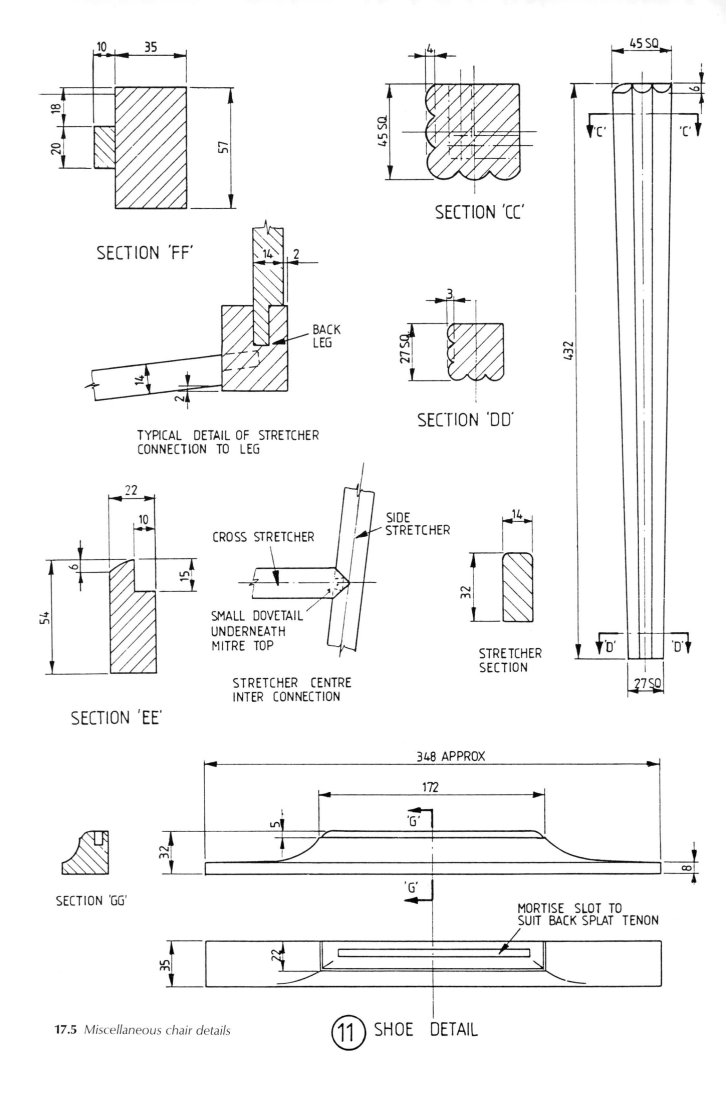

SECTION 'FF'

SECTION 'CC'

BACK LEG

TYPICAL DETAIL OF STRETCHER
CONNECTION TO LEG

SECTION 'DD'

CROSS STRETCHER

SIDE
STRETCHER

SMALL DOVETAIL
UNDERNEATH
MITRE TOP

STRETCHER CENTRE
INTER CONNECTION

STRETCHER
SECTION

SECTION 'EE'

348 APPROX

172

'G'

'G'

MORTISE SLOT TO
SUIT BACK SPLAT TENON

SECTION 'GG'

17.5 *Miscellaneous chair details*

(11) SHOE DETAIL

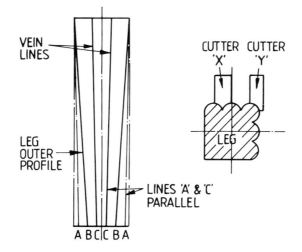

17.6 *Cutting leg taper reeds*

Parts list

Item	No	Material	Dimensions (mm)
1 Front rail	1	Mahogany	54 × 76 × 530 long
2 Side rail	1	Mahogany	54 × 38 × 430 long
3 Back rail	2	Mahogany	57 × 35 × 430 long
4 Front leg	2	Mahogany	45sq × 440 long
5 Back leg/stile	2	Mahogany	110 × 42 × 900 long
6 Cross stretcher	1	Mahogany	32 × 14 × 500 long
7 Side stretcher	2	Mahogany	32 × 14 × 470 long
8 Back stretcher	1	Mahogany	32 × 14 × 400 long
9 Crest rail	1	Mahogany	120 × 30 × 480 long
10 Splat	1	Mahogany	230 × 30 × 500 long
11 Shoe	1	Mahogany	35 × 32 × 350 long
12 Seat frame (front)	1	Beech	110 × 19 × 500 long
13 Seat frame (side)	2	Beech	80 × 19 × 400 long
14 Seat frame (back)	1	Beech	75 × 19 × 440 long
15 Support strip	1	Mahogany	20 × 10 × 400 long
16 Seat cover	1	Material	Quantity to suit
17 Hessian cover	—	Hessian	Quantity to suit
18 Stuffing	—	Horsehair	Quantity to suit
19 Webbing	—	Webbing	50 wide, length to suit

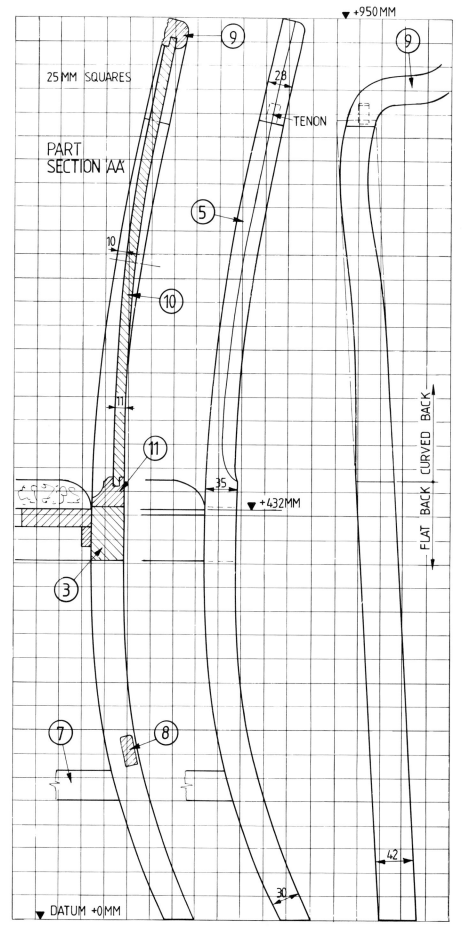

▼ +950MM

25MM SQUARES

28

TENON

PART
SECTION 'AA'

⑨

⑤

10

⑩

11

35

▼ +432MM

⑪

FLAT BACK — CURVED BACK

③

⑨

⑦

⑧

30

42

▼ DATUM +0MM

17.7 *Chair back leg details*

114

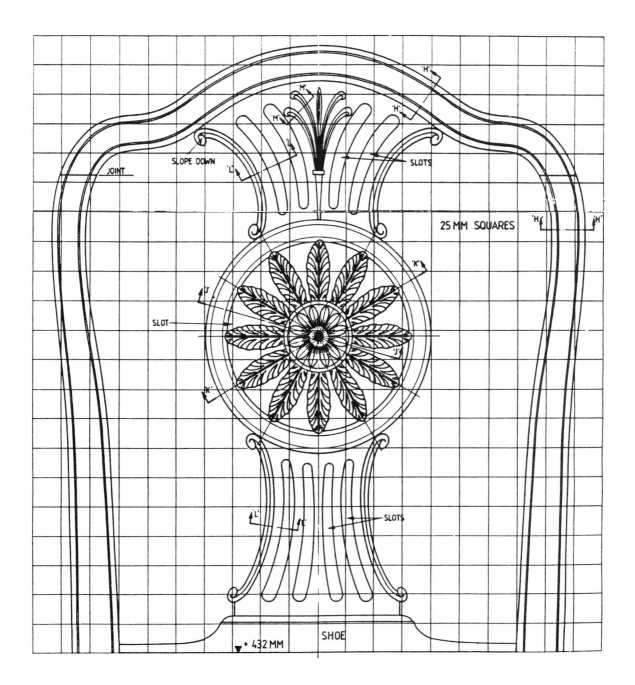

JOINT   SLOPE DOWN   'M'   'M'   'H'   'H'

'L'   SLOTS

25 MM SQUARES   'H'   'H'

SLOT   'K'   'J'

'J'   'K'

'L'   SLOTS

SHOE

▽ + 432 MM

SECTION 'JJ'
19
11

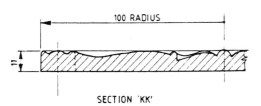
SECTION 'KK'
100 RADIUS
11

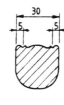
SECTION 'HH'
30
5   5

SECTION 'LL'
11

RAISED HONEYSUCKLE PATTERN

SECTION 'MM'

17.8 *Chair back details*

115

17.9 *Back splat centrepiece*

17.10 *Chair leg, flute detail*

Chapter 18

Double chest

The American Room in Capesthorne Hall is furnished from a house near Philadelphia, USA, belonging to the late Lady Bromley-Davenport. The furniture includes a mahogany desk and bookcase with swan neck pediment (c. 1750), a piecrust tripod table (c. 1775), a mahogany folding table with flap over top and reeded legs, and an eighteenth-century mahogany frame wing chair. Also in this room is a Boston four-post bed with tester (c. 1790), and a fine quality Virginia walnut double chest (c. 1775).

The double chest is a two-tier arrangement with ten graduated drawers, a cavetto cornice and ogee feet. The bottom chest has three drawers, and the top one seven, including an upper row of three. The drawer fronts are in solid Virginia walnut, with cedar linings (used for its worm resistant properties and sweet smell), and have swan neck handles on curvilinear backing plates.

The quality of double chests depends upon a number of factors, such as the wood, the bracket feet, the crest details and the brasswork. As always with antique furniture, the wood colour and patination is one of the most important aspects. Chests made of curl or flame grain hardwood, or with applied burr veneers, are more desirable than those with a plainer grain. On simpler arrangements the crest decoration features a moulded cornice, often of cavetto, dentil or fluted form. Those of a higher order have a more complicated structure such as a canted corner, or swan neck pediment, with fretted pattern work in between. Plainer chests stand on square form bracket feet, while better ones have an ogee profile. These have an S-shaped contour, and are more complicated to make.

The brasswork is variable: it may consist of a simple swan neck handle on twin button mounts, or it may be more elaborate with a curvilinear, or pierced backing plate, as in the double chest design. Brasswork is also an indicator of date, for example towards the end of the eighteenth century the pattern changed towards stamped round or oval rosette style backing plates. On eighteenth-century American furniture, the brasswork was often imported from England.

18.1 *Double chest*

Construction

The general arrangement of the double chest is given in Fig 18.2, and sectional details in Figs 18.3 and 18.4. The constructional work is largely cabinet work, and a small amount of veneering on the sides is required.

Chippendale dining chair

Oyster veneer chest

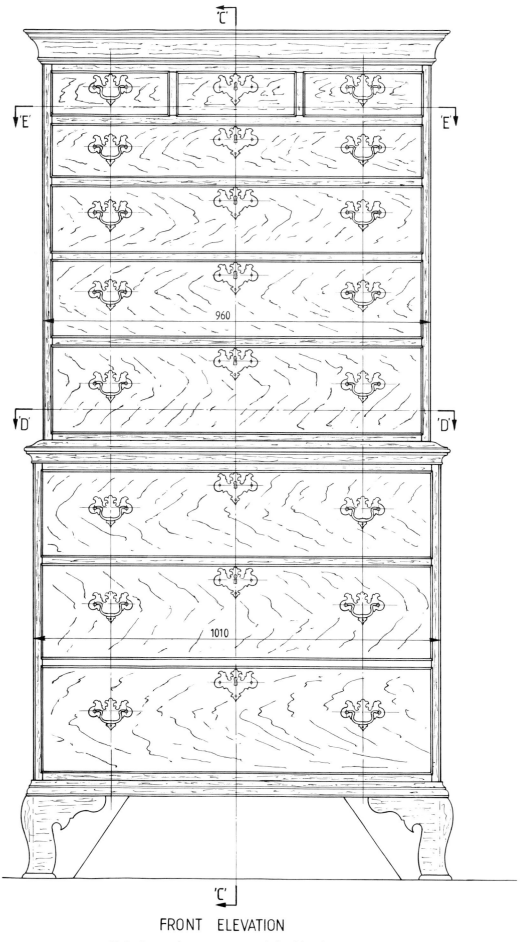

'C'

'E'   'E'

'D'   'D'

960

1010

'C'

FRONT ELEVATION

18.2 *General arrangement of double chest*

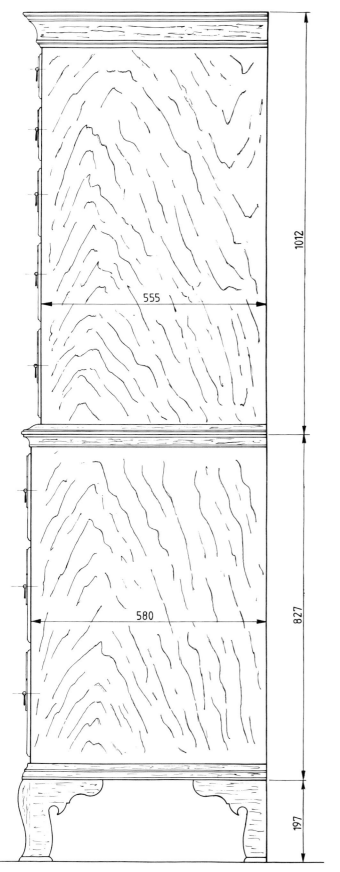

SIDE ELEVATION

Each chest is built as a separate entity, commencing with the bottom one and progressing upwards.

Chest carcases

The bottom chest consists of carcase panels (16), (17) and (18), dovetail jointed. From inspection of the original, these slot horizontally into the top and bottom boards (Fig 18.4). Prepare the side panels (17) with all necessary grooving etc, to accept the front rails, drawer runners, dust boards and back, (19), (20), (21) and (22). Grooves are not required for drawer runners (23). The side panels (17) are veneered in Virginia walnut with applied hardwood edging strips at the front to conceal the end grain (Fig 18.5). The upper chest construction follows a similar format to the lower one with slightly smaller panel members. It has additional division strips (11) partitioning the upper row of three drawers.

Ogee feet

Details of the ogee feet for the lower chest are given in Fig 18.5, drawn on a squared background for ease of transferring the shape to the hardwood. The feet are built up round a centre leg support (27), resting on a pad foot (29), with externally applied ogee shape pieces (28). These items are then added to the bottom chest, making it free standing.

Cover strips

A number of mouldings need to be prepared and added. These are the crest cover strip (14), the base cover strip (26), and the chest joint line cover strips (15), (25). Moulding (14) is often referred to as a cavetto cornice, because of its concave shape. The cover strip (15) serves to locate the upper chest relative to the lower one. Routing techniques should be employed to make these mouldings.

Drawers

Drawer details are given in Fig 18.5, and are of dovetail construction. A table is given with the dimensions specific to each drawer.

Brasswork

Details of the swan neck brass plate handles are given in Fig 18.4, and these are commercially available if required.

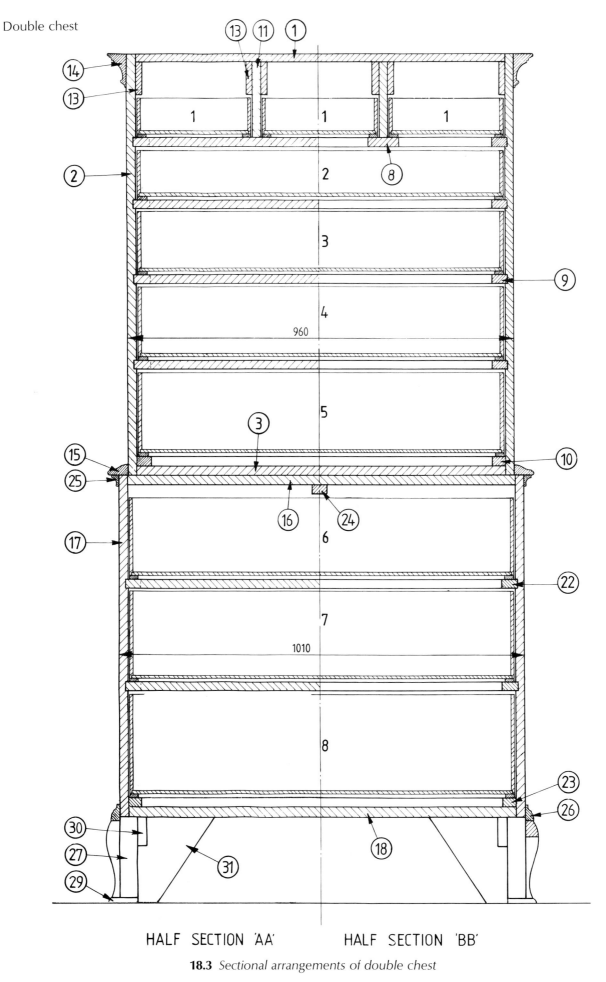

HALF SECTION 'AA'   HALF SECTION 'BB'

18.3 *Sectional arrangements of double chest*

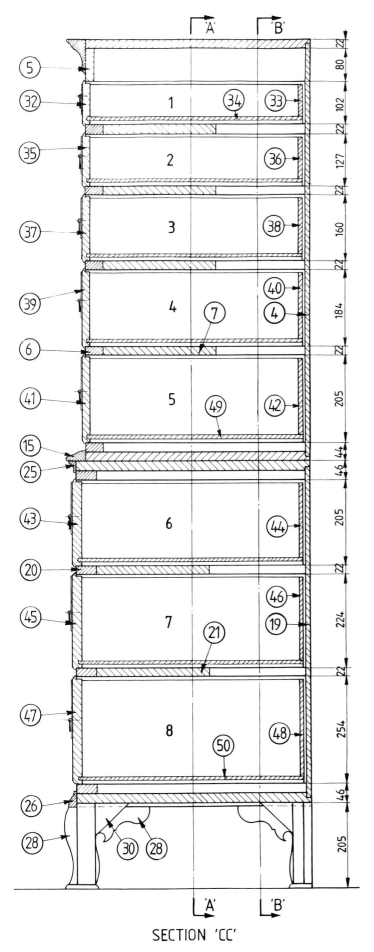

SECTION 'CC'

Parts list

Item	No	Material	Dimensions (mm)
1 Carcase top	1	Pine	555 × 22 × 960 long
2 Carcase side	2	Pine	555 × 22 × 1012 long
3 Carcase bottom	1	Pine	555 × 22 × 960 long
4 Back	1	Pine	350 × 12 × 3000 long total
5 Fascia strip	1	Virginia walnut	80 × 22 × 960 long
6 Front rail	5	Virginia walnut	45 × 22 × 960 long
7 Dust board	4	Pine	280 × 22 × 960 long
8 Runner strip (1)	2	Pine	76 × 22 × 240 long
9 Runner strip (2)	8	Pine	35 × 22 × 240 long
10 Runner strip (3)	2	Pine	42 × 22 × 525 long
11 Drawer partition	2	Pine	182 × 22 × 532 long
12 Edging strip	1	Virginia walnut	22 × 12 × 2400 long total
13 Drawer tip stop	6	Pine	80 × 16 × 520 long
14 Crest cover strip	1	Virginia walnut	85 × 48 × 1300 long total
15 Joint cover strip (1)	1	Virginia walnut	50 × 25 × 2400 long total
Lower chest			
16 Carcase top	1	Pine	580 × 25 × 1010 long
17 Carcase side	2	Pine	580 × 22 × 827 long
18 Carcase bottom	1	Pine	580 × 24 × 1010 long
19 Back	1	Pine	290 × 12 × 3100 long total
20 Front rail	4	Virginia walnut	50 × 22 × 1010 long
21 Dust board	2	Pine	280 × 22 × 1010 long
22 Runner strip (4)	4	Pine	35 × 22 × 260 long
23 Runner strip (5)	2	Pine	42 × 22 × 545 long
24 Support strip	1	Pine	38 × 22 × 545 long
25 Joint cover strip	1	Virginia walnut	27 × 18 × 2400 long
26 Bottom edge cover strip	1	Virginia walnut	38 × 20 × 2400 long total
27 Leg strut	4	Pine	45sq × 195 long

Double chest

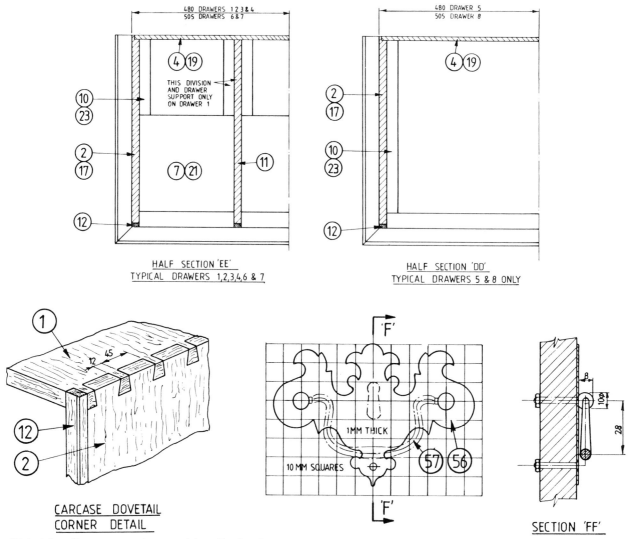

HALF SECTION 'EE'
TYPICAL DRAWERS 1,2,3,4,6 & 7

HALF SECTION 'DD'
TYPICAL DRAWERS 5 & 8 ONLY

CARCASE DOVETAIL
CORNER DETAIL

SECTION 'FF'

18.4 *Miscellaneous sections and handle details*

Item	No	Material	Dimensions (mm)
28 Ogee cover strip	6	Virginia walnut	189 × 32 × 250 long
29 Pad foot	4	Virginia walnut	85sq × 10 thick
30 Fillet support	6	Pine	70 × 22 × 300 long total
31 Back support fillet	2	Pine	190 × 22 × 195 long
Drawer 1			
32 Front	3	Virginia walnut	108 × 20 × 305 long
33 Lining	3	Cedar	88 × 9 × 1400 long
34 Bottom	3	Cedar	300 × 9 × 540 long
Drawer 2			
35 Front	1	Virginia walnut	133 × 20 × 940 long
36 Lining	1	Cedar	113 × 9 × 2020 long total
Drawer 3			
37 Front	1	Virginia walnut	166 × 20 × 940 long
38 Lining	1	Cedar	146 × 9 × 2020 long total
Drawer 4			
39 Front	1	Virginia walnut	190 × 20 × 940 long
40 Lining	1	Cedar	170 × 9 × 2020 long total
Drawer 5			
41 Front	1	Virginia walnut	211 × 20 × 940 long
42 Lining	1	Cedar	191 × 9 × 2020 long total

Item	No	Material	Dimensions (mm)
Drawer 6			
43 Front	1	Virginia walnut	211 × 20 × 940 long
44 Lining	1	Cedar	191 × 9 × 2120 long total
Drawer 7			
45 Front	1	Virginia walnut	230 × 20 × 940 long
46 Lining	1	Cedar	210 × 9 × 2120 long total
Drawer 8			
47 Front	1	Virginia walnut	257 × 20 × 940 long
48 Lining	1	Cedar	240 × 9 × 2120 long total
Common drawer items			
49 Bottom	4	Cedar	305 × 9 × 1650 long total
50 Bottom	3	Cedar	330 × 9 × 1750 long total
51 Runner	20	Cedar	22 × 9 × 570 long
Metalwork items			
52 Handle/lock back plate	24	Brass	80 × 120 × 1 thick
53 Swan neck handle	17	Brass	Purchase to suit
54 Lock	10	Brass	Purchase to suit

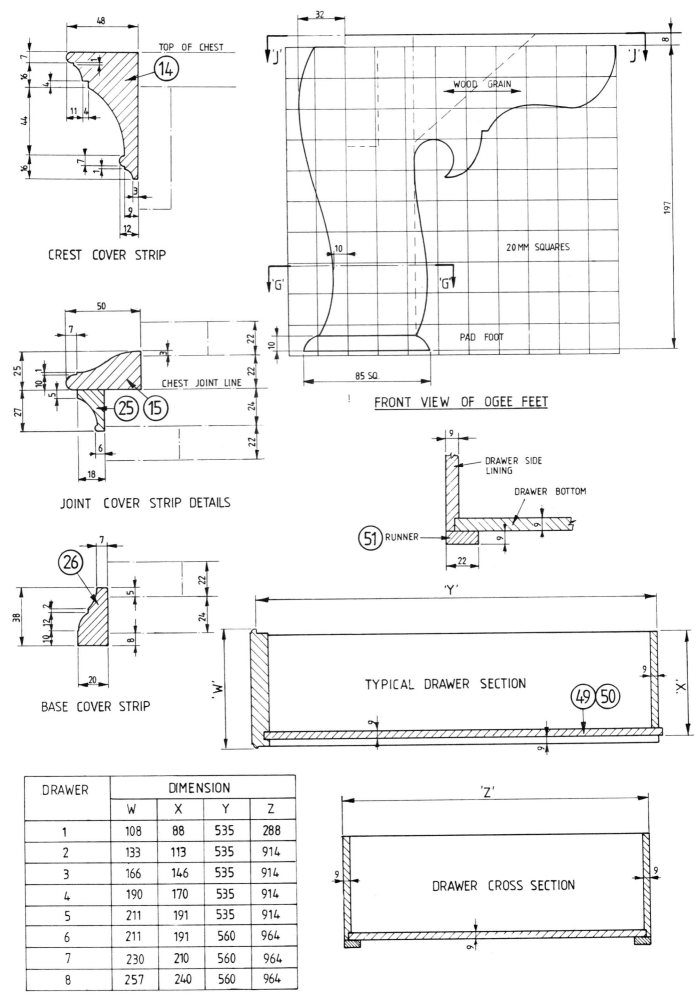

CREST COVER STRIP

JOINT COVER STRIP DETAILS

BASE COVER STRIP

FRONT VIEW OF OGEE FEET

WOOD GRAIN

20 MM SQUARES

PAD FOOT

85 SQ.

DRAWER SIDE LINING

DRAWER BOTTOM

RUNNER

TYPICAL DRAWER SECTION

DRAWER CROSS SECTION

TOP OF CHEST

CHEST JOINT LINE

DRAWER	DIMENSION			
	W	X	Y	Z
1	108	88	535	288
2	133	113	535	914
3	166	146	535	914
4	190	170	535	914
5	211	191	535	914
6	211	191	560	964
7	230	210	560	964
8	257	240	560	964

18.5 *Ogee feet and drawer details*

Thrown chair

Chippendale dining chair

Oyster veneer chest

Walnut side table

Mahogany tray

Queen Anne dining chair

Quartetto tables

Satinwood Pembroke table

Sheraton elbow chair

Kent Hall chair

Bedside cupboard

Sheraton dressing table (closed)

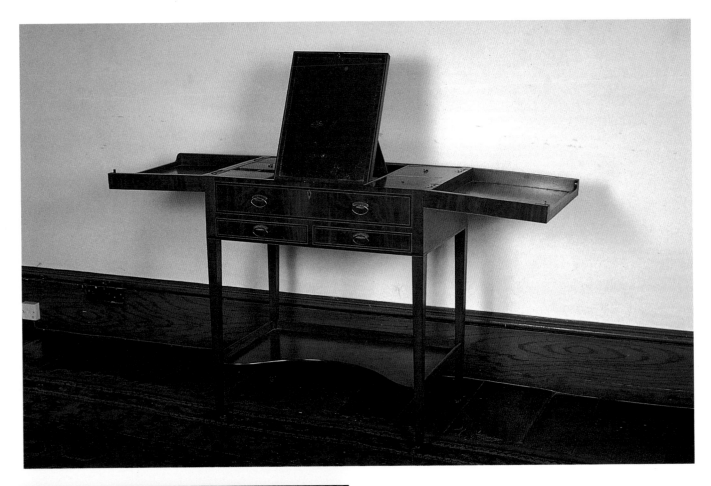

Sheraton dressing table (open)

Silver table

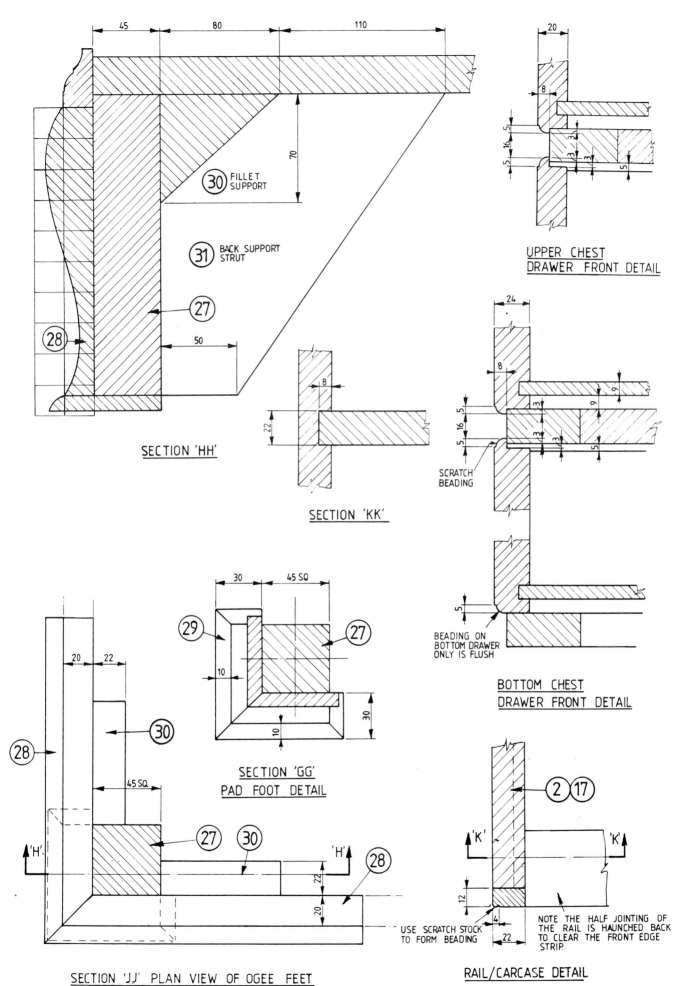

SECTION 'HH'

30 FILLET SUPPORT

31 BACK SUPPORT STRUT

27

28

70

50

45 · 80 · 110

UPPER CHEST
DRAWER FRONT DETAIL

20

8

SECTION 'KK'

8

22

BOTTOM CHEST
DRAWER FRONT DETAIL

24

8

9

9

16

5

5

5

3

3

3

3

SCRATCH
BEADING

5

BEADING ON
BOTTOM DRAWER
ONLY IS FLUSH

29 27

SECTION 'GG'
PAD FOOT DETAIL

30 45 SQ

10

10

30

28

20 22

30

45 SQ

'H'

27 30

'H' 28

22

20

USE SCRATCH STOCK
TO FORM BEADING

SECTION 'JJ' PLAN VIEW OF OGEE FEET

RAIL/CARCASE DETAIL

2 17

'K' 'K'

12

4

22

NOTE THE HALF JOINTING OF
THE RAIL IS HAUNCHED BACK
TO CLEAR THE FRONT EDGE
STRIP.

Chapter 19

Mahogany dining table

Peover Hall (pronounced 'Peever'), an imposing mansion just south of Knutsford in Cheshire, is where we find the next furniture design, a George III mahogany dining table. Originally a half-timbered building, the hall was owned by the Mainwaring family, and was completely rebuilt about 400 years ago as an Elizabethan manor. It was eventually sold to Mr Harry Brooks, a Manchester furniture tycoon, in 1940. The present squire, Mr Randle Brooks, has sympathetically restored the hall over the last 25 years. During the Second World War the house was used as a headquarters by General Patton of the US army, and the church nearby commemorates this with a flag. Adjoining Peover Hall is a Grade II listed coach house and stables, which is architecturally more important than the house.

The house interior reveals some impressive furniture. In a corner of the baronial style Great Hall, once a sunken kitchen, is a most ornate bobbin or 'thrown' chair. Usually these chairs have suffered one way or another due to their age, but this one is quite magnificent, and probably dates from around 1600. There is also an early Victorian sideboard, possibly made around the time of the Great Exhibition in 1851, upon which stands a carved scene of King John signing the Magna Carta at Runnymede. The study sports an architect's table, and in the long gallery

19.1 *Peover Hall*

19.2 *George III mahogany dining table*

there is an early hooded rocking cradle (c. 1650).

In the dining room attention is drawn to the centrepiece mahogany dining table. This is of similar type to the Gillow extending table discussed in Chapter 13, though not nearly so long. Smaller and less conspicuous is a George III mahogany dining table, another type of extending table, which is based on a modular form of assembly.

It consists of three units, a centre gate-leg section and two D-shaped end tables, and is sometimes alternatively referred to as a D-end dining table. The D-ends may serve as individual side tables, say in a drawing room or hall, and the gate-leg centre section folds down neatly to make a compact unit, which can be stored against a wall, perhaps under a window.

The units can be assembled together end to end to produce a table 2750mm long, as shown in Fig 19.2, which will comfortably seat twelve people. Its versatility does not finish here, because you can make use of the gate-leg section on its own as a table 1560mm long, to accommodate about eight people. The two D-ends can also be joined together as a pair to make a circular dining table for four or six people.

So this is a table to suit a variety of purposes, yet is easily split up into its individual units for storage. The design would suit a modern house. Figs 19.3 and 19.4 show the table in its separate units. The original D-end table is from the late George III period.

19.3 *D-end table*

19.4 *Gate-leg table*

Construction

The general arrangement is given in Fig 19.7. The construction is principally a joinery exercise with a small amount of external veneer work. Dimensions of the D-ends are given in Fig 19.5, and of the gate-leg centre section in Fig 19.6.

D-end table

The D-end table uses the brick construction method for the circular end rails, ie four layers of mahogany strip wood 24mm thick with staggered jointing. The rail connection with the intermediate legs is probably a bridle joint, while that with the corner legs is a mortise and tenon. The external face of the curved rail is veneered in the space between the legs. The table top is screw-fixed to the rails.

Gate-leg table

In the original gate-leg table the top, besides being screw-fixed to the rails from the underside (similar to the D-end table), also has a number of wood blocks glued underneath for additional support. The table flaps pivot on rule joints which require some care in making to ensure that the hinges are not visible during the motion. The gate legs supporting these flaps swing out on knuckle joints. The gate-leg table and the D-ends are aligned by three tongue-and-groove pieces set in the abuting table top edges. The units are linked together with table forks/connectors (see Fig 19.6), which can be purchased.

Leg profile and pitch

The leg section profile (Fig 19.5) is a moulded shape typical of the Hepplewhite era (see Hepplewhite chair, Chapter 17). It is therefore possible that the D-end table may also date from about 1780.

The similarity between the table and chairs may prompt you to consider matching these two items together. However, attention is drawn to a problem which can occur with D-end dining tables. The leg pitching can present difficulties with the sitting position at the table. Unlike the Gillow dining table, where the legs tuck away nicely underneath, D-end tables always have their legs on the edge. If the leg pitch is smaller than the width of the chair you intend to put under it, there is a limit as to how close you can sit up against the table.

If you want to use the Hepplewhite chairs paired with the D-end table design here, it might be worth considering making some adjustment to the table size to accommodate them. An increased table width of 1370mm would help. Alternatively the D-ends could be made squarer, as indicated in Fig 19.7, to space out the legs a little. If you are interested in variations on the theme of D-end dining tables there is a slightly different design worthy of inspection at Adlington Hall, a few miles away from Peover.

Parts list

Item	No	Material	Dimensions (mm)
'D-end' table			
1 Table top	1	Mahogany	600 × 22 × 1200 long
2 Leg	4	Mahogany	45sq × 708 long
3 Back rail	1	Mahogany	100 × 16 × 1200 long

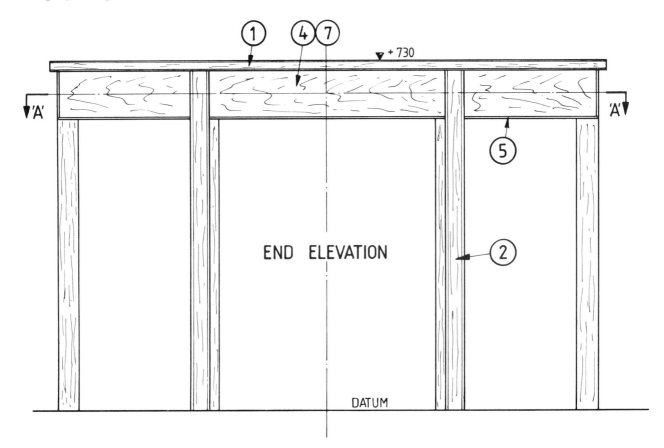

END ELEVATION

DATUM

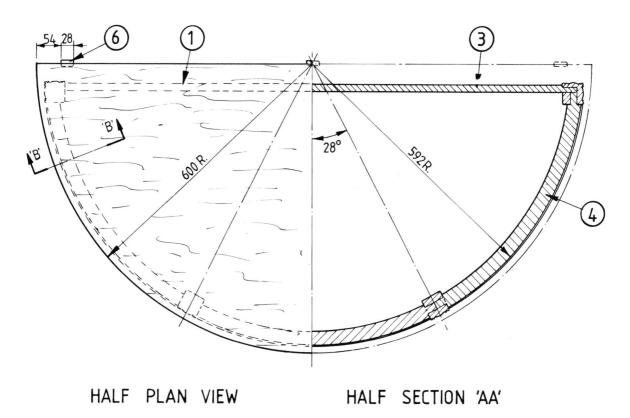

HALF PLAN VIEW   HALF SECTION 'AA'

19.5 *D-end table details*

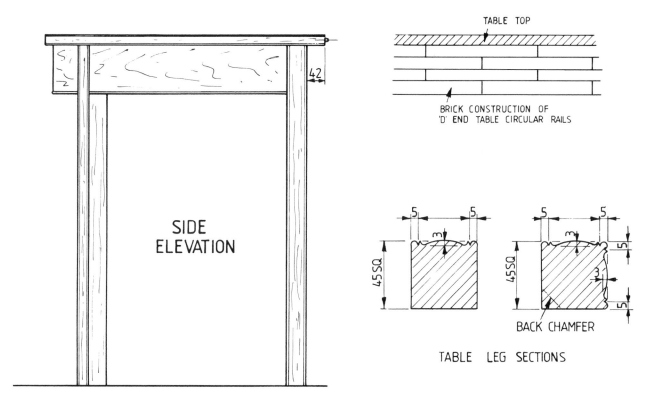

SIDE ELEVATION

42

TABLE TOP

BRICK CONSTRUCTION OF 'D' END TABLE CIRCULAR RAILS

45 SQ

45 SQ

BACK CHAMFER

TABLE LEG SECTIONS

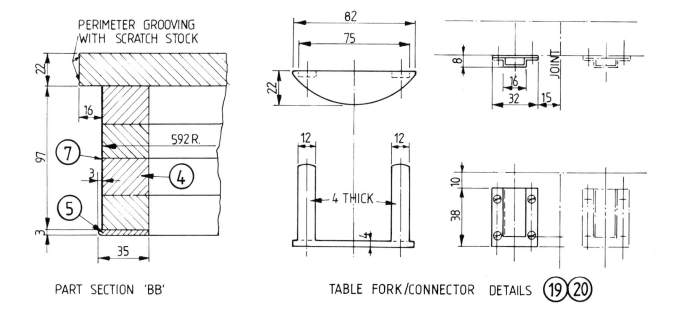

PERIMETER GROOVING WITH SCRATCH STOCK

22

16

97

3

3

35

592 R.

⑦

④

⑤

PART SECTION 'BB'

82

75

22

12

12

4 THICK

8

16

32

15

JOINT

10

38

TABLE FORK/CONNECTOR DETAILS ⑲⑳

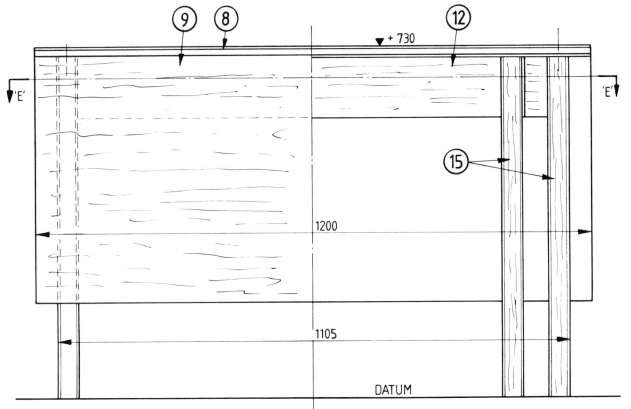

END ELEVATION   END ELEVATION (FLAP REMOVED)

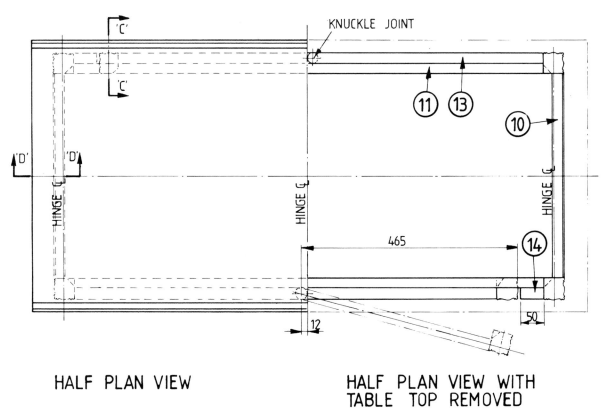

HALF PLAN VIEW   HALF PLAN VIEW WITH
TABLE TOP REMOVED

19.6 *Gate-leg table details*

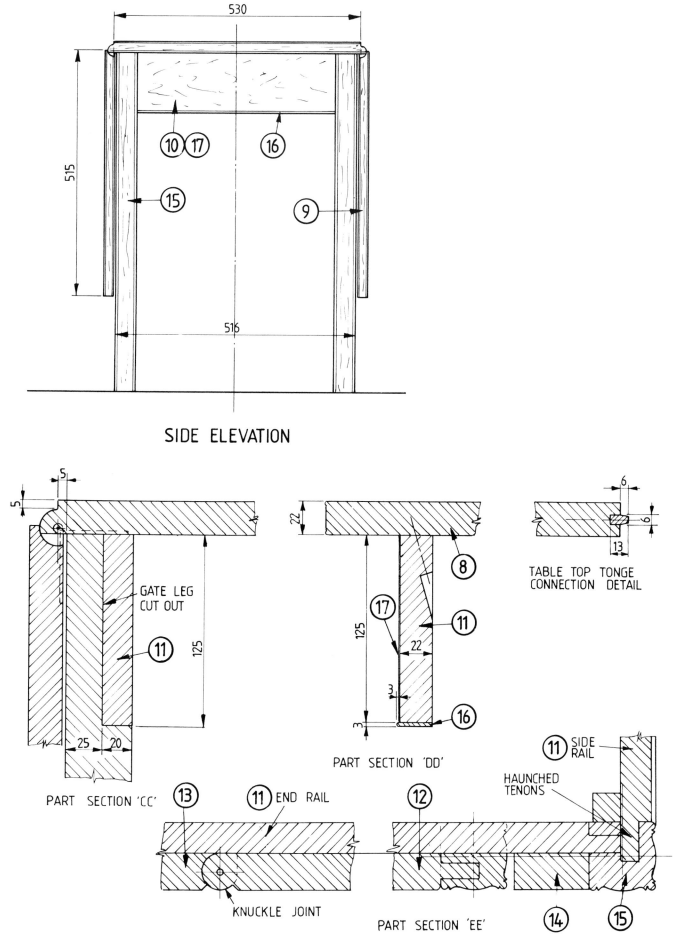

530

515

516

SIDE ELEVATION

5

5

GATE LEG
CUT OUT

125

25   20

PART SECTION 'CC'

22

125

22

3

3

PART SECTION 'DD'

6

6

13

TABLE TOP TONGE
CONNECTION DETAIL

KNUCKLE JOINT

END RAIL

PART SECTION 'EE'

SIDE
RAIL

HAUNCHED
TENONS

Item	No	Material	Dimensions (mm)
4 Curved rail	1	Mahogany	25 × 30 × 320 long; pieces assembled in brick fashion
5 Edge beading	1	Mahogany	200 × 3 × 540 long
6 Tongue piece	3	Mahogany	13 × 6 × 28 long
7 Veneer	1	Mahogany	130 wide × 1800 long total length
Gate-leg table			
8 Table top	1	Mahogany	565 × 22 × 1200 long
9 Table flap	2	Mahogany	515 × 22 × 1200 long
10 Side rail	2	Pine	125 × 22 × 530 long
11 End rail	2	Pine	125 × 20 × 1100 long
12 Gate rail	2	Pine	125 × 25 × 480 long

Item	No	Material	Dimensions (mm)
13 Dummy rail	2	Pine	125 × 25 × 520 long
14 End block	2	Pine	125 × 25 × 50 long
15 Leg	6	Mahogany	45sq × 708 long
16 Edge beading	1	Mahogany	25 × 3 × 450 long
17 Veneer	1	Mahogany	125 wide × 900 long total length
Metalwork items			
18 Hinge	6	Brass	38 × 50 long
19 Table connector	4	Brass	From 1.5 thick plate
20 Table fork	4	Brass	Fabricate to suit
21 Screws	–	Brass	To secure table tops to frame and for hinges

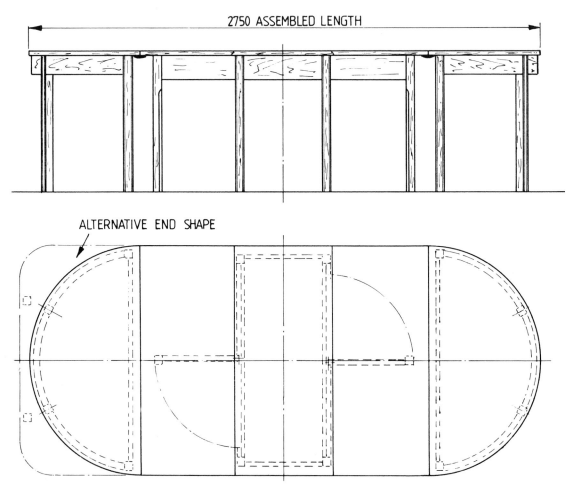

19.7 *General arrangement of table*

Chapter 20

Sheraton elbow chair

20.1 *Tatton Park*

There were two very good reasons for me to include furniture designs from Tatton Park, the seat of the Tattons and Egertons. First, the hall is one of the largest National Trust properties, and contains many furniture items of interest to woodworkers and historians; and second, I live close by! The house is set in 1700 acres of parkland, and besides the hall and gardens, the mere and the Old Hall, there are numerous other attractions throughout the year to interest the visitor.

In the Middle Ages the manor belonged to the Tattons, and in 1598 the estate passed to Sir Thomas Egerton. The architecture, decoration and furnishings of the present house are largely due to later descendants, William Tatton Egerton (1749–1806), and his son Wilbraham (1781–1856). They engaged the architect Samuel Wyatt and later his nephew Lewis Wyatt to restyle Tatton in the neo-classical manner.

The last Baron Egerton of Tatton (1874–1958) was a pioneer in motor cars and aviation, and knowledgeable on early wireless transmission. He was renowned for his exploits on safari, and the Tenant's Hall contains many exhibits of his world-wide travels. The 4th Lord Egerton was unmarried and the Baronetcy became extinct when he died. He bequeathed Tatton Park to the National Trust, since when it has flourished to become the showpiece it is today. One of the added attractions for woodwork enthusiasts are the adjoining gardens which contain a wide variety of trees, some of them rare. If you look hard enough you will find a pocket handkerchief tree.

Much of the fine quality furniture in the house is by the firm of cabinet makers Gillow, who were employed there during 1780–1813 while the hall was being restyled. Of particular note in the drawing room, set out in resplendent pink with ornate gilt style furniture, are some Gillow sofas with their frames carved in high relief, and in the library are some superb bookcases supplied by the firm in 1811.

The dining room, dating from about 1750, is set out in magnificent rococo style which contrasts with the neo-classicism of the other rooms. The furniture

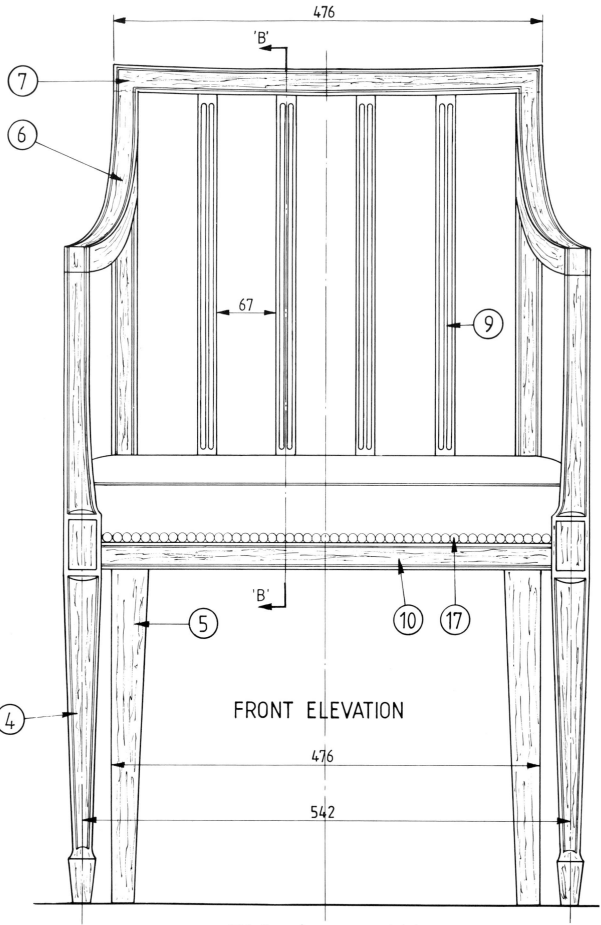

FRONT ELEVATION

20.2 *General arrangement of chair*

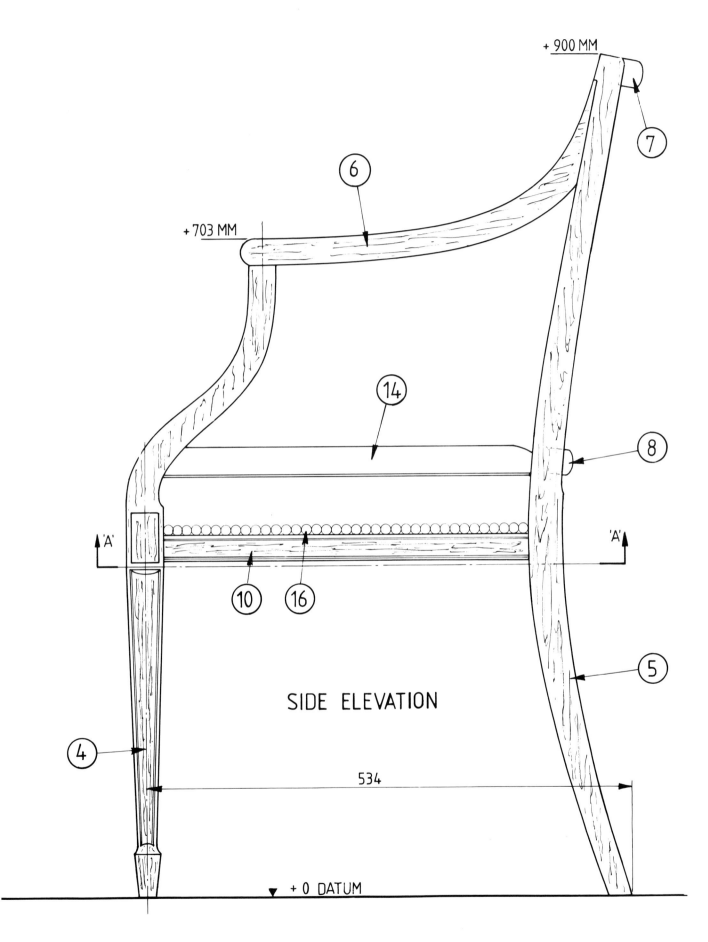

+ 900 MM

⑦

⑥

+ 703 MM

⑭

⑧

'A'   'A'

⑩ ⑯

⑤

SIDE ELEVATION

534

④

▼ + 0 DATUM

20.3 *Sheraton elbow chair*

includes two eighteenth-century mahogany ladder-back chairs in the Chippendale style, and a Sheraton mahogany sideboard c. 1790. The centrepiece is an early nineteenth-century mahogany dining table, and

20.4 *Back slat detail*

20.5 *Seat detail*

surrounding this is a set of Sheraton style elbow chairs, possibly of slightly later date. There are 20 chairs in the set. The front legs are in the typical Sheraton style, tapering down to square spade ends, and the chair back support is in the form of four fluted slats (Fig 20.4). The seats are stuff-over, covered in crimson leather (Fig 20.5).

Construction

The general arrangement of the chair is given in Fig 20.2, and sections through the seat in Fig 20.6. The construction is principally a joinery exercise plus seat upholstery, with a minor amount of carving on the front legs. The seat rails are of oak, and connected to the mahogany front and rear legs by mortise-and-tenon joints. The framework is strengthened by corner brace pieces (12). The oak rails are concealed on the front and sides by mahogany cover strips (10) with beaded edges, and at the back by a mahogany veneer strip (11).

Legs and splats

Details of the front and rear legs (4) and (5), and the arm rests (6), are given in Figs 20.7, 20.8 and 20.9. Dimensions for the curved members are set out on a square background to aid transfer of the design to the wood. Miscellaneous chair details are given in Fig 20.10, including sections through the legs showing the beaded corners and the fluted back splats. Routing or scraping techniques can be used to form these.

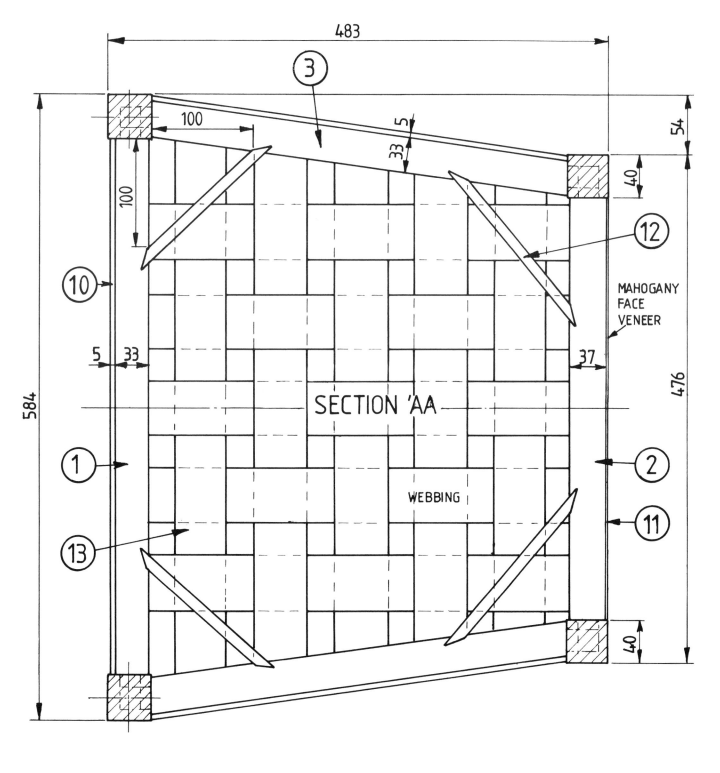

483

3

100

33 5

54

40

100

12

10

MAHOGANY
FACE
VENEER

5 33

476

37

SECTION 'AA

1

2

WEBBING

11

13

40

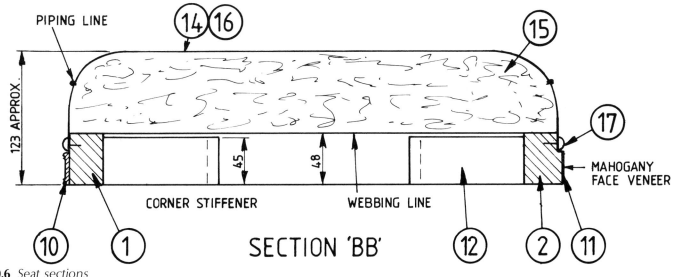

PIPING LINE

14 16

15

123 APPROX.

45

48

17

MAHOGANY
FACE VENEER

10

1

CORNER STIFFENER

WEBBING LINE

12

2

11

SECTION 'BB'

20.6 *Seat sections*

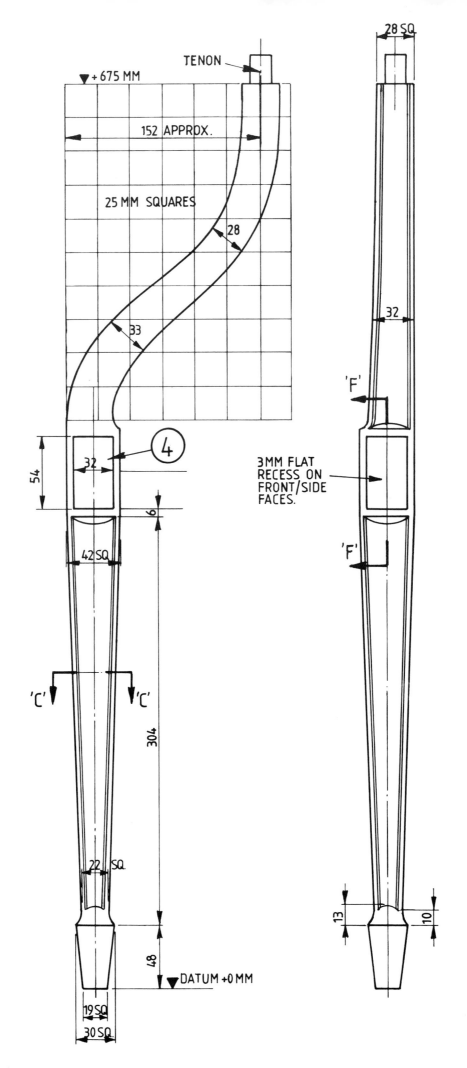

TENON

+ 675 MM

152 APPROX.

25 MM SQUARES

28

33

TENON

28 SQ

32

'F'

3 MM FLAT
RECESS ON
FRONT/SIDE
FACES.

'F'

④

54

32

6

42 SQ.

'C'   'C'

304

22 SQ.

13   10

48

DATUM +0 MM

19 SQ
30 SQ.

20.7 *Front leg details*

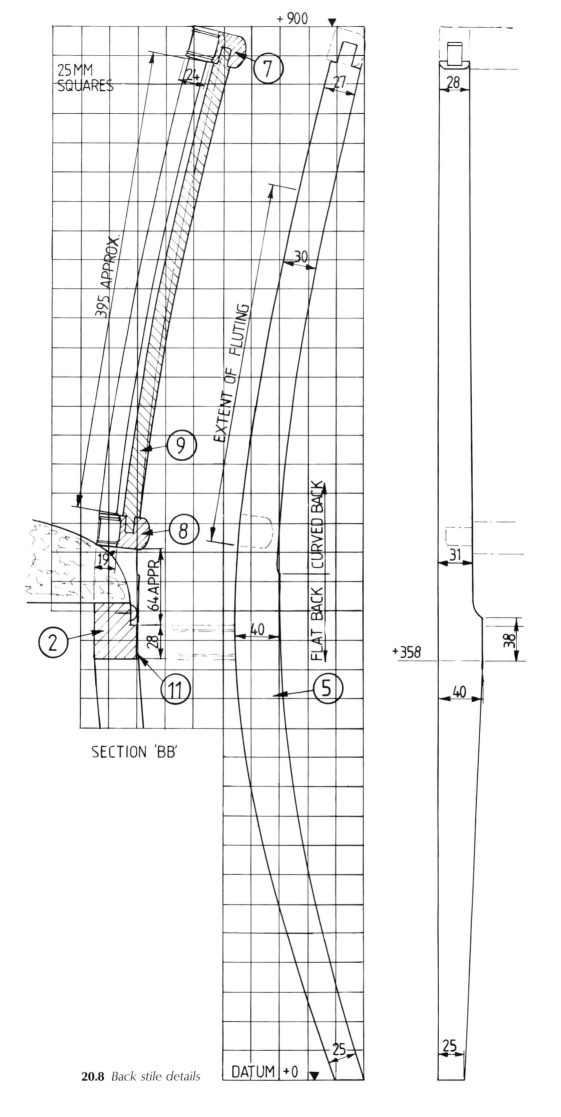

+ 900

25 MM
SQUARES

395 APPROX.

EXTENT OF FLUTING

⑦
⑨
⑧

⑤

⑪

⑫

27

30

19

64 APPR.

28

40

25

CURVED BACK

FLAT BACK

+358

SECTION 'BB'

DATUM +0

20.8 *Back stile details*

28

31

38

40

25

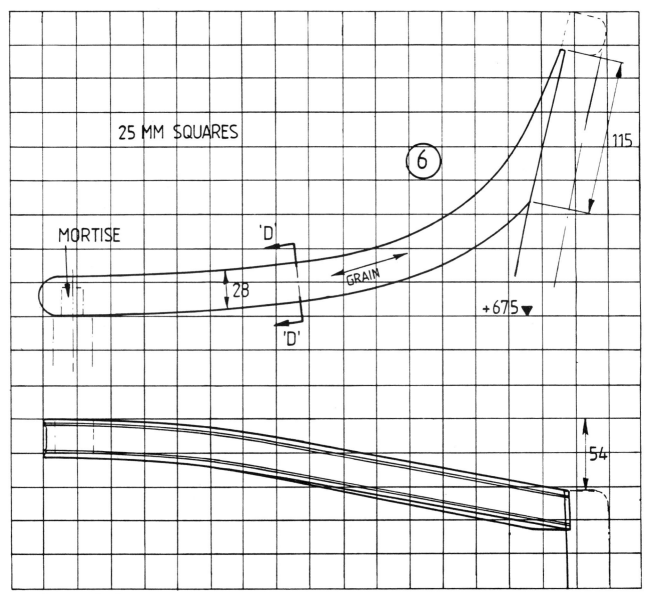

25 MM SQUARES

⑥

MORTISE   'D'

28

GRAIN

'D'

+675 ▼

115

54

20.9 *Arm rest details*

Seat

The stuff-over seat upholstery follows the usual pattern, ie webbing over the frame, hessian lining, stuffing, and leather cover. It may be worth investing in a basic upholsterer's kit, including a webbing strainer, needles, strong scissors and a trimming knife, and perhaps an upholsterer's hammer. A source for upholsterer's materials is given on p. 218. You will find the chairs very comfortable to sit in and that the back nicely moulds to the human form.

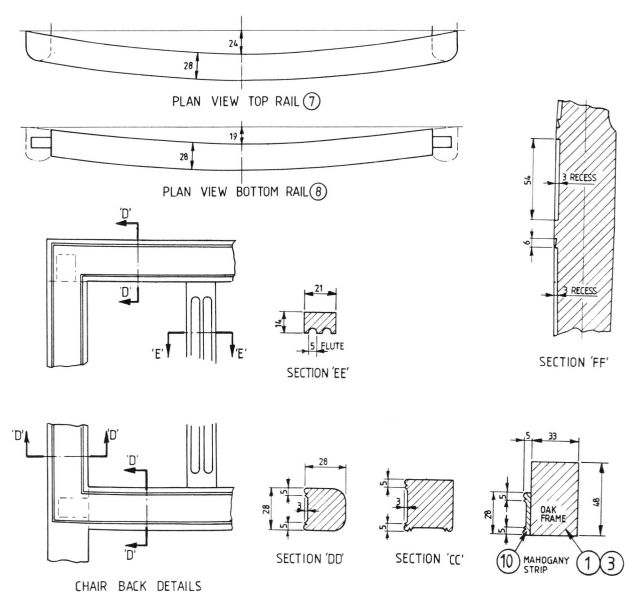

PLAN VIEW TOP RAIL ⑦

PLAN VIEW BOTTOM RAIL ⑧

SECTION 'EE'

SECTION 'FF'

CHAIR BACK DETAILS

SECTION 'DD'

SECTION 'CC'

OAK FRAME

⑩ MAHOGANY STRIP ① ③

20.10 *Miscellaneous details*

Parts list

Item	No	Material	Dimensions (mm)
1 Front seat rail	1	Oak	48 × 33 × 600 long
2 Back seat rail	1	Oak	48 × 37 × 480 long
3 Side rail	2	Oak	48 × 33 × 500 long
4 Front leg	2	Mahogany	240 × 42 × 720 long
5 Back leg/ style	2	Mahogany	175 × 40 × 925 long total
6 Arm rest	2	Mahogany	170 × 45 × 520 long
7 Crest rail	1	Mahogany	55 × 30 × 500 long
8 Bottom rail	1	Mahogany	50 × 30 × 500 long
9 Fluted splat strip	4	Mahogany	21 × 25 × 450 long

Item	No	Material	Dimensions (mm)
10 Cover strip	3	Mahogany	28 × 5 × 1350 total
11 Veneer strip	1	Mahogany	28 wide × 410 long
12 Corner brace	4	Oak	45 × 10 × 190 long
13 Webbing	–	Webbing	Length to suit
14 Leather seat cover	1	Leather	Area to suit, mahogany red
15 Stuffing	–	Horsehair	Purchase to suit
16 Hessian cover	–	Hessian	Purchase to suit
17 Chair nail	–	Brass	Purchase to suit: approx 180 will be needed

Chapter 21

Rosewood octagon worktable

The second furniture design from Tatton Park is in the music room, and is a fine quality Rosewood octagon worktable (c. 1815). This Regency period table stands on a pedestal column carried by four splayed legs on brass castors. The drawers, column and legs are inlaid with brass stringing. The table top displays fine marquetry work, inlaid with a variety of octagonal wood specimens, with perimeter stringing and crossbanding round the border. It was originally supplied by Gillow complete with a damask leather cover.

The Lancaster furniture maker Gillow can be firmly linked with this table at Tatton as the firm prepared a design in 1804 for an octagonal writing table of very similar size and shape (See Nicholas Goodison & John Hardy, *Gillows at Tatton Park*). Historical records suggest that it has three drawers, one running straight through and the other two swivelling. This is difficult to confirm as the drawers were unfortunately locked, and had not been opened within memory of the last craftsman who carried out minor restoration work on this table some years ago.

Nevertheless, it is possible from a study of the pin nails seen in the table underside to establish fairly precisely the position of the inside frame members (3).

21.1 *Rosewood octagon worktable*

Other checks suggest that the through drawer is more likely two separate ones. In the reconstructed drawings this is how it is shown. There is still some uncertainty on the design of the swivel drawers, and because these are an unknown quantity, the drawing shows these as false drawer faces.

When researching at Holker Hall in Cumbria for other furniture items in this book, by a stroke of luck I happened to chance upon a circular library table, also by Gillow, made in about the same period as the table at Tatton. This also has triangular drawers that swivel from one of the front corners, and these could be viewed. This suggests that Gillow was using a common design feature of the time, and the pivoting drawers on the octagon work-table are most likely very similar. The probable extent of the triangular drawer is indicated on Fig 21.3, section 'CC'.

Construction

The general arrangement is given in Fig 21.2, and various sections in Fig 21.3. The construction can be split into two aspects: the table top, and the column and legs. The skills needed are basic carcase work, a minor amount of woodturning, and the patience to do some fine veneer and inlay work.

Table top and marquetry inlay

The table top construction is evident from Figs 21.2 and 21.3. The parts of the carcase work that can be seen are made in mahogany, and it must be assumed that the table top (1) is also of this material.

To achieve a creditable result with the marquetry inlay work, it is important to set out the diagonal dimensions of the work top accurately, otherwise when you come to lay out the octagonal wood pieces in the centre, it may be difficult to get an even match. Note that the table edges along the drawer fronts are slightly longer than the adjoining table faces at 45°. The octagonal veneer pieces of miscellaneous timber varieties are randomly placed,

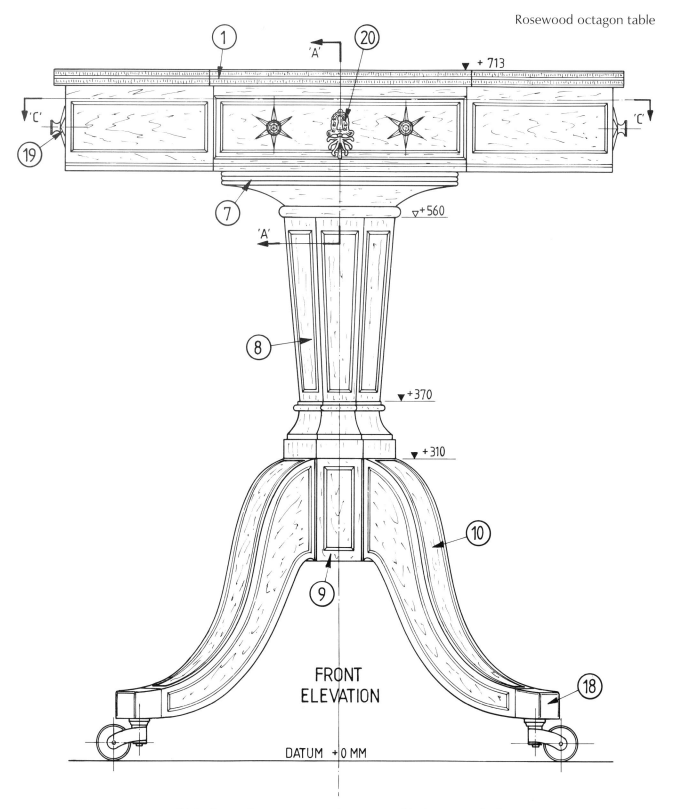

21.2 *General arrangement of octagon table (cont. overleaf)*

except that the middle appears to start off with a centrepiece in sycamore surrounded by four octagonal pieces of ebony. Figs 21.4 and 21.5 give the veneer work details.

Drawers

The construction of the drawers cannot be seen, but they are probably of similar style and quality to, for example, those on the Pembroke table design in

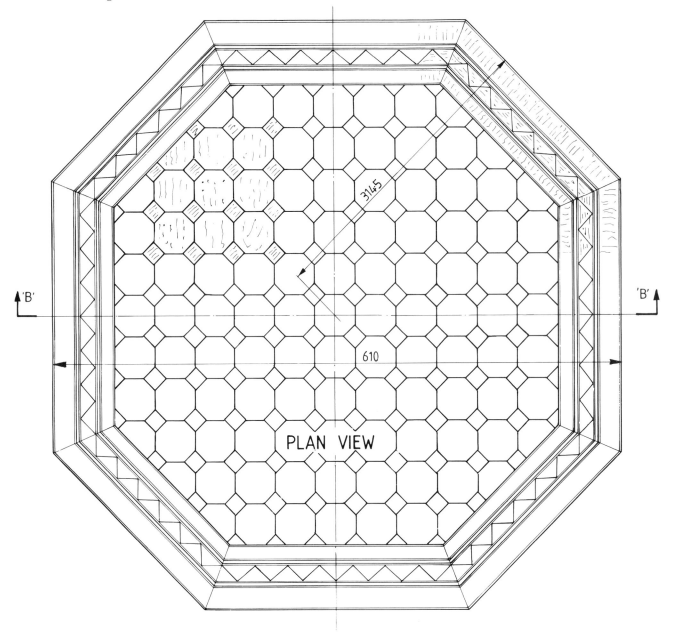

'B'   'B'

314.5

610

PLAN VIEW

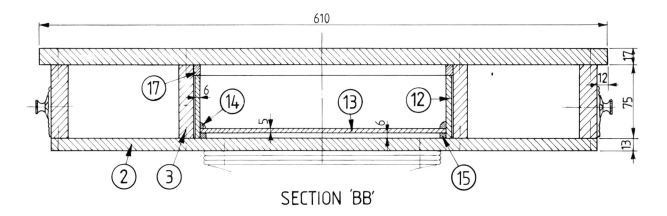

SECTION 'BB'

21.2 *(cont.)*

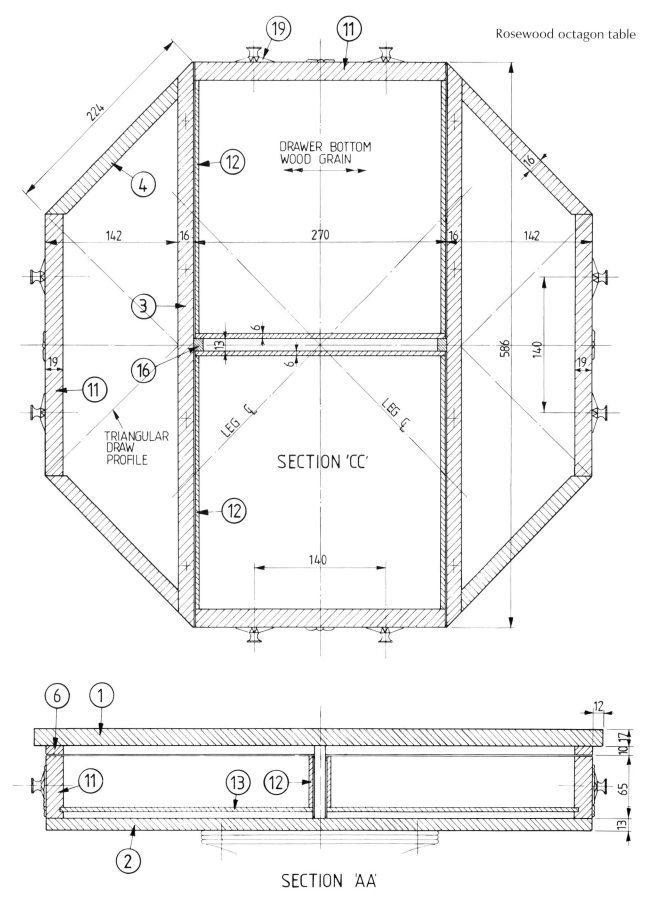

Rosewood octagon table

DRAWER BOTTOM
WOOD GRAIN

SECTION 'CC'

TRIANGULAR
DRAW
PROFILE

LEG ₵

LEG ₵

SECTION 'AA'

21.3 *Sections through octagon table*

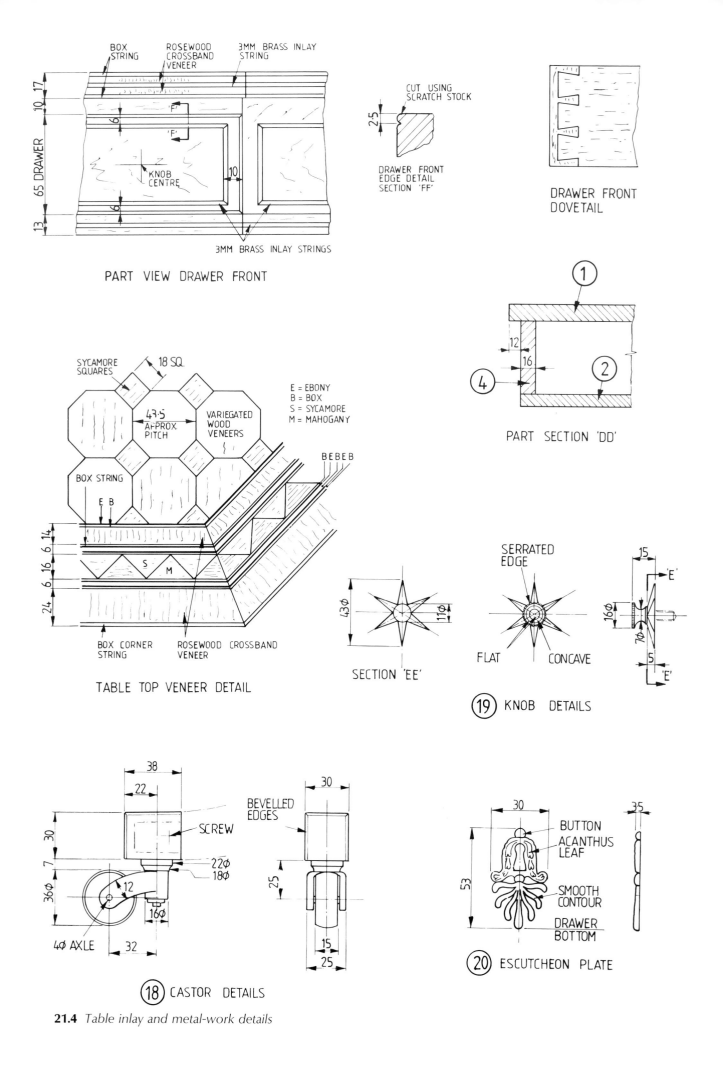

BOX STRING
ROSEWOOD CROSSBAND VENEER
3MM BRASS INLAY STRING

10 17

65 DRAWER

13

6

6

KNOB CENTRE

'F'
'F'

10

3MM BRASS INLAY STRINGS

PART VIEW DRAWER FRONT

CUT USING SCRATCH STOCK

2·5

DRAWER FRONT EDGE DETAIL SECTION 'FF'

DRAWER FRONT DOVETAIL

1
4
2

12
16

PART SECTION 'DD'

SYCAMORE SQUARES
18 SQ.

43·5 APPROX. PITCH

VARIEGATED WOOD VENEERS

E = EBONY
B = BOX
S = SYCAMORE
M = MAHOGANY

B E B E B

BOX STRING

E B

14
6
16
6
24

S   M

BOX CORNER STRING
ROSEWOOD CROSSBAND VENEER

TABLE TOP VENEER DETAIL

43∅
11∅

SECTION 'EE'

SERRATED EDGE

FLAT   CONCAVE

15
'E'
16∅
7∅
5
'E'

19 KNOB DETAILS

38
22
30
7
36∅

SCREW

22∅
18∅

12

16∅

4∅ AXLE
32

BEVELLED EDGES

30

25

15
25

18 CASTOR DETAILS

30

BUTTON
ACANTHUS LEAF

53

SMOOTH CONTOUR

DRAWER BOTTOM

35

20 ESCUTCHEON PLATE

21.4 *Table inlay and metal-work details*

21.5 *Table top inlay*

Chapter 15, and it is suggested that the same format is followed. It has been assumed that the drawers are oak. Drawer front inlay details are given in Figs 21.4 and 21.6. These and the legs display brass inlay, a common feature of Regency period furniture. Some notes on the fitting of brass inlay are given in the quartetto table design in Chapter 16, which also uses this form of string work.

21.6 *Drawer*

Column and legs

The column and leg details are given in Figs 21.7, 21.8 and 21.9. Again, a little detective work was required to discover the construction of the octagonal column section. It was originally thought that the column was of solid rosewood. However, on further inspection, and bearing in mind the column size, it is believed that the core is more likely mahogany with applied thin rosewood pieces or veneer on the outside. It will certainly be much cheaper to construct in this way today. It is uncertain as to whether the column is in one or two pieces. For convenience of working, the

drawing shows it split into two, but you could make it from one piece of mahogany if you prefer.

The legs are puzzling, as inspection suggests they are of solid rosewood, with rosewood veneer on the side faces. However I could be mistaken on this. A piece of solid rosewood with the grain as indicated would probably do without any additional veneer. The legs are connected to the column with dovetails, and should be tight fitting to counter any later relaxation that might occur. Many antique tables with this method of jointing have later had to be strengthened with metal strips applied underneath, as is the case with this table. Castor details are given in Fig 21.4, along with other miscellaneous metalwork items. These are commercially available, but some compromise may be necessary on the knob pattern (19) and escutcheon plate (20).

Parts list

Item	No	Material	Dimensions (mm)
1 Table top	1	Mahogany	305 × 17 × 1250 total
2 Table bottom	1	Mahogany	305 × 13 × 1250 total
3 Division	2	Mahogany	75 × 16 × 600 long
4 Table side piece	4	Mahogany	75 × 16 × 240 long
5 False drawer front	2	Mahogany	75 × 19 × 270 long
6 Cover strip	2	Mahogany	19 × 10 × 270 long
7 Table support disc	1	Mahogany	270sq × 55 thick
8 Column	1	Mahogany	125sq × 300 long
9 Column base	1	Mahogany	125sq × 190 long
10 Leg	4	Mahogany	120 × 45 × 400 long
11 Drawer front	2	Oak	65 × 19 × 270 long
12 Drawer lining	2	Oak	65 × 6 × 850 per drawer
13 Drawer bottom	2	Oak	140 × 5 × 560 per drawer
14 Edge moulding	2	Oak	8 × 560 per drawer
15 Runner	2	Oak	6sq × 560 per drawer
16 Back stop	2	Oak	13 × 10 × 75 long
17 Tip stop	4	Oak	10 × 8 × 280 long
18 Castor	4	Brass	Regency style, purchase to suit
19 Knob	8	Brass	Star pattern

Rosewood octagon table

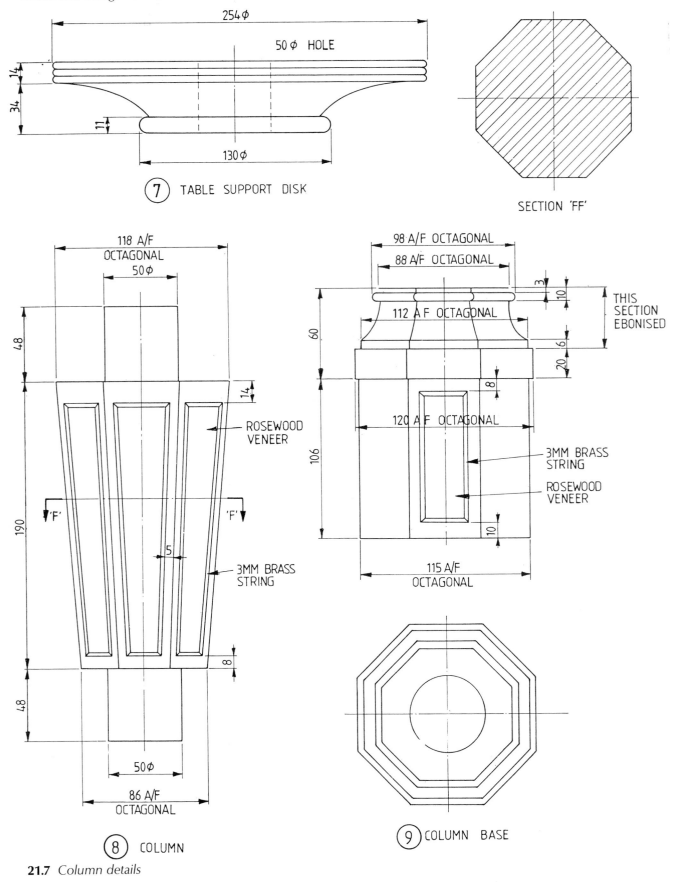

254 ⌀

50 ⌀ HOLE

14

34

11

130 ⌀

⑦ TABLE SUPPORT DISK

SECTION 'FF'

118 A/F
OCTAGONAL

50 ⌀

48

14

ROSEWOOD
VENEER

190

'F'   'F'

5

3MM BRASS
STRING

48

8

50 ⌀

86 A/F
OCTAGONAL

⑧ COLUMN

98 A/F OCTAGONAL

88 A/F OCTAGONAL

3

10

THIS
SECTION
EBONISED

112 A F OCTAGONAL

60

20   6

8

120 A F OCTAGONAL

3MM BRASS
STRING

106

ROSEWOOD
VENEER

10

115 A/F
OCTAGONAL

⑨ COLUMN BASE

21.7 *Column details*

148

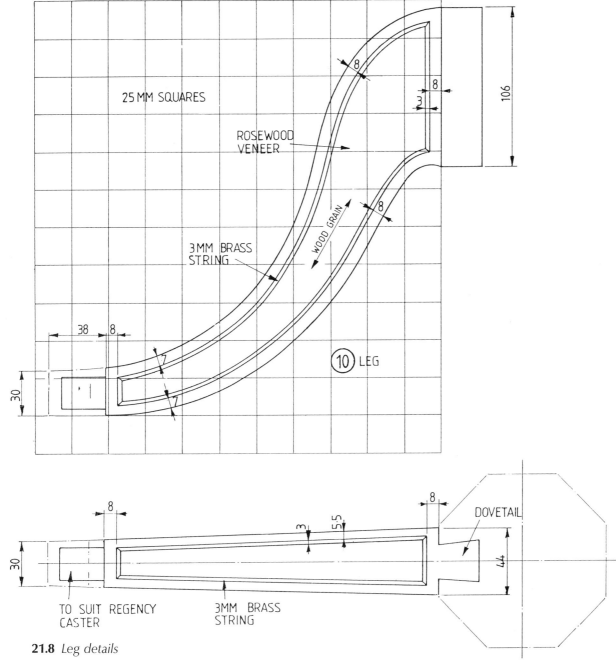

25 MM SQUARES

ROSEWOOD VENEER

WOOD GRAIN

3 MM BRASS STRING

⑩ LEG

8

8

3

106

38

8

30

7

7

8

3

5·5

8

DOVETAIL

30

44

TO SUIT REGENCY CASTER

3MM BRASS STRING

21.8 *Leg details*

Item	No	Material	Dimensions (mm)
20 Escutcheon plate	4	Brass	Bell shaped with honeysuckle motif
21 Rosewood veneer	–	Rosewood	Purchase quantity to suit
22 Strings/ crossbanding	–	Principally, box, ebony and rosewood	
23 Table top veneer	–	Various woods	Purchase to suit
24 Brass stringing	–	Brass	3sq section

21.9 *Leg and column*

149

Chapter 22

Kent Hall chair

Chatsworth in Derbyshire, the home of the 11th Duke of Devonshire, is a house of majestic proportions, and contains some of England's finest treasures. This immense building fronts on to the river Derwent, which meanders through the estate parkland. It has 175 rooms, many of them very large, some with magnificent Louis Laguerre painted ceilings, and the state rooms are of palatial proportions with superb giltwork. The music room has the famous violin door painted by Jan van der Vaart, so deceptive that you feel you want to reach out and touch it. The adjoining gardens, laid out by Joseph Paxton after 1826, feature a breathtaking cascade waterfall and the 'emperor fountain' which can reach a height of 85m on a calm day.

The building of the original house by 'Bess of Hardwick' and her second husband, Sir William Cavendish, began in 1552. In the late seventeenth century the 3rd Duke of Devonshire almost completely rebuilt the house much as it is seen today. He also commissioned the architect and designer William Kent to reconstruct Devonshire House in Piccadilly in 1733, and for the furniture for this house. When Devonshire House was sold in 1920, much of

the furniture was removed to Chatsworth. This included the Kent Hall chairs now in the North Entrance Hall and adjoining North Corridor, one of which I have selected as the first furniture design from Chatsworth.

William Kent (1685–1748) spent ten years of his life in Italy, and this influenced many of his designs. One of his friends and associates was Lord Burlington, the architect and connoiseur. Kent worked largely in the Palladian style, and his furniture generally is of baroque form. His hall chairs, in the simple baroque style, were made in a number of variants including one with an architectural apex back, another with a circular back, and a third two-seater chair design with unusual twin legs at the front corners. For the design I have selected the circular back chair, as I feel it is the most aesthetically pleasing.

This hall chair stands on scroll pattern legs and has a flat seat with egg-and-dart carving beneath the perimeter edge. In spite of the flat form the chairs are surprisingly comfortable. The circular back has foliate carving around the edge with crossed ribbons at top and bottom. The front legs feature carving typical of the period, with a foliate pattern on the knee section,

22.1 *Chatsworth*

and lower down an overlapping circular shell motif. The scroll-ended arm rests are carved with a fish-scale pattern, as are the back stiles above the seat level.

Construction

The general arrangement of the Kent chair is given in Fig 22.6, and further details of the seat sections, etc, in Fig 22.7. The skills needed to make it are joinery, and reasonable competence in carving.

22.2 *Kent Hall chair*

22.3 *Chair leg*

22.4 *Chair back carving*

22.5 *Arm rest carving*

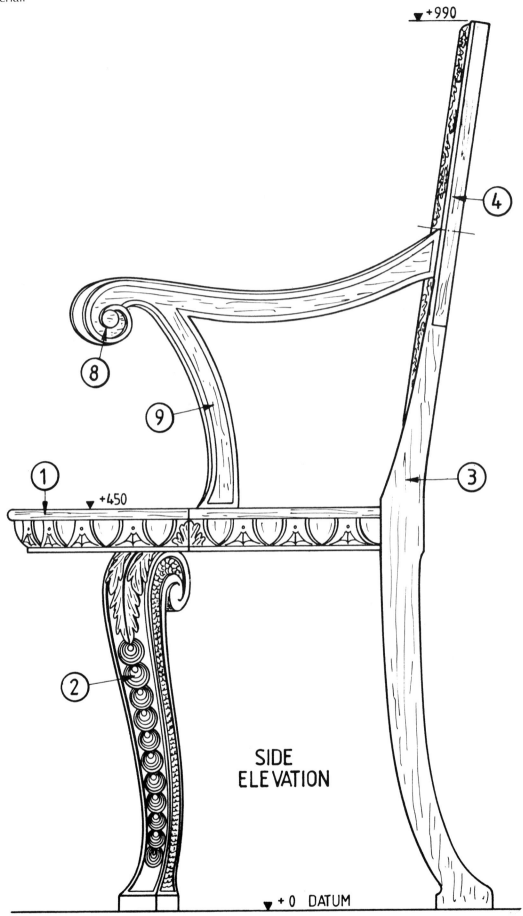

▼ +990

④

①

▼ +450

④

③

⑧

⑨

②

SIDE
ELEVATION

▼ +0 DATUM

22.6 *General arrangement of Kent Hall chair*

Parts list

Item	No	Material	Dimensions (mm)
1 Leg	4	Mahogany	35sq × 760 long
2 Back	1	Mahogany	188 × 15 × 705 long
3 Front	1	Mahogany	124 × 15 × 705 long
4 Side	2	Mahogany	188 × 15 × 450 long
5 Bottom	1	Mahogany	420 × 8 × 675 long
6 Support block	1	Mahogany	10 × 6 × 850 long total
7 Platform	1	Mahogany	450 × 9 × 705 long
8 Platform edging	1	Mahogany	38 × 14 × 1600 long total
9 Compartment division	2	Mahogany	106 × 15 × 450 long
10 Drawer division	1	Beech	73 × 15 × 425 long
11 Fascia piece	1	Mahogany	35 × 15 × 75 long
12 Side strip	2	Beech	73 × 20 × 450 long
13 Drawer front strip	1	Mahogany	45 × 9 × 700 long
14 Carcase veneer	–	Mahogany curl	To cover carcase and drawer fronts
15 Stringing/ banding and misc. veneer	–	Various woods	Order as shown on drawings

Boxes and compartment linings

Item	No	Material	Dimensions (mm)
16 Lid (1), (2), (3)	3	Mahogany	114 × 5 × 171 long
17 Lid (4), (5)	2	Mahogany	206 × 5 × 171 long
18 Box side	1	Mahogany	85 × 5 × 1900 long for all boxes
19 Box bottom (3)	1	Mahogany	114 × 5 × 171
20 Box bottom (4), (5)	2	Mahogany	206 × 5 × 171 long
21 Lid edging (3), (4), (5)	1	Mahogany	12 × 5 × 1900 long for all boxes
22 Lid register	1	Mahogany	210 × 2 × 240 long total
23 Compartment lining	1	Mahogany	106 × 3 × 4000 long total
24 Beading		Mahogany	6 × 850 long total for compartments (1), (2)
25 Lipping (1)	1	Box	3sq × 3100 long total rounded top

Item	No	Material	Dimensions (mm)
26 Lipping (2)	2	Box	6 × 3 × 450 long double rounded top
27 Stop	12	Mahogany	30 × 15 × 4 thick nominal

Mirror frame and slide details

Item	No	Material	Dimensions (mm)
28 Mirror slide	1	Mahogany	220 × 15 × 310 long
29 Mirror frame	1	Mahogany	24 × 18 × 1500 long
30 Mirror	1	Glass	395 × 290
31 Backing board	1	Mahogany	290 × 5 × 395 long
32 Mirror stay	1	Mahogany	30 × 5 × 700 long total
33 Back support piece	2	Mahogany	35 × 12 × 162 long
34 Dust board	1	Mahogany	220 × 3 × 310 long

Drawers and associated components

Item	No	Material	Dimensions (mm)
35 Drawer front	2	Mahogany	55 × 15 × 310 long
36 Drawer lining	1	Mahogany	55 × 6 × 1200 long per drawer
37 Drawer bottom	2	Mahogany	420 × 3 × 310 long
38 Slip strip	4	Mahogany	4 × 3 × 420 long
39 Front fill strip	2	Mahogany	10 × 3 × 310 long
40 Runner	4	Beech	9 × 6 × 400 long
41 Tip stop	4	Beech	10 × 6 × 370 long
42 Back stop	4	Beech	10 × 15 × 60 long

Lid details

Item	No	Material	Dimensions (mm)
43 Lid top	2	Mahogany	450 × 10 × 352 long
44 Lid edge	1	Mahogany	40 × 15 × 1170 total per lid
45 Centrepiece	2	Mahogany	40 × 10 × 450 long

Metalwork items

Item	No	Material	Dimensions (mm)
46 Drawer handle	4	Sheffield plate	1 thick plate and 2mm diameter wire
47 Dutch round handle	6	Brass	Purchase to suit
48 Castor	4	Brass	Purchase to suit
49 Lid hinge	4	Brass	12 × 60 long
50 Mirror hinge	2	Brass	10 × 35 long
51 Backstay hinge	2	Brass	2 × 22 long
52 Escutcheon	1	Brass	30 × 15 × 2 thick
53 Lock	1	Brass	Purchase to suit
54 Lid catch	2	Brass	Purchase to suit lock

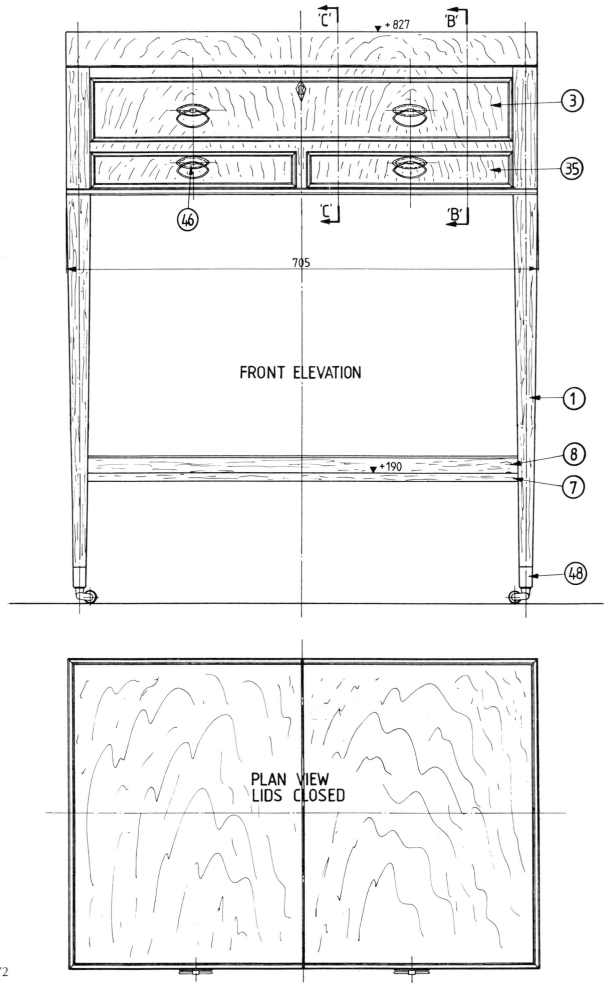

FRONT ELEVATION

PLAN VIEW
LIDS CLOSED

25.2 *General arrangement of dressing table*

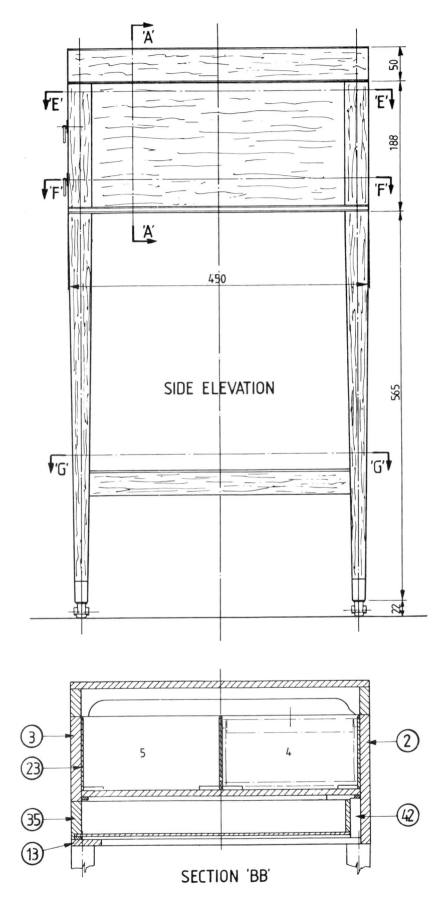

SIDE ELEVATION

SECTION 'BB'

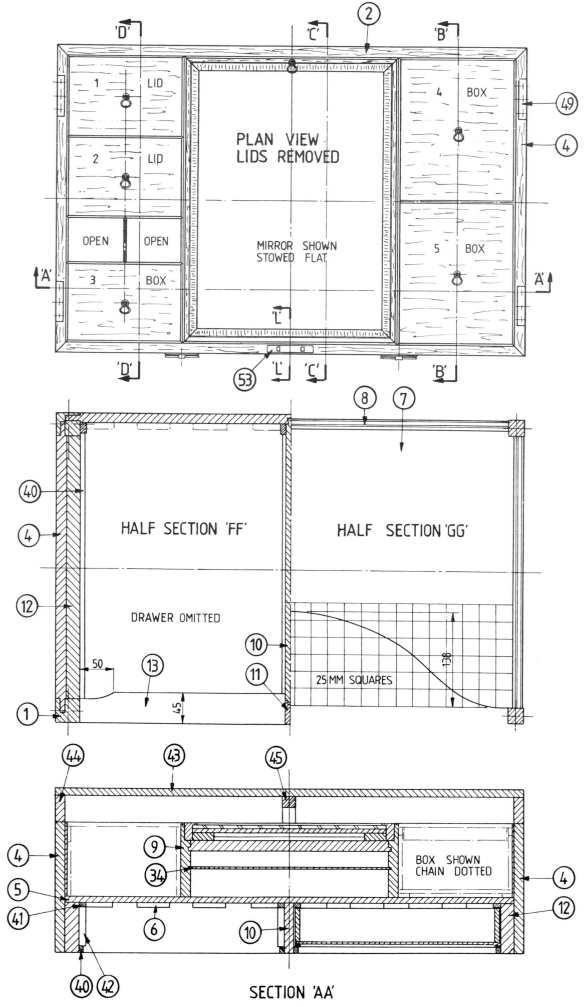

25.3 *Sections through dressing table*

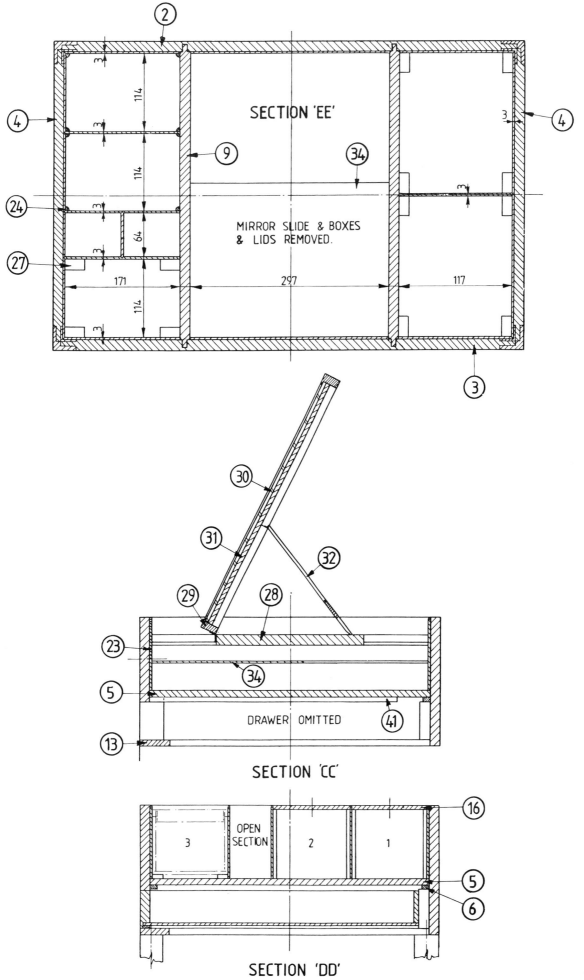

SECTION 'EE'

MIRROR SLIDE & BOXES
& LIDS REMOVED.

SECTION 'CC'

DRAWER OMITTED

OPEN SECTION

SECTION 'DD'

175

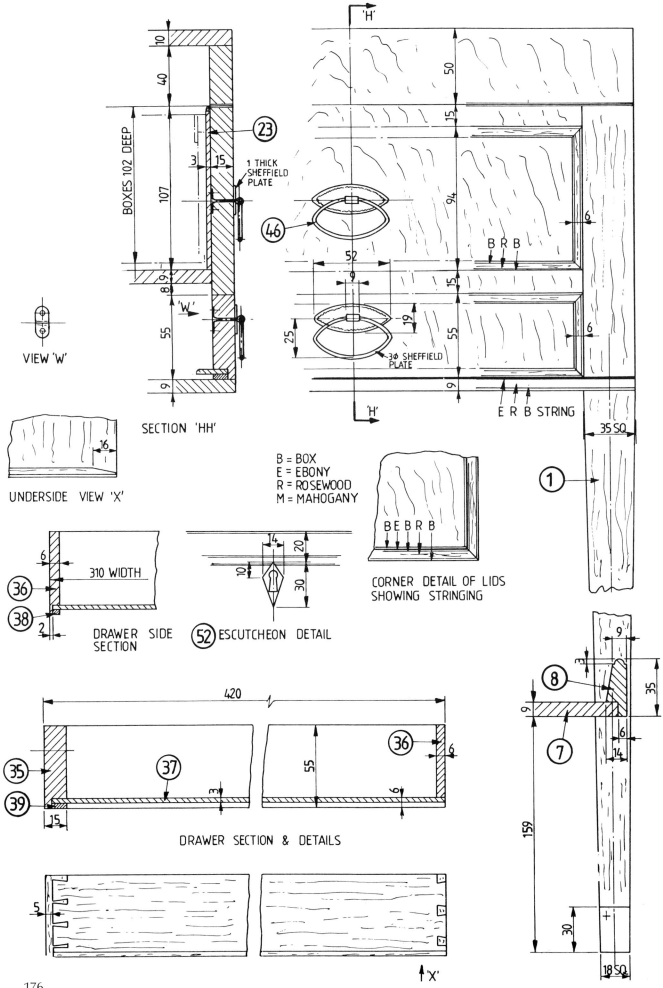

VIEW 'W'

BOXES 102 DEEP

1 THICK
SHEFFIELD
PLATE

23

46

3∅ SHEFFIELD
PLATE

E R B STRING

'H'

SECTION 'HH'

35 SQ

1

UNDERSIDE VIEW 'X'

B = BOX
E = EBONY
R = ROSEWOOD
M = MAHOGANY

B R B

CORNER DETAIL OF LIDS
SHOWING STRINGING

36

38

310 WIDTH

DRAWER SIDE
SECTION

52 ESCUTCHEON DETAIL

8

7

35

420

35

37

36

39

DRAWER SECTION & DETAILS

159

18 SQ

'X'

176

25.4 *Leg and drawer details*

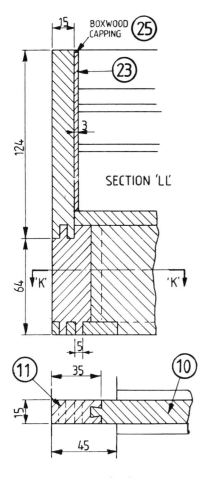

15

BOXWOOD
CAPPING (25)

(23)

124

SECTION 'LL'

3

64   'K'   'K'

5

(11)   35   (10)

15

45

SECTION 'KK'

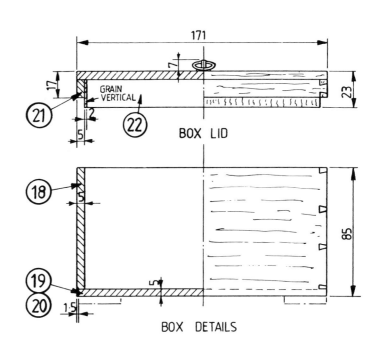

171

17   7

(21)   GRAIN
VERTICAL   23

2   (22)

5   BOX LID

(18)   5

85

(19)

(20)   1·5

BOX   DETAILS

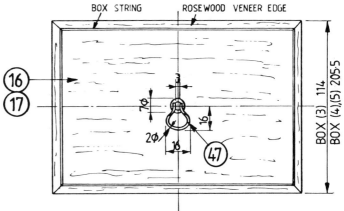

BOX STRING   ROSEWOOD VENEER EDGE

(16)

(17)   3

7Ø

16

2Ø   (47)

16

BOX (3) 114

BOX (4),(5) 205·5

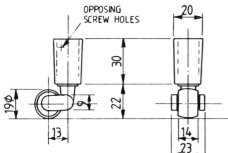

OPPOSING
SCREW HOLES   20

30

22

19Ø   9

13   14

23

(48) CASTER
DETAILS

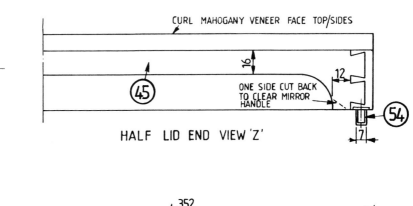

CURL MAHOGANY VENEER FACE TOP/SIDES

16

(45)   12

ONE SIDE CUT BACK
TO CLEAR MIRROR
HANDLE   (54)

7

HALF LID END VIEW 'Z'

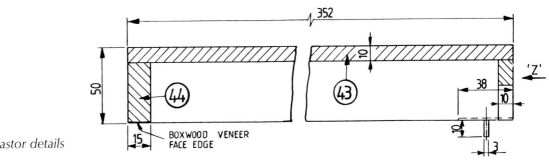

352

10   'Z'

50   (44)   (43)   38

10

BOXWOOD VENEER
FACE EDGE   10

15   3

25.5 *Box and castor details*

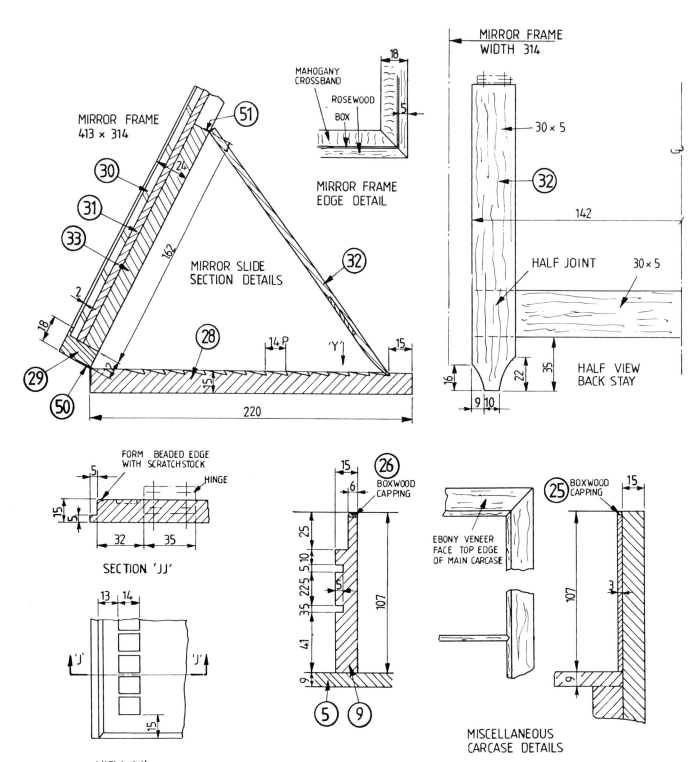

25.6 *Mirror easel details*

edging (8) at the back and sides, and the arrangement is stiffened by a curvilinear shelf (7).

The carcase is completed by fitting the drawer division pieces (10), (11), (13), and the compartment divisions (9). It is difficult to be sure how item (9) is connected to the front and back rails, but it is thought that dovetail joints are used. For assembly reasons the compartment divisions should not be

glued to place until after the mirror slide (28) and dust board (34) have been fitted, since these slide in grooves in item (9).

Drawers and fold-over lids

Details of the drawers are given in Fig 25.4, and a dovetail construction is used. Note that the wood grain of the bottom (37) is across the drawer width. Dimensions of the fold-over lids are given in Fig 25.5. At the conclusion of this work it should be possible to consider the veneer and string work applied to these items and the carcase. The original has an applied mahogany curl veneer mirrored about the vertical centre line (Fig 25.2). The front veneer is from two such pieces carried down from the lid face to the bottom drawers, with stringing and banding applied afterwards. In the original the back and sides are not veneered.

Mirror easel

The mirror easel details are given in Fig 25.6. It consists of a mirror slide, frame and back stay. The back stay fits into a row of serrated notches cut either side in the mirror slide (28), enabling the mirror tilt to be adjusted. There is a small amount of veneer and string work around the edge of the mirror. The mirror folds flat for storage, when it is required to close the fold-over lids.

Boxes

The details of the internal boxes and lids are given in Fig 25.5. The fine quality of the original dressing table is revealed particularly by the precision with which the internal boxes and compartments were made. The fitting of boxes (4) and (5) in their compartments is so accurate, that pushing one down will lift the other by the air pressure underneath, as there is a small hole in the bottom of the division lining (23) between the compartments to allow air to pass through. Fig 25.7 shows the left-hand compartment boxes.

Handles

The handles on the front of the dressing table are of Sheffield plate, with details as in Figs 25.4 and 25.8. I know of no commercial source for these. An alternative is to consider oval Sheraton style brass handles, which are more easily obtainable. Sheffield plate, by the way, is rather like bi-metal strip, and consists of a centre plate of copper with a thin plate of silver soldered on either side. The bar is then passed between heavy rollers and thinned to the

25.7 *Lidded boxes in left-hand compartment*

25.8 *Drawer front inlay and Sheffield plate handles*

required thickness. The process was discovered by Thomas Bolsover of Sheffield in 1743.

Finish

It is suggested that the dressing table is french polished.

Chapter 26

Silver table

Holker Hall nestles on the southern edge of the Lake District near Grange-over-Sands, and is the home of the Cavendish family. The hall has an extremely fine furniture collection, and from these I have picked three desirable pieces. The hall itself originated in the sixteenth century when, after the dissolution of the monasteries, part of the old Cartmell Priory estate was acquired by George Preston, a wealthy local landowner. He built the first house on the present site in 1604.

In 1697 the estate passed by marriage to the Lowther family, and in the 1720s they were responsible for rebuilding much of the house and adding a north wing. Sir William Lowther (1727–56) died unmarried, and it is through his father Sir Thomas Lowther's marriage to Lady Elizbeth Cavendish, daughter of the 2nd Duke of Devonshire, that Holker Hall eventually became a Cavendish possession. Lord George Augustus Cavendish, who inherited Holker, and later members of the family, made several additions to the house in the modern Gothic style.

In March 1871, disaster struck when early one morning fire completely destroyed the west wing, and

26.1 *Holker Hall*

26.2 *Silver table*

many irreplaceable paintings, statues, books and furniture were lost. Undaunted, the 7th Duke of Devonshire immediately began a programme of reconstruction on an even grander scale. It is this impressive Elizabethan style red sandstone building, which is the visitor's first glimpse of Holker Hall today.

On entering Holker Hall, one is immediately struck by the spaciousness and fine interior craftsmanship in all the rooms. The entrance hall is particularly impressive with its lofty proportions, wainscot panelling and splendid oak staircase. The adjoining library has more than 3500 books, including many that survived the fire, and others brought over from Chatsworth. This room bears testament to Henry Cavendish (1731–1810), a renowned but reclusive scientist to whom we owe the discoveries of nitric acid, the properties of hydrogen and a calculation of the density of the earth.

I have mentioned that Holker Hall has an extremely fine furniture collection, and the first design that I have selected is from the drawing room: a rare Chinese Chippendale silver table (c. 1780).

Chinoserie is the art of applying the Chinese

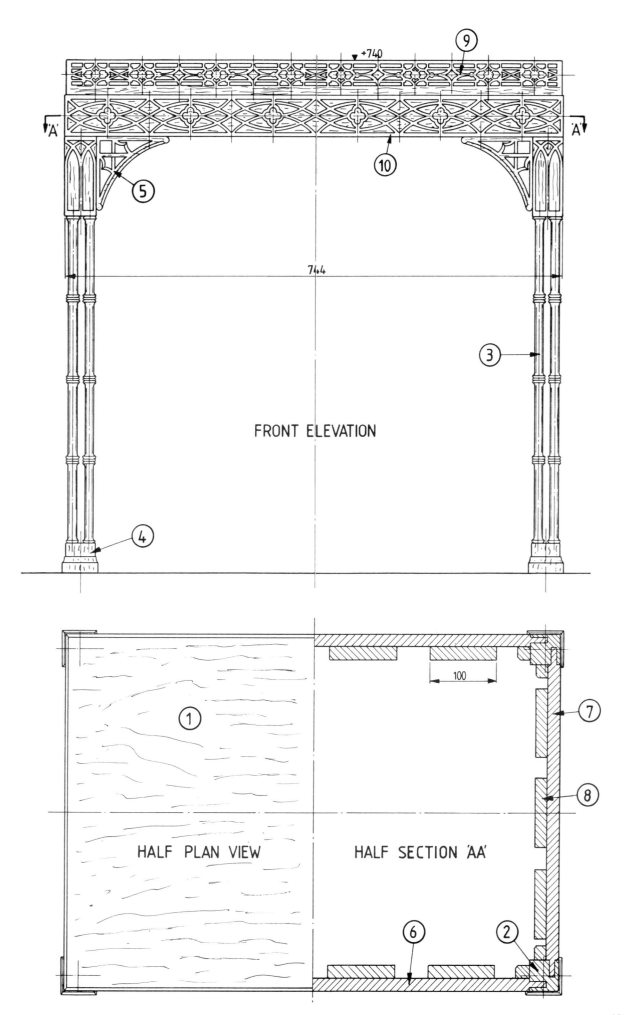

FRONT ELEVATION

HALF PLAN VIEW

HALF SECTION 'AA'

26.3 *General arrangement of silver table (cont. overleaf)*

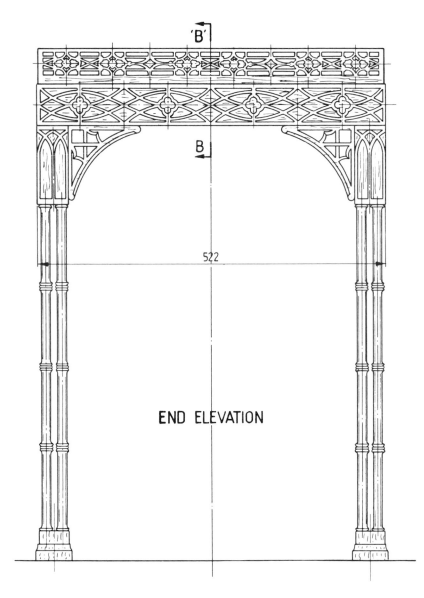

'B'

B

522

END ELEVATION

26.3 (cont.)

decorative manner on to European style furniture, and was very popular in the Rococo period. Pagoda shapes and sharp angular fretwork are common features of such furniture. The chinoserie on the silver table is in the form of geometric fretwork tracery applied to the frieze, and above this is a finely cut fretwork gallery. Thomas Chippendale, in his pattern book *The Gentleman and Cabinet Maker's Director*, gives designs for Chinese and Gothic fretwork and there are similarities to be noted with those on the silver table.

Complementing this are the legs in characteristic Chippendale cluster column form, each consisting of four finely-turned spindles standing on a guttae foot. Scroll brackets, also in fretted Chinese style, strengthen the table at each corner. All these features, together with the superb workmanship, make this little table a very desirable, fine-quality piece of furniture.

Construction

The general arrangement drawings are given in Fig 26.3, with elevations and plan sections, etc. The constructional skills required are woodturning, joinery and fretwork. The project needs some patience, and the ability to work accurately, but the craftsman will be rewarded with an enviable piece of furniture. The table top is made first, followed by the fretwork and then the legs.

The table framework consists of side and end rails (6), (7), mortise-and-tenon jointed into corner blocks (2). While the corner blocks are loose, the opportunity should be taken to pre-machine the spigot holes for the spindle leg ends. The original table top (1) is a single sheet of high quality mahogany, something you may find difficult to purchase today. An acceptable compromise could be to apply a mahogany curl veneer on top of a plainer mahogany base, with possibly a balancing veneer on the underside to

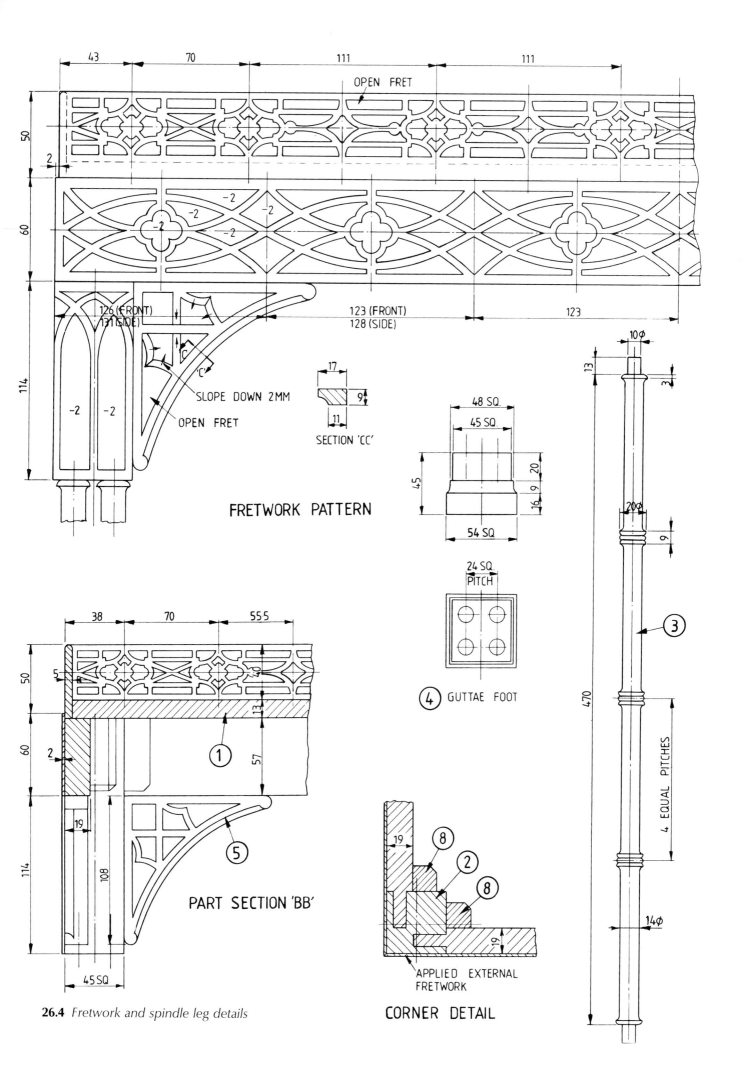

OPEN FRET

FRETWORK PATTERN

126 (FRONT)
131 (SIDE)

123 (FRONT)
128 (SIDE)

123

SLOPE DOWN 2MM

OPEN FRET

SECTION 'CC'

48 SQ.
45 SQ.
54 SQ.

24 SQ.
PITCH

④ GUTTAE FOOT

PART SECTION 'BB'

45 SQ

CORNER DETAIL

APPLIED EXTERNAL
FRETWORK

④ EQUAL PITCHES

10∅

20∅

14∅

470

26.4 *Fretwork and spindle leg details*

stabilize against warping. If it is proposed to veneer both sides of the table top, a blockboard centre might even be considered.

Chinese fretwork

The fretwork is without doubt the most demanding aspect of the job. In measuring up the original, it was thought that the frieze decoration was carved into the table rails (6) and (7), but closer inspection revealed this to be a thin sheet of mahogany 2mm thick, which is cut first and then glued to place along each table rail.

Details of the fretwork patterns are given in Fig 26.4, and to achieve a creditable result these need to be transferred accurately on to the mahogany strips. It may help to tackle the thicker gallery fretwork first to gain some confidence, before moving on to the thinner frieze work. It should be noted that the pitch of the fretwork on the end frieze is marginally larger than that on the front.

Some experimentation may be necessary on scrap pieces before proceeding with cutting out the final fret strips. A suggestion for tackling the thin fretwork is to stick it first on to a thicker waste strip, using a dissolvable glue. This way the risk of the fretwork accidently breaking whilst being cut will be minimized. The two strips are then gently parted. The fretwork is illustrated in Fig 26.5.

26.5 *Chinese fretwork*

Cluster column legs

Each corner leg consists of a group of four finely-turned mahogany spindles spigotted at either end to fit into corner blocks (2) and guttae feet (4). These cluster column legs are long and slender, so a lathe steady will be required while machining in order to achieve a good finish. The leg dimensions are given in Fig 26.4. When these and the guttae feet are completed they can then be added to the table top, and the corner scroll pieces finally glued to place. You may find it worthwhile french polishing the leg spindles before they are finally assembled.

Parts list

Item	No	Material	Dimensions (mm)
1 Table top	1	Mahogany	508 × 13 × 730 long
2 Corner block	4	Mahogany	45sq × 171 long
3 Spindle leg	16	Mahogany	25sq × 520 long
4 Guttae foot	4	Mahogany	54sq × 45 long
5 Scroll bracket	8	Mahogany	108 × 17 × 520 long total
6 Side rail	2	Mahogany	57 × 19 × 740 long
7 End rail	2	Mahogany	57 × 19 × 520 long
8 Support block	22	Mahogany	19sq × 2000 long total
9 Fretwork gallery	1	Mahogany	53 × 5 × 2600 long total, for table edge perimeter
10 Frieze fretwork	1	Mahogany	60 × 2 × 2600 long total, for table side perimeter

Chapter 27

Dumb waiter

I have previously discussed a design for a Chippendale style dining chair from Rufford Old Hall (Chapter 4), so it would be wrong to present another. However, I cannot pass without mentioning the extremely fine set of Harlequin Chippendale dining chairs in the dining room and other rooms at Holker Hall. Their quality exudes the grandeur of the house, and their diversity includes many with square leg/stretcher pattern, others with ball-and-claw feet, seats of both stuff over and drop in type, and a variety of back splat patterns. Also in the dining room at Holker is the second furniture design I have chosen, a fine-quality dumb waiter (c. 1780).

There are two dumb waiters in the dining room, one of two-tier form and the other three-tier. The design selected is the smaller, two-tier one, because it seemed more attractive and better suited to the modern house. In addition, the three-tier dumb waiter is mounted on brass castors which you might find difficult to obtain. The two-tier version does not have this problem, as it is supported on graceful Queen Anne style legs.

The general period for dumb waiters is between 1740 and 1840, although they are known to have existed before this. They are invariably supported on

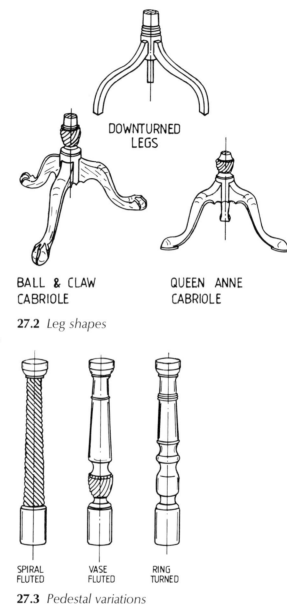

DOWNTURNED LEGS

BALL & CLAW CABRIOLE

QUEEN ANNE CABRIOLE

27.2 Leg shapes

SPIRAL FLUTED

VASE FLUTED

RING TURNED

27.3 Pedestal variations

27.1 *Dumb waiter*

three legs, and in this respect have some commonality with the design of tripod tables of the same period (ie George III). These are often of the cabriole shape, either the ball-and-claw pattern, or, as here, the more slender Queen Anne style with its undulating S-shape. The legs can also be downswept, as in the Holker three-tier dumb waiter. Occasionally they may be of downturned Z-form, and, if you are interested, there are a pair of lamp tables in the library at Erddig (NT) with legs of this shape. Fig 27.2

shows these leg pattern variants. Some are fitted with castors, and others are not; the Holker Hall dumb waiters feature one of each type.

Common forms for pedestals are illustrated in Fig 27.3. These are the vase reed, spiral reed and ring-turned patterns. The vase reed was a favourite of the Chippendale era (1750–80). The two-tier dumb waiter has a vase reed pattern on each section of the pedestal column. The ring-turned form, is, as its name suggests, simply a spindle-turned column without the added embellishment of vase beading. The three-tier dumb waiter at Holker has a ring-turned pedestal. A heavily ringed column may date from 1800 or after. A further pedestal variant, sometimes seen, is a vertical reeded or fluted form rather like a Grecian column.

The tray design is almost always circular. The simpler ones are flat, but most are dished shaped with a raised perimeter edge (Fig 27.4). The dish tray design requires more wood to make it and is more desirable,

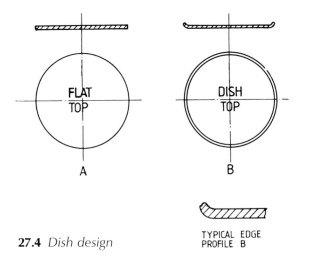

27.4 *Dish design*

while the extra workmanship and quality makes it more valuable. Sometimes the trays have a galleried edge, and occasionally you may see dumb waiters with trays that flap down either side of the centre pedestal. The tier arrangement usually features the smallest dish at the top, increasing in size downwards, this being generally the most aesthetically pleasing. However, some do exist with a reversed tier structure, with the largest dish at the top.

Construction

The construction of the dumb waiter can be conveniently split into three aspects: the legs, the pedestal column and the dish trays. The general arrangement details are given in Fig 27.6 and of the

pedestal column in Fig 27.8. The column is in two sections, spigotted together with the lower dish tray sandwiched in between. The columns are spindle-turned with the vase bead carving added afterwards. The 14 convex beads have a 90° spiral twist, and need careful marking out and then crisp carving. The spiral twist is illustrated in Fig 27.5.

Legs

Details of the Queen Anne style legs are given in Fig 27.9. The pattern is set out on a squared background to facilitate transferring the shape to the hardwood. These legs are a lovely S-shape when properly executed, so do take a little time and patience to complete them. They are connected to the lower pedestal by dovetail joints, and care should be taken to make these accurately. You often find some slackness on old tripod stands due to wear and tear, and they have to be reinforced with steel strips screwed on underneath. The legs are illustrated in Fig 27.7.

Dish machining

Machining of the upper dish (1) and support platform (2), which are of modest size in single pieces of

27.5 *Vase flutework*

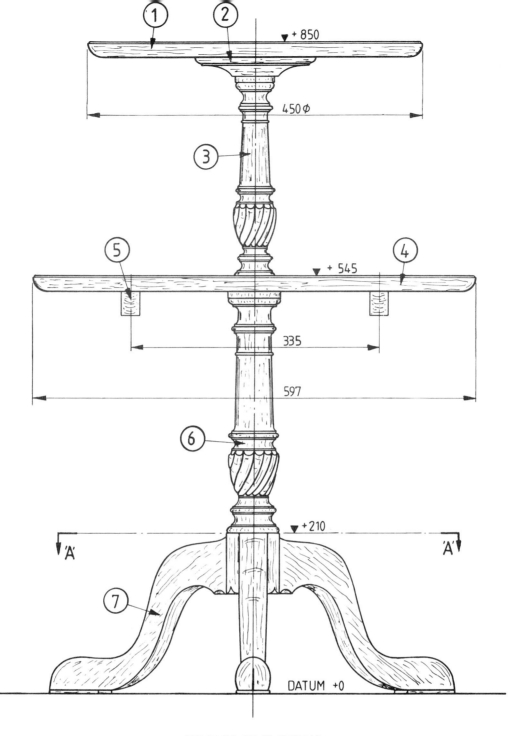

FRONT ELEVATION

27.6 *General arrangement of dumb waiter (cont. overleaf)*

mahogany, should present no problems. They can be screw-fixed in the centre area to the lathe bowl turning head for this purpose. The lower dish (4) could be similarly screw-fixed to the lathe in the centre for machining, but its greater diameter means it is poorly supported, and consequently it may be difficult to achieve a satisfactory turned finish. An improved method of securing it more rigidly to the lathe is as follows.

In the original, the lower dish (4) is made from two pieces of mahogany supported by a pair of lopers (5) underneath. Edge joint the dish blank pieces together, and when the glue is set, plane or glasspaper the underside flat in preparation for mounting on the lathe. Prepare a plywood backing disc, of about 520mm diameter, to act as a sandwich between the dish blank and the bowl turning head. Screw-fix the dish blank/sandwich piece together in the location of

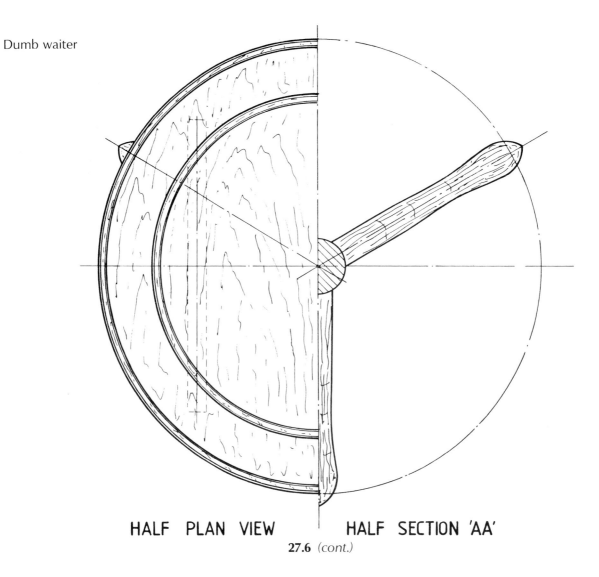

HALF PLAN VIEW   HALF SECTION 'AA'

27.6 (cont.)

the loper positions, ie where the screw holes will not show when the lopers are finally screwed in place. Fix this assembly to the bowl turning head and machine the dish blank to the required size. When finished, separate the dish from the sandwich piece and screw the lopers into place, concealing the holes used for woodturning.

27.7 Queen Anne style leg

Assembly and finish

Assembly should present no special problems, and the dumb waiter should then be finished by french polishing.

Parts list

Item	No	Material	Dimensions (mm)
1 Upper dish	1	Mahogany	460sq × 25 thick
2 Support platform	1	Mahogany	170sq × 30 thick
3 Upper pedestal	1	Mahogany	65sq × 340 long
4 Lower dish	1	Mahogany	610sq × 25 thick; make from strips
5 Loper	2	Mahogany	32 × 25 × 380 long
6 Lower pedestal	1	Mahogany	75sq × 420 long
7 Leg	3	Mahogany	120 × 48 × 375 long

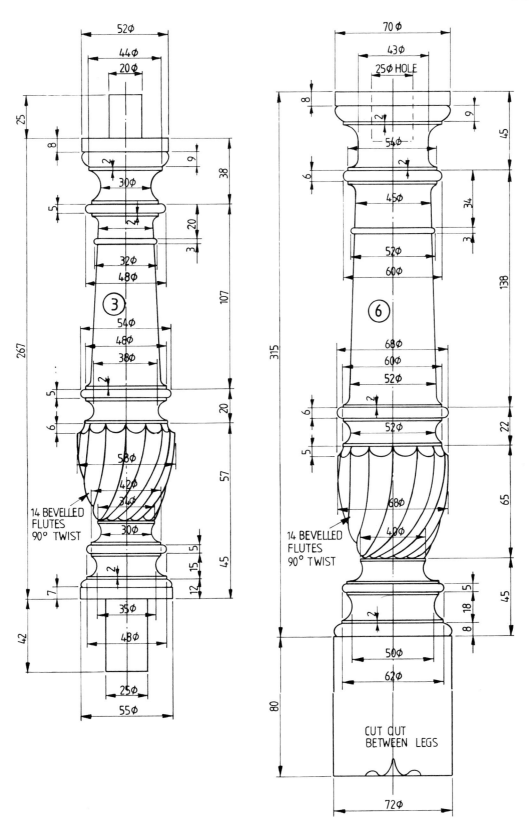

27.8 *Pedestal column details*

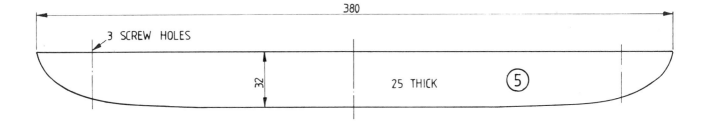

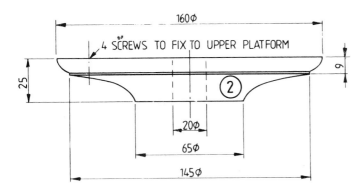

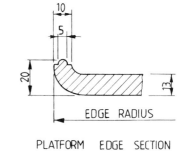

EDGE RADIUS

PLATFORM EDGE SECTION

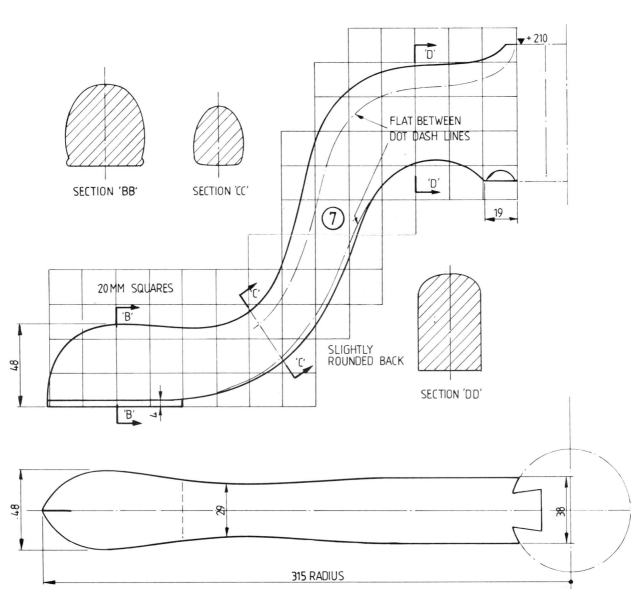

SECTION 'BB'

SECTION 'CC'

FLAT BETWEEN
DOT DASH LINES

SLIGHTLY
ROUNDED BACK

SECTION 'DD'

20 MM SQUARES

315 RADIUS

27.9 *Leg details and miscellaneous items*

Chapter 28

Hepplewhite four-post bed

To find a four-post bed design which would fit in a modern house, with its limited ceiling height of about 2.4m, took some searching amongst our country houses. Many are of vast proportions, custom-made to suit the state bedroom they were intended to go in. Those in Chatsworth, for example, are quite grandiose. However, I found a nicely proportioned Hepplewhite four-post bed (c. 1780), with a full tester arrangement, in the Queen Mary Dressing Room at Holker Hall.

The original, made in mahogany, is only 1220mm wide, compared to today's minimum standard of 1372mm or king size, which is 1525mm wide. I have therefore amended the width to 1372mm and the reader can extend this to king size if desired. Four-post beds were sometimes adapted when they were

28.1 *Hepplewhite four-post bed*

moved to a different room or house, so a careful inspection is needed to check the authenticity of originals.

Construction

The general arrangement, including half-plan sections, is given in Fig 28.2, and additional sections and plan information are detailed in Fig 28.3. The assembly consists of four corner posts, interconnected below mattress level by side and end rails, and at the top by a tester framework.

The suggested order of construction is first to make the corner posts (1), (2) and interconnecting rails (3), (4), then the tester arrangement. In the original the posts are linked by what appear to be large coach bolts. In Fig 28.4 an alternative screw/tie bar arrangement is given. The mattress is supported on eight crossbeams (5), which drop into dovetails in the side rails (3). The headboard (4) fits into rebated grooves in corner posts (1). Having completed this assembly it can be temporarily dismantled while work continues with the tester framework. When this is finished, the bed is reassembled, and the tester frame lifted into position on top of the corner posts. Finally the mattress, tester, coverlet and drapes, etc, are added. The most difficult items to make are the corner posts and tester framework.

Corner posts

The two head posts (1) are easy to make, being of simple square tapered section. By contrast, the foot posts (2), detailed in Fig 28.4, are of more ornamental design. These posts are woodturned at the top and bottom, and between this and the square section at mattress level is a tapered reeded column, above a carved wheat-ear pattern. These features, together with the post length of over 2m, may pose a few constructional problems.

Woodturning

The first difficulty will be in tackling the woodturning. The average amateur woodturning lathe typically

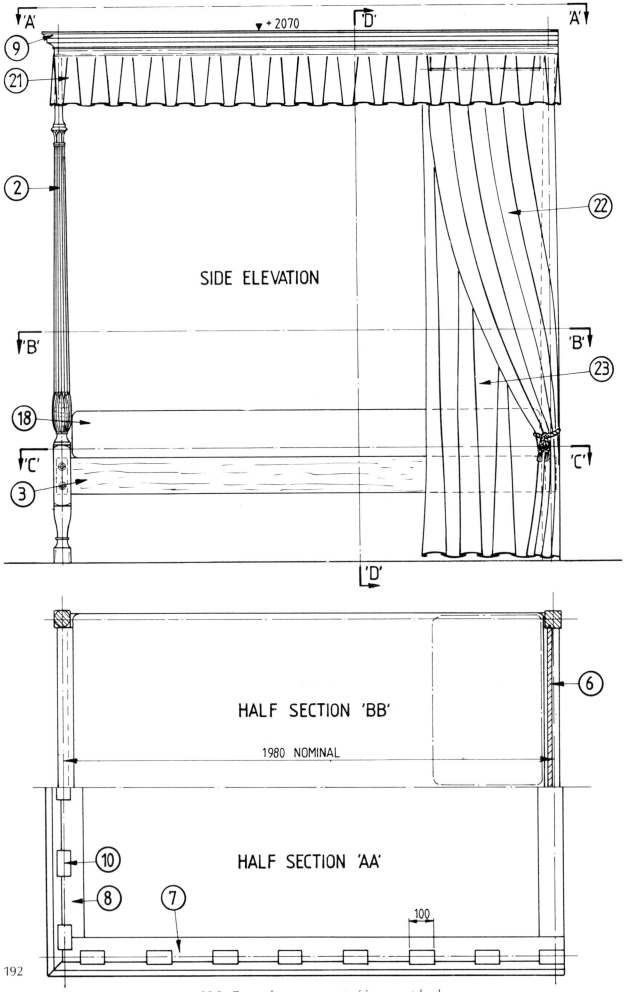

SIDE ELEVATION

▼ +2070

HALF SECTION 'BB'

1980 NOMINAL

HALF SECTION 'AA'

100

28.2 *General arrangement of four-post bed*

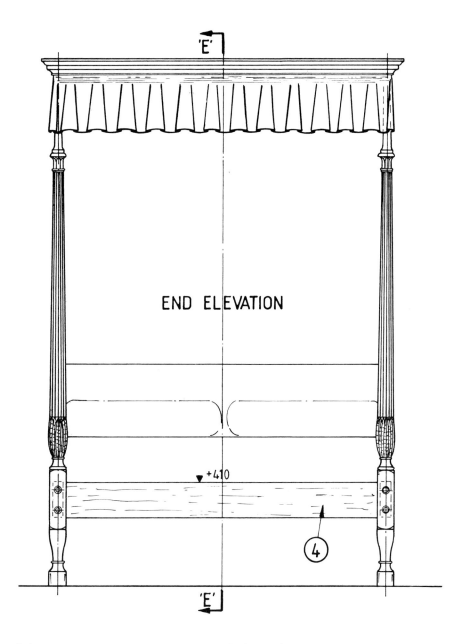

END ELEVATION

+410

④

'E'

accepts spindle-work between centres of 600mm and 1200mm. Thus, unless you have an unusually long lathe, some adaption will be needed to extend the bed length to accommodate a post 2100mm long. Alternatively, you may consider splitting the post into two lengths at an inconspicuous point, although there is no easy point to make the split.

Opting for the lathe extension solution will mean relocating the tailstock, and devising some method of enabling the tool rest to be adjusted/clamped along the length to be turned. With some ingenuity it should not be too difficult to devise a workable arrangement. However, it may well be easier and more practical to consider purchasing longer lathe bed rails. If the length is still too great for the lathe manufacturer to help, you could visit your local steel stockholder. He might have a steel section which could be adapted for the purpose. By extending a

lathe in this way, you have the bonus of a permanent facility to machine very long spindles. One other necessary piece of woodturning equipment is a lathe steady: the post length is too great to be done successfully without this.

Reeding

The completion of the woodturning will have prepared the groundwork for the reeded column section. Details of the latter are given in Fig 28.4 (section 'GG'). This will require machine routing facilities, using a pointed round engraving cutter to form the beaded shape. A robust framework jig should be made to hold the column centred at either end, and with provision to carry the spindle router sliding on a runner either side. This must align the cutter accurately on the post centre line, and there

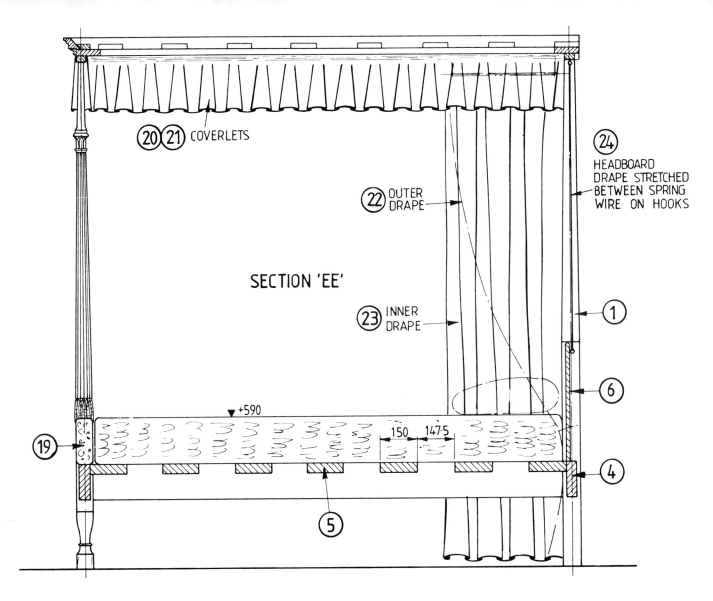

(20)(21) COVERLETS

(24) HEADBOARD DRAPE STRETCHED BETWEEN SPRING WIRE ON HOOKS

(22) OUTER DRAPE

SECTION 'EE'

(23) INNER DRAPE

(1)

(6)

▼ +590

(19)

150   147·5

(4)

(5)

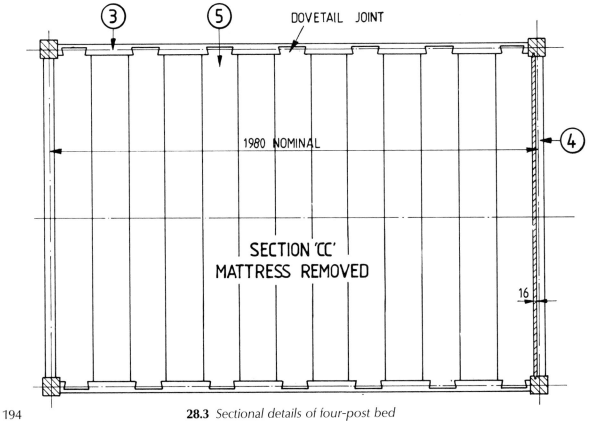

(3)   (5)   DOVETAIL JOINT

(4)

1980 NOMINAL

SECTION 'CC'
MATTRESS REMOVED

16

   28.3 *Sectional details of four-post bed*

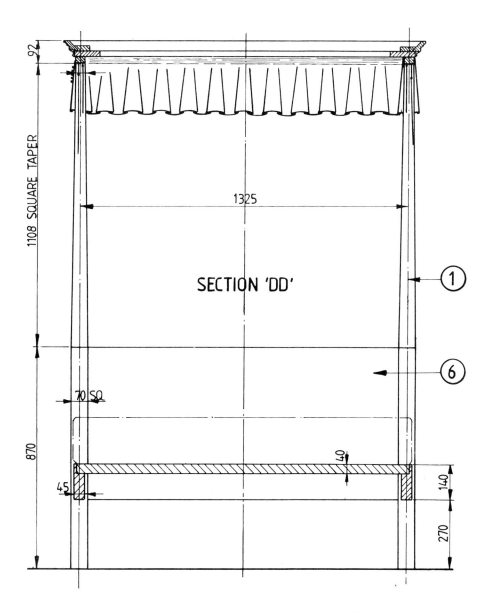

SECTION 'DD'

1108 SQUARE TAPER

92

1325

870

70 SQ

45

40

140

270

① ⑥

should be no slackness to permit the router to wobble, as this would produce an uneven reed. A scheme such as in Fig 28.6 could be considered. The jig also needs provision to allow incremental rotation of the post so that each bead can be cut in turn. If you have a lathe with an indexing head facility, you could consider building a temporary routing box jig around the lathe bedplate. It is suggested that you experiment first with a dummy post to check that the reed form is satisfactory.

Carving

Having completed the reeding exercise, there is only the carving on the corner posts to finish. There are short carved sections either end of the reeded length. The upper carving is a six-fluted petal detail, and the lower carving is a twelve-lobed wheat-ear motif mentioned earlier. Carving details are given in Figs 28.4 and 28.7.

Tester framework

Details of the tester framework are given in Fig 28.5. It consists of a side and end frame (7) and (8) joined by mortise-and-tenons. On to this is added a crest rail (9), support blocks (10), a coving strip (13), and Grecian key fretwork (12). Routing facilities will be needed to form the curved shape of the crest rail and coving strip. The Grecian fretwork is shown in Fig 28.8.

Drapes

The extent of the inner and outer drapes, and coverlets, etc, is indicated on the general arrangement drawings, etc. On the original these are principally white satin, but the choice of material and colour scheme can of course be adapted to suit your own requirements.

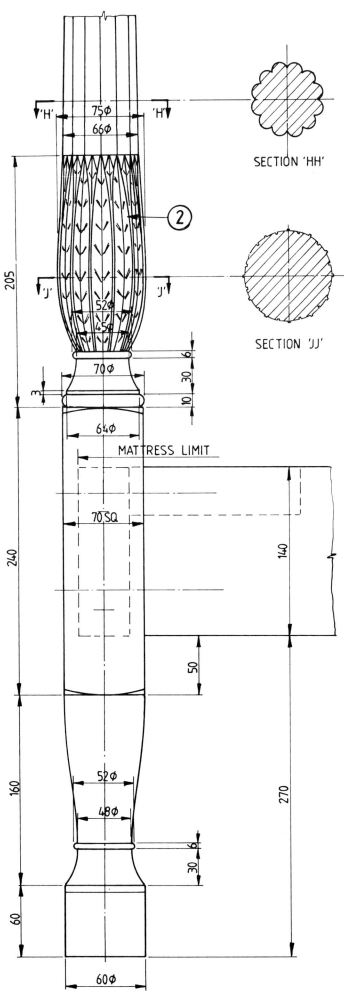

SECTION 'HH'

SECTION 'JJ'

②

MATTRESS LIMIT

70 SQ

140

50

270

28.4 *Miscellaneous foot post details*

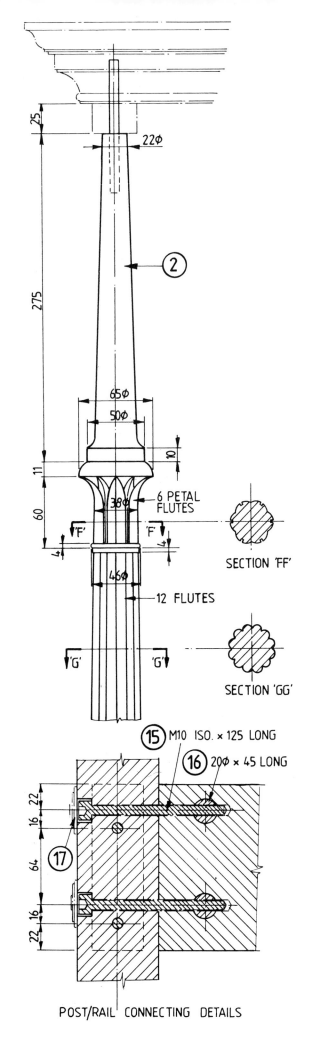

②

6 PETAL
FLUTES

SECTION 'FF'

12 FLUTES

SECTION 'GG'

⑮ M10 ISO. × 125 LONG

⑯ 20⌀ × 45 LONG

⑰

POST/RAIL CONNECTING DETAILS

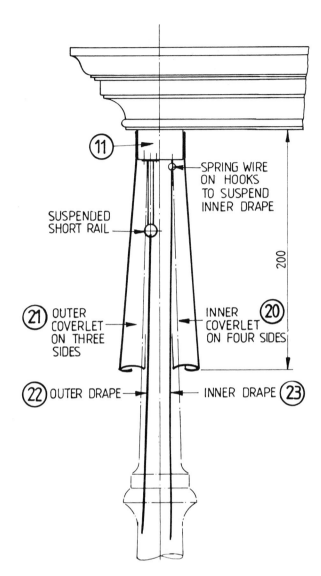

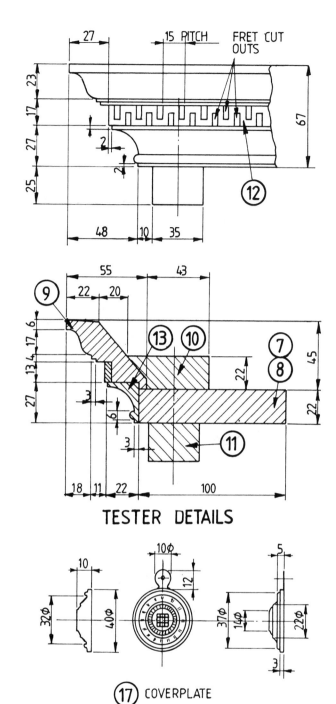

TESTER DETAILS

SPRING WIRE
ON HOOKS
TO SUSPEND
INNER DRAPE

SUSPENDED
SHORT RAIL

(21) OUTER
COVERLET
ON THREE
SIDES

(20) INNER
COVERLET
ON FOUR SIDES

(22) OUTER DRAPE

INNER DRAPE (23)

28.5 *Tester framework details*

(17) COVERPLATE

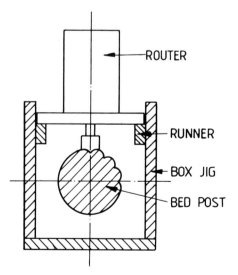

ROUTER

RUNNER

BOX JIG

BED POST

28.6 *Spindle moulding jig to form foot post reeds*

Parts list

Item	No	Material	Dimensions (mm)
1 Head post	2	Mahogany	70sq × 2000 long
2 Foot post	2	Mahogany	80sq × 2100 long
3 Side rail	2	Mahogany	140 × 45 × 1910
4 End rail	2	Mahogany	140 × 45 × 1255
5 Cross beam	7	Mahogany	150 × 40 × 1370
6 Headboard	1	Mahogany	460 × 16 × 1325
7 Tester side frame	2	Mahogany	100 × 22 × 2040 long
8 Tester end frame	2	Mahogany	100 × 22 × 1375 long
9 Crest rail	1	Mahogany	75 × 22 × 5800 long total
10 Support block	21	Mahogany	55 × 22 × 100 long
11 Coverlet strip	1	Mahogany	35 × 25 × 6900 long total
12 Grecian fret strip	1	Mahogany	13 × 5 × 5700 long total
13 Coving strip	1	Mahogany	27 × 22 × 5700 long total
14 Post rod	4	Steel	8 diameter × 130 long
15 Connecting bolt	8	Steel	M10 isometric × 125 long
16 Screw bar	8	Steel	20 diameter × 45 long
17 Coverplate	16	Brass	40 dia pressed plate
18 Mattress	1	—	1372 wide × 1905 long
19 End pad	1	Foam	175 × 75 × 1255 long. Fix with 'Velcro' strip
20 Inner coverlet	1	White satin	Make up to suit. Fix with 'Velcro' strip
21 Outer coverlet	1	White satin	Make to suit. Fix with 'Velcro' strip
22 Outer drape	2	Fabric	Purchase/make to personal choice
23 Inner drape	2	White satin	Purchase/make to personal choice
24 Headboard drape	1	White satin	Purchase/make to personal choice
25 Valance	1	Fabric	Purchase/make to personal choice

28.7 *Foot post carving*

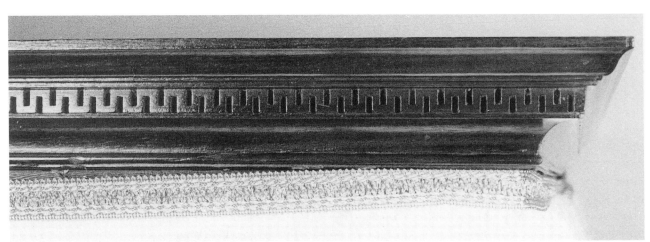

28.8 *Tester Grecian fretwork*

Chapter 29

Sofa table

I chose Arley Hall in Cheshire for the last two furniture designs in this book. The first known settler at Arley was Adam of Dutton, during the eleventh century. He owned many thousands of acres in various localities, including land at Aston-by-Budworth nearby and Warburton to the north, and the family eventually adopted the Warburton name. In 1469 Piers Warburton moved his principal seat south to Arley, where he built the first medieval great hall with adjoining wings, the west to accommodate his family and the east for the kitchens, servants' quarters, etc. Some time later a grand south front was added, linking the east and west wings and making the building quadrangular.

In 1758 the hall was recorded to have been in a draughty, decaying condition, and much patching and mending was required. Sir Peter Warburton decided to solve the problem by encasing the old building within new walls of brick and stucco. This proved only to be a temporary solution, and when his son Rowland Egerton-Warburton inherited Arley, he commissioned a completely new Elizabethan style house to replace the older one. The building was constructed in two phases between 1832 and 1845, using over half a million bricks, and over £1000 worth of oak timbers. The impressive Elizabethan façade of the south front, completed in the second phase between 1840 and 1845, is Arley Hall as the visitor sees it today.

Arley Hall remained a Warburton stronghold for more than 500 years until 1891, when through marriage with the Flower family it eventually came into the possession of Lord and Lady Ashbrook, whose elder son Michael Flower is now the present squire.

The most notable furniture items are in the library, drawing room and gallery. The library contains a fine set of pinnacled bookcases by H. Wood, a Regency drum table with leather top, and a fine quality long case clock by John Long. In the drawing room is a virginal (1675) by Stephen Keene, reputed to be one of the oldest surviving English keyboard instruments. The gallery includes a fine quality Victorian rosewood Sutherland table, an eighteenth-century Chinese

29.1 *Arley Hall*

black and gold lacquer games table, an eighteenth-century scarlet lacquer cabinet (also Chinese), a walnut side table with oyster veneer and floral marquetry, and a Rosewood sofa table (c. 1820).

Low back settees were introduced towards the end of the eighteenth century, and sofa tables were often placed behind them. It is from this association that they get their name. The earliest sofa tables date from about 1780, and their production probably spans a time of about 40 years to the end of the Regency period.

Sofa tables can be considered as longer versions of Pembroke tables (see Chapter 16), with a small drop-leaf table flap at either end, and fitted with two drawers instead of one. Their length is commonly between 1500 and 1700mm with flaps extended, and width about 600–700mm. Their support arrangement differs, and instead of having four corner legs the table is carried at either end by a paired set of legs joined to a column, usually referred to as an end standard.

The arrangements vary, but one commonly seen is a square section column joined by a pair of downswept, undulating, or notched style legs, according to the date. Sometimes the end standard is carried at the base by a crossbeam, to which the feet are then separately connected, as in the Arley Hall

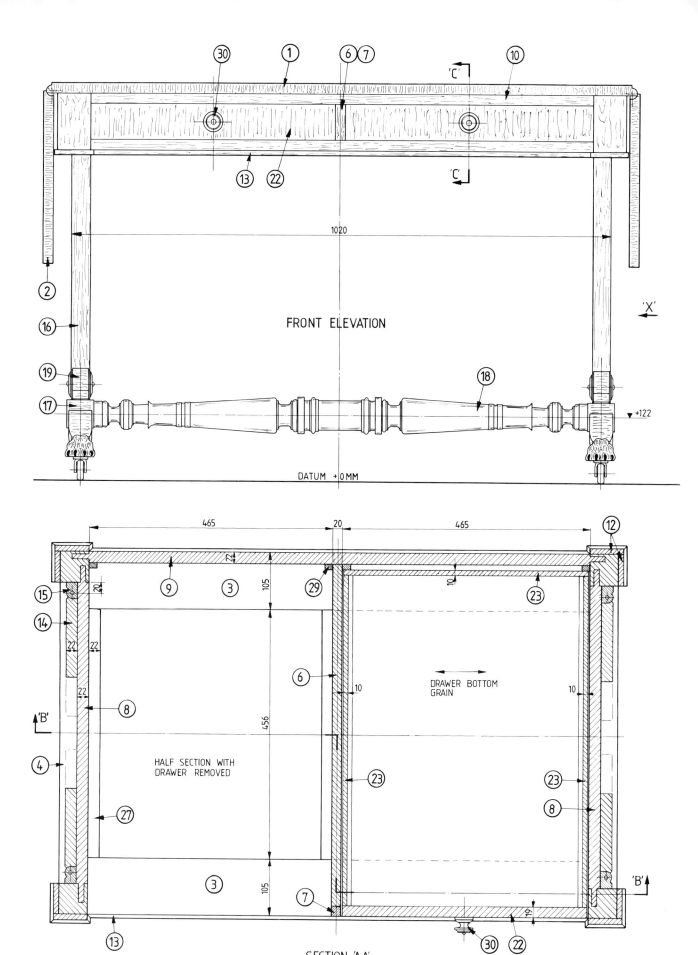

29.2 *General arrangement of sofa table*

FRONT ELEVATION

1020

DATUM +0MM

+122

SECTION 'AA'

HALF SECTION WITH
DRAWER REMOVED

DRAWER BOTTOM
GRAIN

465 · 20 · 465

22 · 105 · 456 · 105

20 · 22 · 22 · 22

10 · 10 · 10 · 19

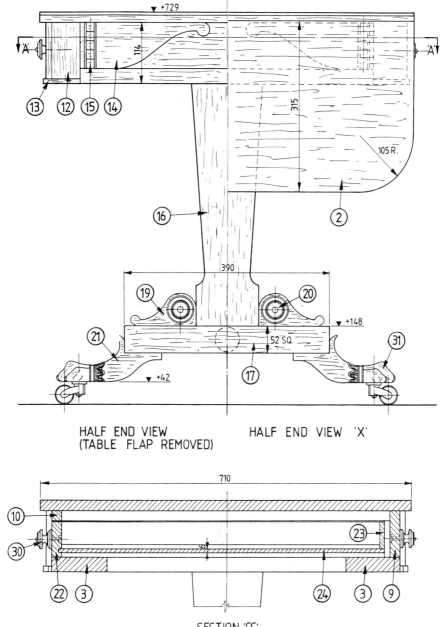

HALF END VIEW
(TABLE FLAP REMOVED)

HALF END VIEW 'X'

SECTION 'CC'

SECTION 'BB'

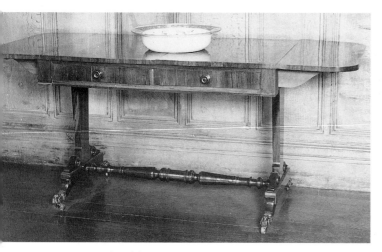

29.3 *Sofa table*

29.4 *Claw foot*

example. Another variant, also using a crossbeam support, is for the end standards to be spindle turned, and just occasionally you will find a sofa table which is carried by a centre pedestal similar to Regency period games tables. Sometimes the leg pairs are linked by a centre stretcher to give added strength. If the reader is interested in viewing other sofa tables, there are further examples in the Green Saloon at Dunham Massey (NT), one in the Queen of Scots Apartments at Chatsworth with an impressive lyre end standard, and a mahogany sofa table with satinwood inlay at Wythenshawe.

Construction

The general arrangement of the sofa table is given in Fig 29.2. Its construction is principally joinery, with some veneer work and a small amount of woodturning. The suggested order of work is first to make the table top carcase, then the columns and legs, and finally the table top itself.

Table top and drawers

The carcase underframe is shown in Fig 29.5, and consists of interconnecting timber items (3), (4) and (5).

On to this is added corner blocks (11) connected by side, back and front rails (8), (9) and (10) using mortise-and-tenon joints. These are softwood items in the original, but could be changed to beech or mahogany if desired. The structure is completed by adding the drawer division pieces (6), (7), the swivelling table flap details (14), (15), and the external rosewood strips and veneer facework. The mahogany drawers have applied rosewood veneer to the front, and the grain direction of the drawer bottom is across the width. The back rail (9) is veneered to simulate a false drawer arrangement as at the front.

Columns and legs

Details of the table supports and stretchers are given in Fig 29.7, and for the legs, etc, in Fig 29.8. If lathe limitations prevent you machining the stretcher (18) in one piece, then consideration could be given to making it in two halves spigotted together. If this alternative is used, the split should not be at the centre, but at one of the shoulders 40mm to one side where it will not be noticed.

Brasswork

The only brasswork required is the claw pattern castors. Dimensional information for these is given in Fig 29.8. These are available commercially, although you may not be able to match the design precisely. You may therefore have to adapt the sofa table leg (21) slightly to accommodate this.

Table top

The table top is made as a separate entity complete with end flaps, and is screw-fixed. Cracked table tops are occasionally experienced with original sofa tables where the grain is across the table width to match the end flaps. This is due to seasoning reducing the length of the table top until the end flaps in the down position touch the carcase frame. Further reduction beyond this point places a substantial strain on the table top, and it cracks across the middle. With this in mind, and although some will decry it, the table top (1) is probably best made from either plywood or blockboard, which will give good stability. Another advantage is that plywood can be purchased mahogany faced. The table flaps (2), however, should be made in mahogany in order that the rule joint does not disclose any plywood edging. For the same reason, the matching ends of the table top (1) should also be edged in mahogany.

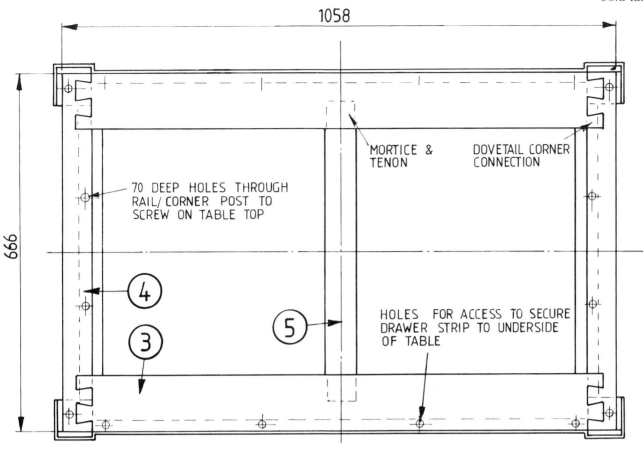

1058

666

70 DEEP HOLES THROUGH RAIL/ CORNER POST TO SCREW ON TABLE TOP

MORTICE & TENON

DOVETAIL CORNER CONNECTION

④

③

⑤

HOLES FOR ACCESS TO SECURE DRAWER STRIP TO UNDERSIDE OF TABLE

UNDERSIDE FRAME VIEW

29.5 *Underside frame view*

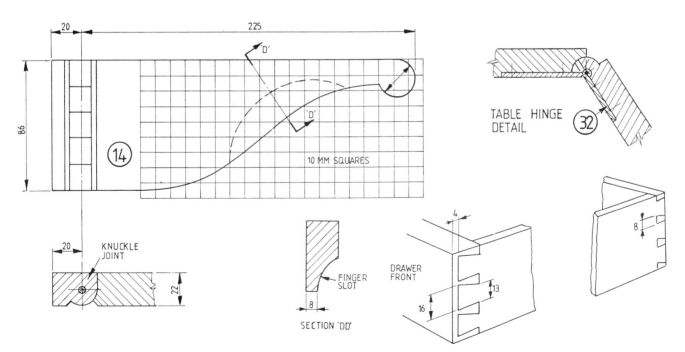

20

225

'D'

'D'

10 MM SQUARES

86

⑭

20

KNUCKLE JOINT

22

FINGER SLOT

8

SECTION 'DD'

4

DRAWER FRONT

13

16

TABLE HINGE DETAIL ㉜

8

29.6 *Table flap support details*

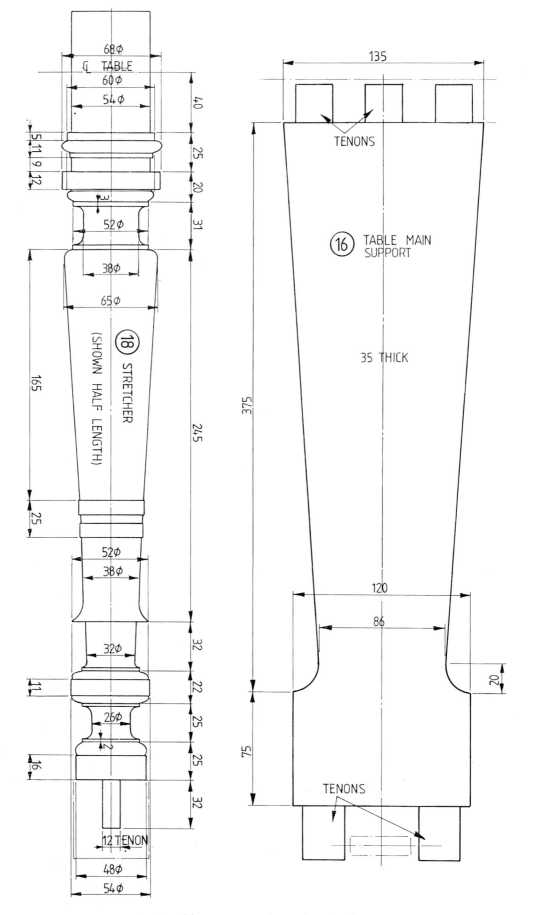

29.7 *Table support and stretcher details*

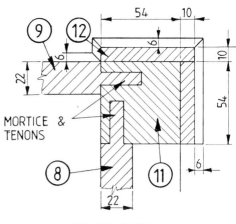

54 10

6

6

22

10

54

6

22

MORTICE &
TENONS

⑨ ⑫

⑧ ⑪

CORNER DETAIL

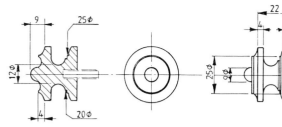

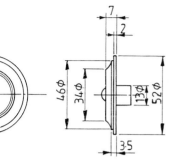

9 25Φ

12Φ

4

20Φ

22

4 4

25Φ

9Φ

36

㉚ KNOB

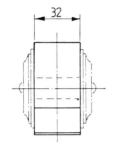

10 10

22Φ

10Φ

7

2

46Φ

34Φ

13Φ

52Φ

3·5

⑳ FINIAL

TABLE TOP

30

40

LOCAL
CUT OUT

124

16Φ

30R

13Φ HOLE

11

60

32

⑲ SCROLL PIECE

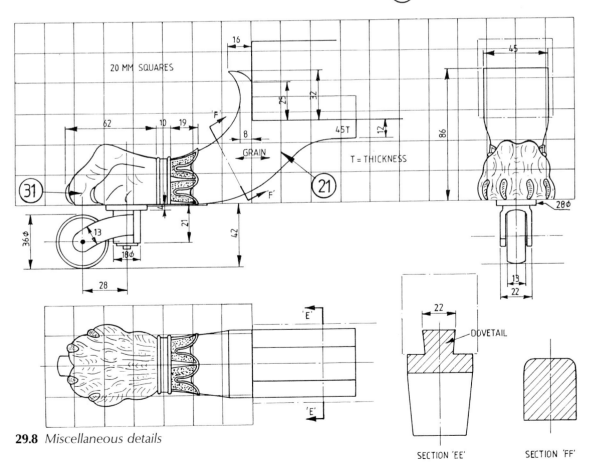

20 MM SQUARES

16

25

32

45

62

10 19

F

8

GRAIN

45T

12

86

T = THICKNESS

㉛

F'

㉑

28Φ

36Φ

13

18Φ

21

42

28

13

22

'E'

22

DOVETAIL

'E'

29.8 Miscellaneous details

SECTION 'EE'

SECTION 'FF'

205

Parts list

Item	No	Material	Dimensions (mm)	Item	No	Material	Dimensions (mm)
1 Table top	1	Plywood	800 × 520 × 19 thick	20 Finial	8	Rosewood	52sq × 35 long
				21 Leg	4	Rosewood	90 × 45 × 160 long
2 Table end flap	2	Mahogany	320 × 19 × 710 long	22 Drawer front	1	Mahogany	67 × 19 × 470 long
				23 Drawer lining	2	Mahogany	67 × 10 × 1750 long
3 Front/back frame	2	Softwood	105 × 28 × 1050 long	24 Drawer bottom	2	Mahogany	160 × 6 × 1900 long per drawer
4 Side frame	2	Softwood	54 × 28 × 700 long	25 Beading	4	Mahogany	8 × 600 long
5 Frame cross piece	1	Softwood	60 × 28 × 570 long	26 Drawer slipper	4	Mahogany	10 × 6 × 620 long
6 Division	1	Softwood	86 × 20 × 660 long	27 Runner	2	Softwood	28 × 22 × 460 long
7 Edging strip	1	Rosewood	19sq × 100 long	28 Tip stop	4	Softwood	19 × 10 × 630 long
8 Side rail	2	Softwood	86 × 22 × 650 long	29 Back stop	4	Softwood	16 × 10 × 70 long
9 Back rail	1	Softwood	86 × 19 × 1050 long	30 Knob	4	Rosewood	40sq × 200 long total
10 Front strip	1	Softwood	19sq × 1050 long	31 Claw foot castor	4	Brass	Purchase to suit
11 Corner block	4	Softwood	54sq × 90 long				
12 Corner cover piece	8	Rosewood	70 × 10 × 120 long	32 Table top hinge	6	Steel	Purchase to suit
13 Fascia strip	1	Rosewood	10 × 6 × 2800 total length	33 Rosewood veneer	–	Rosewood	Quantity to suit table top and other items
14 Flap support	4	Mahogany	86 × 22 × 250 long				
15 Knuckle joint piece	4	Mahogany	86 × 22 × 50 long	34 Ebony string	–	Ebony	2200 long, required for false drawer effect
16 End standard	2	Rosewood	135 × 35 × 520 long				
17 Cross beam	2	Softwood	52sq × 390 long				
18 Stretcher	1	Rosewood	75sq × 1020 long	35 Screws	–	Steel	Miscellaneous
19 Scroll piece	4	Rosewood	60 × 32 × 124 long				

Chapter 30

Rosewood centre table

Apart from the 'D-end' dining table in Chapter 19, I have not yet featured any circular form tables in this book, so for the last furniture design I decided to select a centre table. At Arley Hall there are two such tables of interest: one is an impressive Victorian mahogany centre table, crossbanded in rosewood and cherrywood, with massive carved tripod form legs, and the other is a smaller Rosewood centre table (c. 1820) in the library. I have chosen the earlier table as a design, mainly on account of its more compact size.

The rosewood centre table is 830mm in diameter, features a tilt top, and is supported on a pedestal column carried by four sabre form legs with foliate pattern brass castors. Special features are the proliferation of beading, sometimes termed 'reeling', on the table perimeter and the pedestal, the foliate carving on the column, and the notched leg form.

The legs on the centre table illustrate the changing mood during the transitional years of 1790 to 1820. Just as fashion changes today, so too did the leg form vary on pedestal supported tables. In the 1790s the prevailing taste was for the simple downswept form as in Fig 30.3(a). By about 1805 this had changed to an undulating S-shape, as in Fig 30.3(b). An example of this is the octagon worktable design in Chapter 21. By 1820 this shape had been modified yet again and the rounded upper section had developed pronounced notches, lumps or 'toothache' as it is sometimes called in the antique trade (Fig 30.3(c)). This feature is noted again on the Regency games table in Chapter 24, this time in the form of overturned nodules at the top end of the legs.

Construction

The general arrangement of the table is given in Fig 30.2, with additional sections in Fig 30.6. The constructional skills required include joinery, woodturning, carving and veneering. The work can be split into the table top, pedestal column and legs.

Table top

The table top (1) is made from two mahogany pieces supported by lopers (3) and (4) underneath, and the

30.1 *Centre table (front)*

perimeter edge (2) is of the brick construction, using short overlapping hardwood sections. This work should be straightforward, but you might consider some form of routing jig to machine the table top and the brick edging to the circular form. This jig could be used to prepare the rebates ready for the edge beading (22) and (23).

Regency beading

The original edge beading is not machined into the table rim, but consists of small individual beads added to the table perimeter. There are nearly 400 edge beads (22), and about 240 facing beads (23), and they are small and fiddly to make.

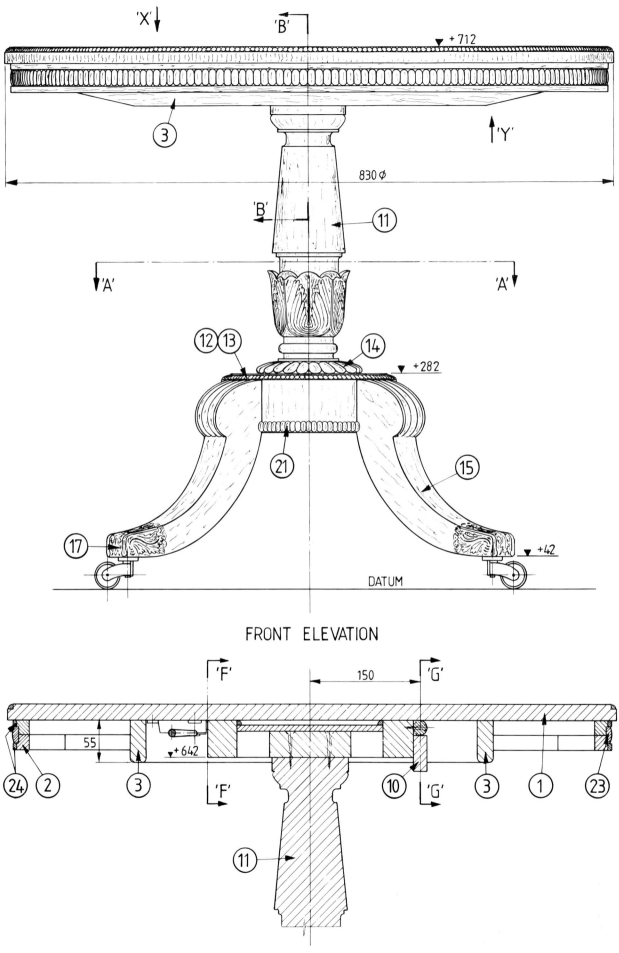

FRONT ELEVATION

SECTION 'BB'

30.2 *General arrangement of centre table*

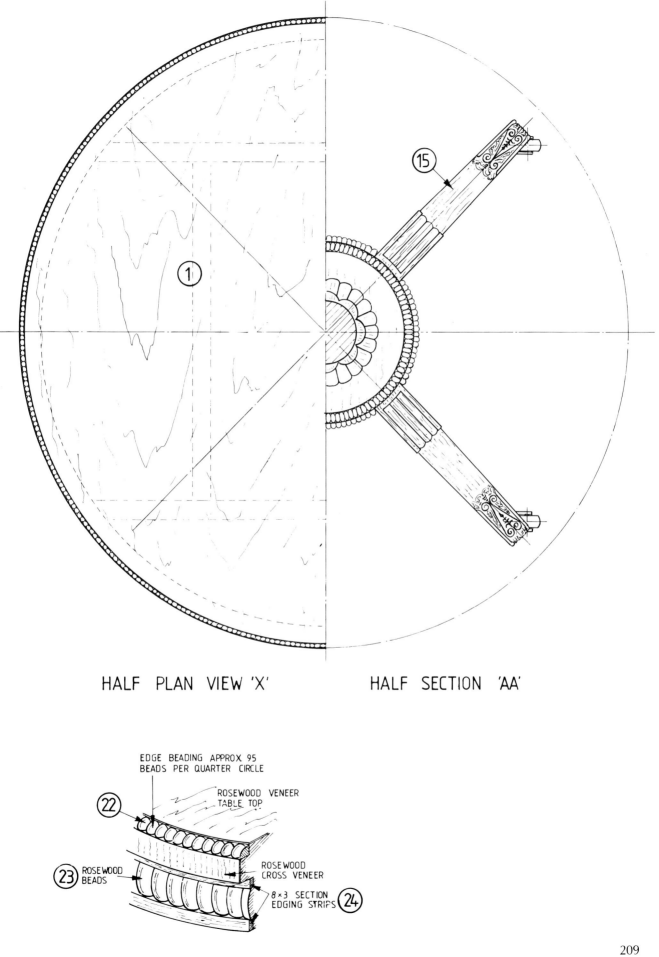

HALF PLAN VIEW 'X'   HALF SECTION 'AA'

EDGE BEADING APPROX 95
BEADS PER QUARTER CIRCLE

ROSEWOOD VENEER
TABLE TOP

ROSEWOOD
BEADS

ROSEWOOD
CROSS VENEER

8×3 SECTION
EDGING STRIPS

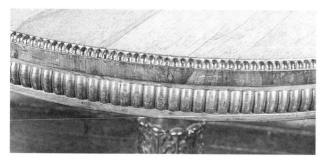

30.3 *Table edge beading*

30.4 *Pedestal column*

30.5 *Foliate castor*

Their preparation requires some ingenuity. It is suggested that spindle-turning techniques are employed to make the beads, as in Fig 30.8. This is the easy part; the difficult bit is to cut them so that they fit the table edge precisely. It may be worth considering a routing technique for this rather than sawing, which will give a ragged finish, and some thought will have to be given to devising a practical method of holding the beads during this operation. Cleaning up the tiny beads by hand will be difficult, so the dicing process should give a good finish ready for them to be glued into place without further work. The bead widths may need marginally trimming to fit evenly round the table perimeter. It is suggested that they are fitted on a segmental basis to even out any irregularities.

Platform and column

Platform and column details are given in Fig 30.7. You may have a problem obtaining the brass pivot hinge (18) for this. An alternative is to adapt the platform tip stop (10) and extend it at the top to include small ear pieces either side to act as pivots. Fit the platform to the table top at the same time as the lopers (4) are secured, as otherwise assembly will not be possible. The column is spindle-turned, and the foliate carving carefully marked out and crisply carved (Fig 30.4).

Hub and legs

Details of the hub and petal piece, etc, are given in Fig 30.10. The original hub has an unusual built-up construction, and readers may prefer to simplify this to a one-piece mahogany design with added rosewood veneer on the side and top. Leg details are shown in Fig 30.9, and a squared background is given to enable the shape to be transferred to the hardwood.

Brasswork

Difficulty may be experienced in obtaining the brass castors (17) with their intricate foliate pattern. Plain rounded toe castors are, however, available commercially and may be an acceptable compromise. Details of the double table catch (19) are given in Fig 30.10. This can also be purchased.

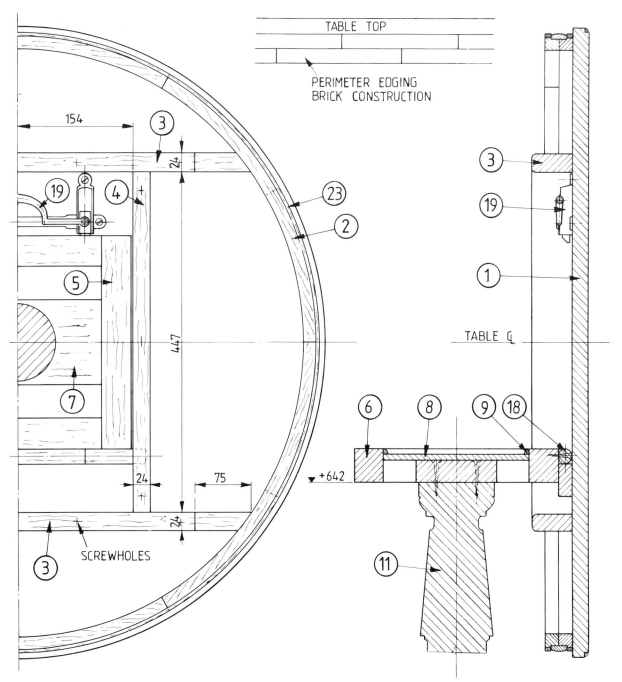

TABLE TOP

PERIMETER EDGING
BRICK CONSTRUCTION

154

24

19

4

5

447

7

24

75

24

SCREWHOLES

3

23

2

TABLE ℄

6   8   9   18

+642

11

1

3

19

UNDERSIDE VIEW 'Y'

SECTION 'BB' (TABLE TIPPED)

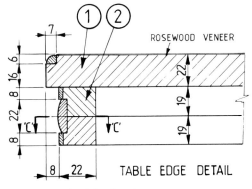

7

6

16

8

22

8

'C'   'C'

8   22

1   2

ROSEWOOD VENEER

22

19

19

TABLE EDGE DETAIL

ROSEWOOD BEADING
APPROX. 60 BEADS
PER QUARTER CIRCLE

3 APPROX

SECTION 'CC'

30.6 *Sectional table details*

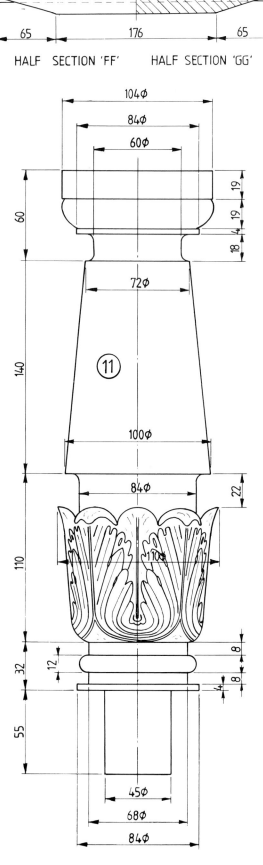

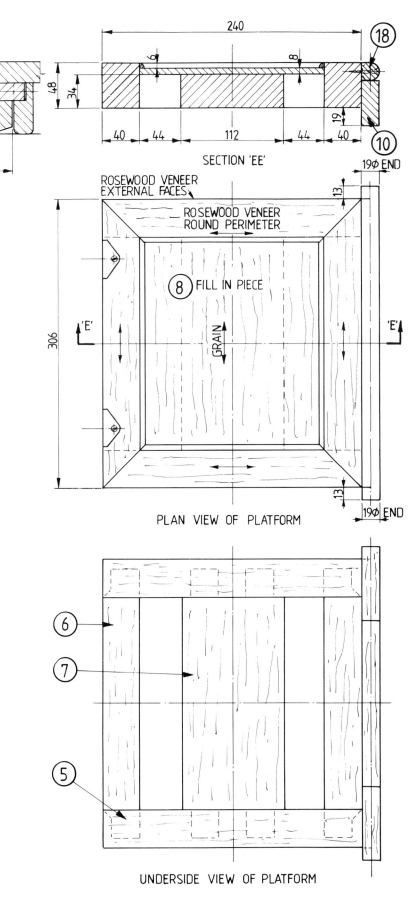

HALF SECTION 'FF'   HALF SECTION 'GG'

PIVOT LINE

SECTION 'EE'

19Ø END

ROSEWOOD VENEER
EXTERNAL FACES

ROSEWOOD VENEER
ROUND PERIMETER

⑧ FILL IN PIECE

GRAIN

'E'   'E'

PLAN VIEW OF PLATFORM

19Ø END

⑥
⑦
⑤

UNDERSIDE VIEW OF PLATFORM

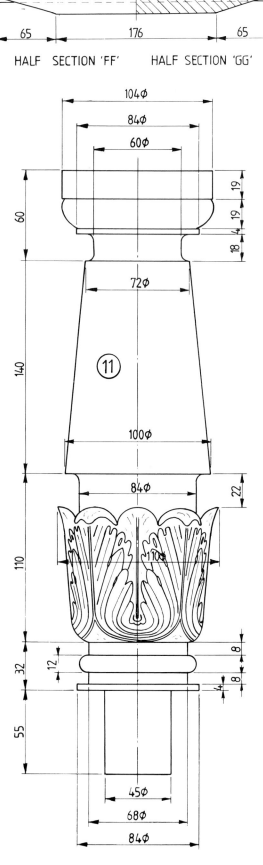

30.7 *Platform and column details*

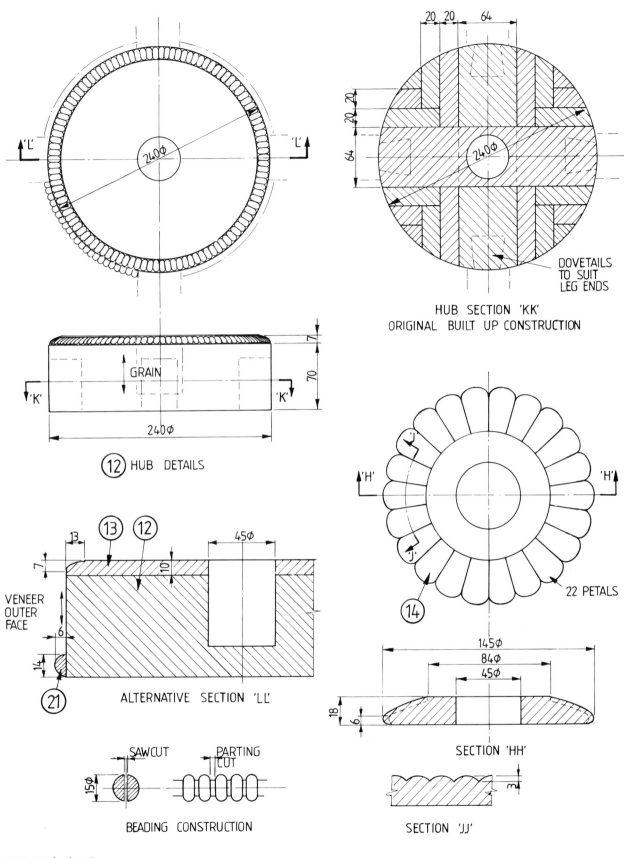

20 20 64

240∅

20 20

64

240∅

HUB SECTION 'KK'
ORIGINAL BUILT UP CONSTRUCTION

DOVETAILS
TO SUIT
LEG ENDS

'L' 'L'

'K' 'K'

7

70

GRAIN

240∅

(12) HUB DETAILS

13 (13) (12)

45∅

7

10

VENEER
OUTER
FACE

6

14

(21)

ALTERNATIVE SECTION 'LL'

SAWCUT PARTING
CUT

15∅

BEADING CONSTRUCTION

'H' 'H'

'J'

'J'

22 PETALS

(14)

145∅

84∅

45∅

18

6

SECTION 'HH'

3

SECTION 'JJ'

30.8 *Hub details*

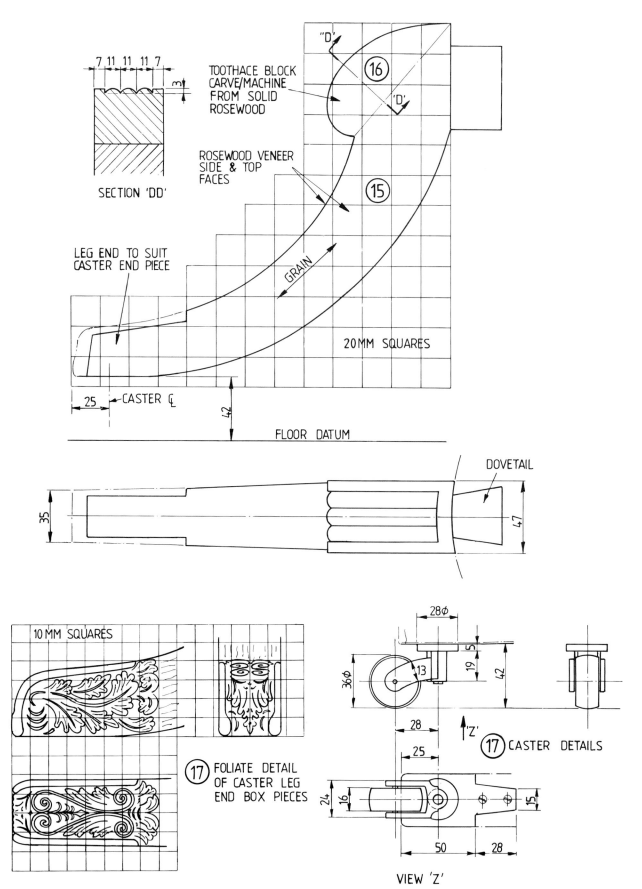

SECTION 'DD'

7 11 11 11 7

TOOTHACE BLOCK
CARVE/MACHINE
FROM SOLID
ROSEWOOD

16

ROSEWOOD VENEER
SIDE & TOP
FACES

15

"D'

'D'

GRAIN

20MM SQUARES

LEG END TO SUIT
CASTER END PIECE

25   CASTER ₵

42

FLOOR DATUM

DOVETAIL

35

47

10 MM SQUARES

17 FOLIATE DETAIL
OF CASTER LEG
END BOX PIECES

28ø

36ø

13

19

42

28

25

'Z'

17 CASTER DETAILS

24

16

15

50   28

VIEW 'Z'

30.9 *Leg and castor details*

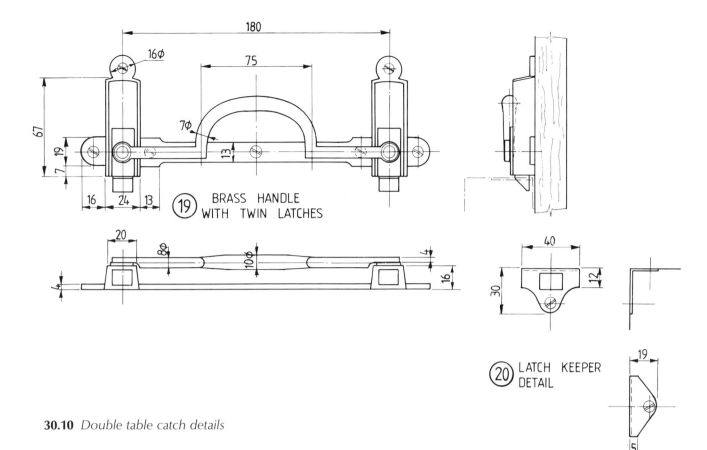

(19) BRASS HANDLE WITH TWIN LATCHES

(20) LATCH KEEPER DETAIL

30.10 *Double table catch details*

Parts list

Item	No	Material	Dimensions (mm)
1 Table top	1	Mahogany	415 × 22 × 1660 total
2 Table edge	1	Mahogany	150 × 19 × 2200 long. Material for 12 segments
3 Loper (1)	2	Mahogany	55 × 24 × 680 long
4 Loper (2)	2	Mahogany	55 × 24 × 500 long
5 Platform side piece	2	Mahogany	48 × 40 × 290 long
6 Platform end piece	2	Mahogany	48 × 40 × 310 long
7 Platform crosspiece	1	Mahogany	112 × 34 × 305 long
8 Fill piece	1	Mahogany	200 × 8 × 230 long
9 Platform beading	1	Mahogany	6 × 900 long total
10 Tip stop	1	Mahogany	48 × 19 × 310 long
11 Column	1	Rosewood	115sq × 450 long
12 Hub	1	Mahogany	250sq × 80 thick
13 Hub cover piece	1	Rosewood	250sq × 15 thick
14 Petal piece	1	Rosewood	155sq × 20 thick
15 Leg	4	Mahogany	100 × 48 × 350 long
16 Toothache block	4	Rosewood	38 × 48 × 110 long

Item	No	Material	Dimensions (mm)
17 Castor	4	Brass	Regency style with foliate pattern. Purchase to suit
18 Pivot hinge	1	Brass	19sq × 332 long with round ends
19 Double table catch	1	Brass	Purchase or make to suit
20 Catch plate	2	Brass	55 × 40 × 1.8 thick or purchase to suit
21 Hub beading	1	Rosewood	20sq × 900 long total
22 Table edge beading	1	Rosewood	10sq × 4000 long approx
23 Table face beading	1	Rosewood	20sq × 500 long approx
24 Table edging strip	2	Rosewood	8 × 3 × 900 long
25 Rosewood veneer	—	Rosewood	To suit table top, edging, legs and hub
26 Screws	—	Brass or steel	To fix lopers/table top and column/platform

Metric/imperial conversion table

Millimetres	Inches	Millimetres	Inches	Millimetres	Inches	Millimetres	Inches
1.5	$\frac{1}{16}''$	25	$1''$	125	$4\frac{15}{16}''$	900	$35\frac{7}{16}''$
3	$\frac{1}{8}''$	30	$1\frac{3}{16}''$	150	$5\frac{7}{8}''$	1000	$39\frac{3}{8}''$
5	$\frac{3}{16}''$	35	$1\frac{3}{8}''$	200	$7\frac{7}{8}''$	1500	$59\frac{1}{16}''$
6	$\frac{1}{4}''$	38	$1\frac{1}{2}''$	300	$11\frac{13}{16}''$	2000	$78\frac{3}{4}''$
8	$\frac{5}{16}''$	40	$1\frac{9}{16}''$	305	$12''$	2500	$98\frac{7}{16}''$
10	$\frac{3}{8}''$	45	$1\frac{3}{4}''$	400	$15\frac{3}{4}''$	3000	$118\frac{1}{8}''$
13	$\frac{1}{2}''$	50	$2''$	500	$19\frac{11}{16}''$	3500	$137\frac{3}{4}''$
16	$\frac{5}{8}''$	60	$2\frac{3}{8}''$	600	$23\frac{5}{8}''$	4000	$157\frac{1}{2}''$
19	$\frac{3}{4}''$	75	$3''$	700	$27\frac{9}{16}''$	4500	$177\frac{1}{8}''$
22	$\frac{7}{8}''$	100	$3\frac{15}{16}''$	800	$31\frac{1}{2}''$	5000	$196\frac{7}{8}''$

Country houses

The following is a list of the country houses whose furniture designs are featured in this book. Most are open between Easter and the end of September, and closed during the winter months. The opening times vary from house to house, so it is suggested that you check beforehand, to avoid a wasted journey.

Address	Opening times and special events
Adlington Hall Macclesfield Cheshire SK10 4LF Contact Mr John Buchanan Telephone 0625 829206	Easter – end September 1400–1730 hrs Su and Bank Hols, Sats in August; also some weekdays. Organ recitals
Arley Hall and Gardens Northwich Cheshire CW9 CNA Contact Cmdr Brian D.B. Gresham Telephone 0565 85353	Easter – end September Tues–Fri and weekends 1400–1800 hrs
Capesthorne Hall Macclesfield Cheshire SK10 4LF Contact Mr John Hegarty Telephone 0625 861221	April – September Sundays 1400–1700 hrs and Tues–Sat depending on month
Chatsworth Bakewell Derbyshire DE4 1PP Contact Mr Eric Oliver Telephone 024688 2204	April – end October Daily 1130–1630 hrs

Address	Opening times and special events
Dunham Massey (NT) Altrincham Cheshire WA14 4SJ Contact Mr Peter Veitch Telephone 061 941 1025	April – end October Daily ex Fri 1300–1730 hrs. Edwardian Extravaganza
Erddig (NT) Nr Wrexham Clwyd LL13 0YT Contact Mr Dillon Telephone 0978 355314	April – mid-October Daily ex Fri 1200–1700 hrs
Gawsworth Hall Nr Macclesfield Cheshire SK11 9RN Contact Mr T. Richards Telephone 0260 223 456	April – early October Daily 1400–1800 hrs. Open air theatre in summer months
Holker Hall and Gardens Cark-in-Cartmel Grange-over-Sands Cumbria LA11 7PH Contact Mrs Carolyn Johnson Telephone 044 853 328	Easter – end October Daily except Sats 1030–1800 hrs

Address	Opening times and special events	Address	Opening times and special events
Leighton Hall Carnforth Lancashire LA5 9ST Contact Mrs C. Reynolds Telephone 0524 73444	May – end September Suns, Bank Hols and Tues–Fri 1400–1700 hrs. Display of birds of prey	Tatton Park (NT) Knutsford Cheshire WA16 6QN Contact Mr David Hardman Telephone 0565 54822	House April – end Oct Daily 1300–1600 hrs. Park land all year; Special events
Levens Hall Kendal Cumbria LA8 0PD Contact Mr T. Schofield Telephone 05395 60321	Easter – mid-October Sun–Thur 1100–1700 hrs	The American Museum in Bath Claverton Manor Bath BA2 7BD Contact Miss J. Elsdon Telephone 0225 60503	April – end October Daily ex Mon 1400–1700 hrs
Peover Hall Knutsford Cheshire Contact Mr R. Brooks Telephone 0565 812135	May – September Mon pm Hall, Gardens and Stables Thu pm Gardens and Stables	Wythenshawe Hall Wythenshawe Road Manchester 23 Telephone 061 998 2331, or contact Mr R. Gray Manchester City Art Gallery, Tel 061 236 9422	Easter – September Weekends pm. Free entry
Rufford Old Hall (NT) Nr Ormskirk Lancashire LA40 1SG Telephone 0704 821254	April – end October Daily ex Friday 1400–1700 hrs		

Bibliography

Furniture history

Geoffrey Beard, *The National Trust Book of English Furniture*, Viking
Arthur Negus talks to Max Robertson, *Going for a Song: English Furniture*, BBC
Robin Butler, *The Arthur Negus Guide to English Furniture*, Hamlyn
Judith and Martin Miller, *The Antiques Directory, Furniture*, Mitchell Beazley
Charles Hayward, *English Period Furniture*, Evans
Therle Hughes, *Old English Furniture*, Lutterworth
W.W. Norton, *Shaker Design*

General woodwork

Alan Peters, *The Technique of Furniture Making*, Batsford

Charles Hayward, *Furniture Repairs*, Evans
George Buchanan, *The Illustrated Handbook of Furniture Restoration*, Batsford

Marquetry and veneering

Charles Hayward, *Practical Veneering*, Evans
W.A. Lincoln, *The Complete Manual of Wood Veneering*, Stobart & Son Ltd

Upholstery

R.J. McDonald, *Upholstery Repair and Restoration*, Batsford
Margery Brown, *Cane and Rush Seating*, Batsford
Mary Butcher, Olivia Elton Barratt and Kay Johnson, *Chair Seating*, Dryad Press

List of suppliers

Metal fittings, castors, hinges, etc
Woodfit
Kem Hill Lane
Whittle le Woods
Chorley
Lancs PR6 7EA
Tel: 02572 66421

Polishing and finishing materials
Henry Flack Ltd
Borough Works
Croydon Road
Elmers End
Beckenham
Kent BR3 4BL

James Jamieson's (Aberdeen) Ltd
10 Whitemyres Avenue
Mastrick Industrial Estate
Aberdeen AB2 6HQ
Tel: 0224 681877

Rush seating materials
J. Burdekin Ltd
Osett
West Yorks WF5 9AQ

Jacobs, Young & Westbury
J.Y.W. House
Bridge Road
Haywards Heath
West Sussex RH16 1TZ

Veneers, inlay and bandings etc
The Art Veneer Co. Ltd
Industrial Estate
Mildenhall
Suffolk IP28 7AY
Tel: 0638 712550

R. Aaronson (Veneers) Ltd
45 Redchurch Street
London E2
Tel: 071 739 3107

Upholstery supplies
Biggs & Co.
Worcester House
Worcester Park
Surrey

Fred Aldous Ltd
37 Lever Street
Manchester
Tel: 0533 510405

Dryad Ltd
PO Box 38
Northgates
Leicester LE1 9BU
Tel: 0533 510405

*Workshop plans: large A0 size
working drawings of all
designs in this book*
David Bryant
4 Grassfield Way
Knutsford
Cheshire WA16 9AF
Tel: 0565 51681

Index